Executions in the Modern Era

From the editors of SunRiver Cartel

LONGSTREET PRESS
Atlanta, Georgia

Published by
LONGSTREET PRESS
2140 Newmarket Parkway
Suite 122
Marietta, GA 30067

Printed in the United States of America

1st printing 2000

Library of Congress Catalog Card Number: 00-105139

ISBN: 1-56352-634-4

Book design by Bill Carson Design

This book presents the factual record preserved by the Texas Department of Criminal Justice for each of the individual offenders executed by the State of Texas in the modern era. The modern era is the period following the June 29, 1972, U.S. Supreme Court ruling in *Furman* v. *Georgia,* which declared capital punishment, as then administered, unconstitutional, and the reinstitution of the death penalty in Texas following passage of House Bill 200 by the Sixty-Third Legislature in Texas, which became effective on June 14, 1973, and satisfied the concerns of the U.S. Supreme Court concerning the unconstitutional nature of the death penalty in Texas.

The entries are listed in order of execution, beginning with #1, Charlie Brooks, and ending with #222, Gary Lee Graham, the last execution to occur before this book went to press on June 25, 2000.

The Texas Department of Criminal Justice (TDCJ) provided all of the information in this book. Those seeking more information are encouraged to visit the Texas Department of Criminal Justice website at www.tdcj.state.tx.us/. Every effort was made to collect photos and complete information on each executed offender. Information not available at press time is marked n/a.

We wish to thank the public relations office at the TDCJ in Huntsville, Texas, particularly Larry Fitzgerald, the public information officer, and Tracy Espinoza, the public information associate. Both Mr. Fitzgerald and Mrs. Espinoza went out of their way to be open, honest, and cooperative. They are true professionals. Without their helpful assistance, this book would not have been possible to produce.

In recent months, the debate over the death penalty has increased in volume and vehemence. It is our hope that the information presented in this book will help educate citizens about publicly funded executions.

Crimes for Which Capital Punishment Is Administered

(Source: Texas Department of Criminal Justice)

Texas Penal Code Acts 1992, 72nd Legislature,
Chapter 12 effective January 1992. PC Sec. 19.03. Capital Murder.

(a) A person commits an offense in which he intentionally or knowingly causes the death of an individual and:

(1) the person murders a peace officer or fireman who is acting in the lawful discharge of an official duty and who the person knows is a peace officer of fireman;

(2) the person intentionally commits the murder in the course of committing or attempting to commit kidnapping, burglary, robbery, aggravated sexual assault, or arson;

(3) the person commits the murder for remuneration or the promise of remuneration or employs another to commit the murder for remuneration or the promise of remuneration;

(4) the person commits the murder while escaping or attempting to escape from the penal institution;

(5) the person, while incarcerated in the penal institution, murders another who is employed in the operation of the penal institution; or

(6) the person murders more than one person;

    (a) during the same criminal transaction; or

    (b) during different criminal transactions but the murders are committed pursuant to the same scheme or course of conduct.

Under the present law, a person convicted of capital murder may be sentenced to one of two sentences – death or life imprisonment. A person must serve at least 35 calendar years of a life sentence if the offense is committed prior to September 1, 1993, or at least 40 years if the offense is committed after this date.

If the jury answers three questions with yes, the sentence is death.
The questions are:

(1) Did the defendant act intentionally and should he have known someone might be killed?

(2) Is there a probability that the defendant would in the future commit criminal acts of violence that would constitute a menace to society?

(3) Was the conduct of the defendant in killing the deceased unreasonable in response to the provocation, if any, of the deceased?

Additional Execution Information

(Source: Texas Department of Criminal Justice)

• The State of Texas authorizes use of electric chair in 1923 and orders all executions to be carried out in Huntsville, Texas. Prior to 1923, Texas counties were responsible for their own executions.

• The electric chair, which was used in Texas from 1924 through 1977, was the original chair built from oak in 1923-24.

• The State of Texas executes first inmate by electrocution on February 8, 1924. On that same date, four additional inmates were executed in the following order:

Charles Reynold	Black	Red River County	Murder
Ewell Morris	Black	Liberty County	Murder
George Washington	Black	Newton County	Murder
Mack Matthew	Black	Tyler County	Murder
Melvin Johnson	Black	Liberty County	Murder

• The State of Texas executes brothers on six occasions. Frank and Lorenzo Noel electrocuted July 3, 1925; S.A. and Forest Robins electrocuted April 6, 1926; Oscar and Mack Brown electrocuted July 1, 1936; Roscoe and Henderson Brown electrocuted May 6, 1938; Curtis Harris by injection July 1, 1993 and Danny Harris by injection, July 30, 1993; Jesse Gutierrez by injection September 16, 1994 and Jose Gutierrez by injection November 18, 1999.

• The State of Texas executes its last inmate by electrocution July 30, 1964. Joseph Johnson (black male) from Harris County for murder.

• Between February 1924 and July 1964, a total of 506 men and women were placed on death row in Texas; of those, 361 died in the electric chair.

Black	229	Murder	259
White	108	Rape	97
Mexican American	23	Armed Robbery	5
Total	361	Total	361

• When capital punishment was declared "cruel and unusual" punishment by the U.S. Supreme Court on June 29, 1972, there were 45 men on death row in Texas and 7 in county jails with a death sentence. All of the sentences were commuted to life sentences by the Governor of Texas, and death row was cleared by March 1973.

• The Texas Legislature revised the Texas Penal Code, and effective January 1, 1974, Texas courts began assessing the death penalty. Under the new statute, the first man was placed on death row on February 15, 1974, John Devrees (white male), born November 19, 1920. Devrees was convicted of murder with malice while committing burglary in Jefferson County. Devrees committed suicide July 1, 1974, by hanging himself with bed sheets.

- Lethal injection consists of:
    Sodium Thiopental (lethal dose – sedates person)
    Pancuronium Bromide (muscle relaxant – collapses diaphragm and lungs)
    Potassium Chloride (stops heartbeat)

- Lethal injection process takes approximately 7 minutes, and the cost per execution for the drugs used is $86.08.

- The State of Texas adopts lethal injection as a means of execution in 1977.

- The State of Texas executes first inmate by lethal injection on December 7, 1982. Charlie Brooks of Tarrant County was executed for the kidnap/murder of a Fort Worth auto mechanic.

- Witnesses: Reporters from community where crime was committed have first choice to witness execution. Members of the Kelley family were the first victim's family allowed to witness an execution on February 9, 1996, under the adoption preamble effective September 26, 1995. The offender executed was Leo Jenkins, who shot the brother and sister of the Kelley family during a robbery at the family-owned Golden Nugget Pawn Shop in Houston, August 29, 1988.

Executions carried out by the State of Texas since death penalty was reinstated:

1982	1983	1984	1985	1986	1987	1988	1989	1990	1991	1992	1993	1994	1995	1996	1997	1998	1999
1	0	3	6	10	6	4	4	4	5	12	17	14	19	3	37	20	35

Texas Execution Statistics
Average Time on Death Row: 9.75 years

Time on Death Row	Name	County	Death Row#	Time on Death Row	Execution
Shortest time	Joe F. Gonzales	Potter	#999177	8 mon. 18 days	09/18/96
2nd shortest time	Aaron Foust	Tarrant	#999268	11 mon 20 days	04/28/99
Longest time	Robert E. White	Collin	#511	24 yrs. 6 mon.	03/30/99
2nd longest time	Joseph Faulder	Gregg	#580	22 yrs. 7 mon.	06/17/99

United States Capital Punishment

• As of February 1, 1996, thirty-seven states have a death penalty statute.

• Texas leads the nation in number of executions since death penalty was reinstated in 1976.

• California has the largest death row population, but ranks almost last in the number of executions carried out.

• There are five methods of execution in the United States: lethal injection, electrocution, lethal gas, hanging, and firing squad.

• Jurisdictions without death penalty statutes: Alaska, District of Columbia, Hawaii, Iowa, Maine, Massachusetts, Michigan, Minnesota, North Dakota, Rhode Island, Vermont, West Virginia, Wisconsin.

Execution Procedures of Inmates Sentenced to Death
(Source: Texas Department of Criminal Justice)

Male inmates under the sentence of death will be housed at the Terrell Unit of the Texas Department of Criminal Justice Institutional Division located east of Huntsville on FM 350 in Livingston, Texas. Female death row inmates will be housed at the Mountain View Unit located in Gatesville, Texas.

• Visitors at the Terrell/Mountain View Units:

MEDIA – Press interviews of condemned prisoners shall be scheduled by the Public Information Office and conducted at the Terrell Unit and Mountain View Unit during specified times. Any media requesting an interview with death row inmates at Terrell Unit or Mountain View Unit should submit names to the Public Information Office prior to the interview date. Requests will not be accepted at the Terrell/Mountain View Units on the day of the interview. The number of inmates requested to be interviewed should be kept within reason.

The inmate may have the following visitors at the Terrell/Mountain View Units: Family member(s) and friend(s) on the list of approved visitors.

An inmate scheduled for execution shall be transported from the Terrell Unit. Mountain View Unit to the Huntsville Unit prior to the scheduled execution.

Transportation arrangements shall be known only to the unit wardens involved, and no public announcement to either the exact time, method, or route of transfer shall be made. The Director's Office and the Public Information Office will be notified immediately after the inmate arrives at the Huntsville Unit.

During transportation and after arrival at the Huntsville Unit, the inmate shall be constantly observed and supervised by security personnel.

The inmate may have the following visitors at the Huntsville Unit:

T.D.C.J. Institutional Division Chaplain(s)

Minister(s)

Attorney(s)

All visits must be approved by the warden. With the exception of chaplain's visits, all visits will be terminated by 12:30 P.M. on the day of the execution. No media visits will be allowed at the Huntsville Unit.

The last meal will be served at approximately 3:30 – 4:00 P.M.

Prior to 6:00 P.M., the inmate may shower and dress in clean clothes. The Huntsville Unite Warden's office will serve as the communications command post and only operations personnel will be allowed entry to this area. All other individuals, including witnesses to the execution, will assemble at approximately 5:54 P.M. in the lounge adjacent to the visiting room. All necessary arrangements to carry out the execution shall be completed at the predetermined time. Shortly after 6:00 P.M., the door will be unlocked, and the inmate will be removed from the holding cell.

The inmate will be taken from the cell area into the execution chamber and secured to a gurney. A medically-trained individual (not to be identified) shall insert an intravenous catheter into the condemned person's arms and cause a saline solution to flow.

At a predetermined time, the witnesses shall be escorted to the execution chamber. Witnesses shall include:

MEDIA – One Texas Bureau representative designated by the Associated Press, one Texas Bureau representative designated by the United Press International, one representative for the Huntsville Item, and one representative each from established separate rosters of print and broadcast media will be admitted to the execution chamber as witnesses, provided those designated agree to meet with all media representatives present, immediately subsequent to the execution. No recording devices, either audio or video, shall be permitted in the unit or in the execution chamber.

Policy allows for up to five pre-approved witnesses requested by the condemned and up to five immediate family members or close friends of the victim to attend.

Once the witnesses are in place, the warden shall allow the condemned person to make a last statement. Upon completion of the statement, if any, the warden shall signal for the execution to proceed. At the time, the designee(s) of the Director, shall induce by syringe, substance and/or substances necessary to cause death. The individual(s) shall be visually separated from the execution by a wall and locked door, and shall also not be identified. After the inmate is pronounced dead, the body shall be immediately removed from the execution chamber, taken to an awaiting vehicle, and delivered to a local funeral home for burial by the family or state. The inmate may request that his body be donated to the state anatomical board for medical research purposes. Arrangements for the body, are to be concluded prior to the execution, shall be made per Vernon's Ann. C.C.P., Article 43.25.

The Director of the Texas Department of Criminal Justice Institutional Division in accordance with Article 43.23 shall return the death warrant and certificate with a statement of any such act and his proceedings endorsed thereon, together with a statement showing what disposition was made of the body of the convict, to the clerk of the court in which the sentence was passed.

Every attempt has been made to report all information for each executed offender.
Information not available at the time of publication is indicated by "n/a."
Lengthy written and spoken last statements have been included in Appendix 1.
An alphabetical listing of inmates is displayed in Appendix 2.

1

Charlie Brooks, Jr.

Executed:
December 7,
1982

Personal Data: *Born:* September 1, 1942. *Race:* Black. *Height:* n/a. *Weight:* n/a. *Education:* n/a. *Prior Occupation:* n/a. *County of Conviction:* Tarrant. *Age at time of execution:* 40.

Sentenced to death for: The December 14, 1976, kidnap-murder of used car lot mechanic David Gregory. Co-defendant Woodie Lourdes was also charged with capital murder in connection with the slaying.

Received at Death Row: April 15, 1978. Time on death row: 1,687 days, (4.62 years).

Last meal: T-bone steak, french fries, catsup, Worcestershire sauce, rolls, peach cobbler, iced tea, and a toothpick.

Last statement: [To witness Vanessa Sapp, his girlfriend] I love you. Be strong.

Pronounced dead: 12:16 A.M.

Note: Brooks was the first person to be executed by lethal injections in the U.S. and the first person executed in Texas following the reinstatement of the death penalty in 1974. Brooks was the sixth person in the U.S. to be executed after the reinstatement.

2

James David Autry

Executed:
March 14, 1984

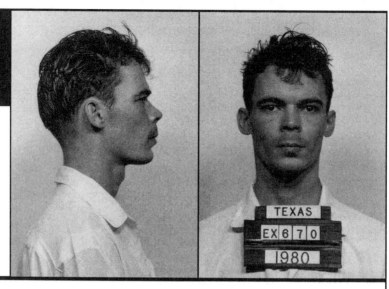

Personal Data: *Born:* September 27, 1954. *Race:* White. *Height:* n/a. *Weight:* n/a. *Education:* n/a. *Prior Occupation:* n/a. *County of conviction:* Jefferson. *Age at time of execution:* 29.

Sentenced to death for: Shot and killed Shirley Crouet, a convenience store clerk, during a robbery on April 20, 1980. The robbery netted one six-pack of beer.

Received at Death Row: October 10, 1980. Time on death row: 1,251 days, (3.43 years).

Last meal: Hamburger, french fries, and Dr Pepper.

Last statement: None.

Pronounced dead: 12:40 A.M.

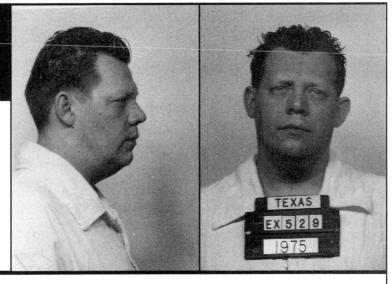

3

Ronald Clark O'Bryan

Executed: March 31, 1984

Personal Data: *Born:* October 19, 1944. *Race:* White. *Height:* 5'10". *Weight:* 215 lbs. *Education:* 14 years. *Prior occupation:* Optician. *County of conviction:* Harris. *Age at time of execution:* 39.

Sentenced to death for: The murder of his son, Timothy O'Bryan, by poisoning his Halloween candy with cyanide.

Note: Ronald O'Bryan was nicknamed in the press The Candy Man.

Received at Death Row: July 14, 1975. Time on death row: 3,183 days, (8.72 years).

Last meal: T-bone (medium to well done), french fries and catsup, whole kernel corn, sweet peas, lettuce and tomato salad with egg and French dressing, iced tea (sweet), saltines, ice cream, Boston cream pie, and rolls.

Last statement: See Appendix 1.

Pronounced dead: 12:48 A.M.

4

Thomas Andy Barefoot

Executed: October 30, 1984

Personal Data: *Born:* February 23, 1945. *Race:* White, *Height:* n/a. *Weight:* n/a. *Education:* 10 years. *Prior occupation:* Cement finisher, oilfield worker, derrick man. *County of conviction:* Bell. *Age at time of execution:* 39.

Sentenced to death for: The August 7, 1978, capital murder of police officer Carl Levin near Killeen, Texas. Barefoot shot Officer Levin with a .25 caliber pistol to avoid arrest. Barefoot was apprehended in Beaumont after bragging about the murder.

Note: Prior to the murder of Levin, Barefoot had been arrested for the rape of the three-year-old daughter of his estranged girlfriend. He escaped from jail by digging himself out with a spoon.

Received at Death Row: November 21, 1978. Time on death row: 2,163 days, (5.93 years).

Last meal: Chef salad with crackers, chili with beans, steamed rice, seasoned pinto beans, corn O'Brien, seasoned mustard greens, hot spiced beets, and iced tea.

Last Statement: I hope that one day we can look back on the evil that we're doing right now like the witches we burned at the stake. I want everybody to know that I hold nothing against them. I forgive them all. I hope everybody I've done anything to will forgive me. I've been praying all day for Carl Levin's wife to drive the bitterness from her heart because the bitterness that's in her heart will send her to hell just as surely as any other sin. I'm sorry for everything that I've ever done to anybody. I hope they'll forgive me. Sharon, tell all my friends goodbye, you know who they are, Charles Bass, David Powell...

Pronounced dead: 12:24 A.M.

5

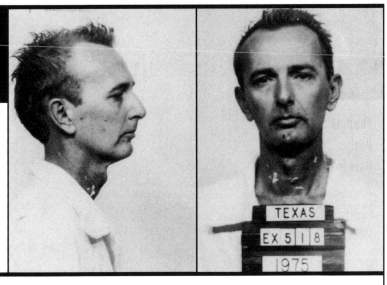

Doyle Skillern

Executed: January 16, 1985

Personal Data: *Born:* April 8, 1936. *Race:* White. *Height:* 5'7". *Weight:* 125 lbs. *Education:* 12 years. *Prior Occupation:* Sales. *County of conviction:* Lubbock. *Age at time of execution:* 49.

Sentenced to death for: Skillern was convicted of capital murder for the October 23, 1974, shooting death of Texas Department of Public Safety narcotics officer Patrick Allen Randel during an undercover drug buy near the town of George West.

Received at Death Row: March 3, 1975. Time on death row: 3,607 days, (9.88 years).

Last meal: Sirloin steak, baked potato, peas, roll, banana pudding, coffee. *Note:* At the end of the meal Skillern said, "My compliments to the chef."

Last statement: I pray that my family will rejoice and will forgive, thank you.

Pronounced dead: 12:23 A.M.

6

Stephen Peter Morin

Executed:
March 13, 1985

TEXAS
EX 7 1 2
1982

Personal Data: *Born*: February 19, 1951. *Race*: White. *Height*: n/a. *Weight*: n/a. *Education*: n/a. *Prior Occupation:* n/a. *County of conviction:* Jefferson and Nueces. *Age at time of execution:* 34.

Sentenced to death for: Convicted of the December 11, 1981, murder of Carrie Marie Scott, 21, who police said was shot in a robbery attempt outside a San Antonio restaurant. This crime was made a capital offense when Morin stole Scott's car after shooting her.

Received at Death Row: April 16, 1982. Time on death row: 1,093 days, (2.99 years).

Last meal: Bread without yeast (unleavened).

Last statement: Heavenly Father, I give thanks for this time, for the time that we have been together, the fellowship of your world, the Christian family presented to me [he called the names of the personal witnesses]. Allow your holy spirit to flow as I know your love has been showered upon me. Forgive them for they know not what they do as I know that you have forgiven me, as I have forgiven them. Lord Jesus, I commit my soul to you, I praise you and I thank you.

Pronounced dead: 12:55 A.M.

7

Jesse de la Rosa

Executed: May 15, 1985

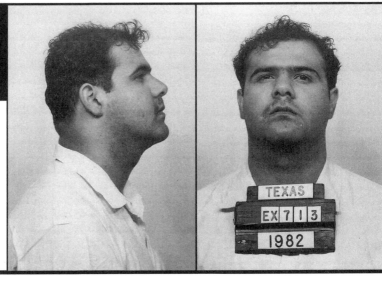

TEXAS
EX 7 1 3
1982

Personal Data: *Born:* September 22, 1960. *Race:* Hispanic. *Height:* 5'9".
Weight: 220 lbs. *Education:* 9 years. *Prior occupation:* Laborer.
County of conviction: Bexar. *Age at time of execution:* 24.

Sentenced to death for: Convicted in the slaying of Masaoud Ghazali, a former captain in the Iranian Air Force, who was shot twice in the head during a robbery at a San Antonio convenience store August 22, 1979. The robbery netted only one six-pack of beer because the cash register could not be opened.

Received at Death Row: May 18, 1982. Time on death row: 1,093 days, (2.99 years).

Last meal: Spanish rice, refried beans, flour tortillas, T-bone steak, tea, chocolate cake, and jalapeno peppers.

Last statement: Gave last statement in Spanish. No record kept.

Pronounced dead: 12:17 A.M.

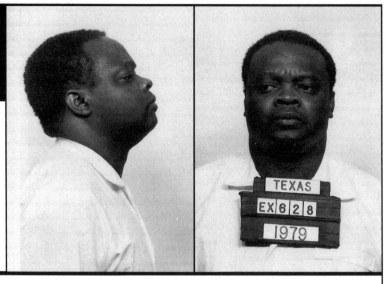

8

Charles Milton

Executed:
June 25,
1985

Personal Data: *Born:* March 15, 1951. *Race:* Black. *Height:* 5'6". *Weight:* 165 lbs. *Education:* 7 years. *Prior Occupation:* Cook. *Age at time of execution:* 34.

Sentenced to death for: Capital murder, for the robbery and murder of liquor store owner Menaree Denton in Fort Worth. Her husband, Leonard Denton, was also shot but survived to testify against Charles Milton.

Received at Death Row: January 18, 1979. Time on death row: 2,350 days, (6.44 years).

Last meal: T-bone steak, french fries, tossed salad with French dressing, catsup, hot rolls, and chocolate cake.

Last statement: There's no God, but Allah and unto thee I belong and unto thee I return. I want to continue to tell my brothers and sisters to be strong.

Pronounced dead: 1:33 A.M.

9

Henry Martinez Porter

Executed:
July 9,
1985

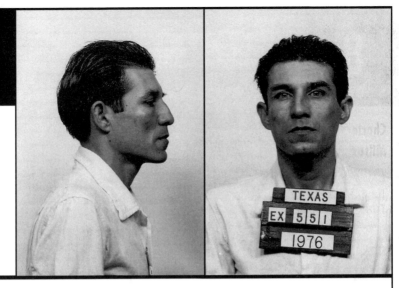

TEXAS
EX 5 5 1
1976

Personal Data: *Born*: December 12, 1941. *Race*: Hispanic. *Height*: 5'6".
Weight: 125 lbs. *Education*: 9 years. *Prior occupation:* Painter's helper.
County of conviction: Tarrant. *Age at time of execution:* 43.

Sentenced to death for: Convicted of capital murder in the November 29, 1975,
shooting death of Henry P. Malloux, a Fort Worth police officer who had
stopped Porter on an investigation of three armed robberies.

Received at Death Row: July 28, 1976. Time on death row: 3,268 days,
(8.95 years).

Last meal: Flour tortillas, T-bone steak, refried beans, tossed salad, jalapeno
peppers, ice cream, and chocolate cake.

Last statement: I want to thank Father Walsh for his spiritual help. I want to thank Bob
Ray [Sanders] and Steve Blow for their friendship. What I want people to know is that
they call me a cold blooded killer when I shot a man that shot me first. The only thing
that convicted me was that I am a Mexican and that he was a police officer. People
hollered for my life, and they are to have my life tonight. The people never hollered for
the life of the policeman that killed a 13-year-old boy who was handcuffed in the back
seat of a police car. The people never hollered for the life of a Houston police officer who
beat up and drowned Jose Campo Torres and threw his body in the river. You call that
equal justice. This is your equal justice. This is America's equal justice. A Mexican's life
is worth nothing. When a policeman kills someone he gets a suspended sentence or probation. When a Mexican kills a police officer, this is what you get. From there you call
me a cold-blooded murderer. I didn't tie anybody to a stretcher. I don't pump any poison
into anybody's veins from behind a locked door. You call this justice. I call this and your
society a bunch of cold-blooded murderers. I don't say this with any bitterness or anger. I
just say this with truthfulness. I hope God forgives me for all my sins. I hope that God
will be as merciful to society as he has been to me. I'm ready, warden.

Pronounced dead: 12:31 AM.

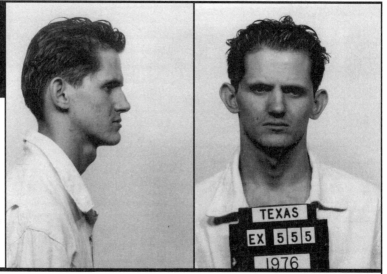

10

Charles Francis Rumbaugh

Executed:
September 11, 1985

Personal Data: *Born*: June 23, 1957. *Race*: White. *Height*: n/a. *Weight*: n/a. *Education*: n/a. *Prior Occupation*: n/a. *County of conviction:* Porter. *Age at time of execution:* 28.

Sentenced to death for: The April 4, 1975, slaying of Michael Fiorillo, 58, during a jewelry store robbery. Rumbaugh was 17 years old at time of offense.

Note: After being sentenced to death in 1976, Rumbaugh threatened to kill the Judge, D.A., bailiff, and his attorney. In February 1983, Rumbaugh was critically wounded in a courtroom after he lunged at a deputy U.S. marshal with a makeshift weapon and shouted, "Shoot me."

Received at Death Row: August 25, 1976. Time on death row: 3,304 days, (9.05 years).

Last meal: One flour tortilla and water.

Last statement: D.J., Laurie, Dr. Wheat, about all I can say is goodbye and for the rest of you, although you don't forgive me for my transgressions, I forgive yours against me. I am ready to begin my journey and that's all I have to say. See Appendix 1 for written last statement.

Pronounced dead: 12:27 A.M.

11

Charles William Bass

Executed: March 12, 1986

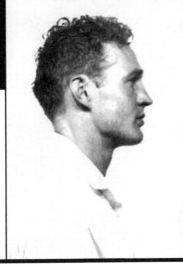 

Personal Data: *Born*: January 10, 1957. *Race*: White. *Height*: 5'6". *Weight*: 135 lbs. *Education*: 9 years. *Prior occupation:* Sheet & metal mechanic. *County of conviction:* Harris. *Age at time of execution:* 30.

Sentenced to death for: Capital murder. On August 16, 1979, Bass robbed a lounge at gunpoint and fled. After going ½ mile from the robbery, he was seen coincidentally by two Houston city marshalls who had a traffic warrant on Bass. Bass was stopped by the officers who noticed his pockets stuffed with rolled coins and dollar bills. Bass pulled out an automatic pistol and shot Officer Baker in the stomach then shot at Baker's partner and missed. He then shot Baker again as Baker lay on the pavement. Bass fled and was arrested four days later in Covington, Kentucky. Officer Baker died.

Received at Death Row: September 9, 1980. Time on death row: 2,072 days, (5.68 years).

Last meal: Plain cheese sandwich.

Last statement: I deserve this. Tell everyone I said goodbye.

Pronounced dead: 12:21 A.M.

12

Jeffery Allen Barney

Executed:
April 16,
1986

PHOTOGRAPHS NOT AVAILABLE

Personal Data: *Born*: March 1, 1958. *Race*: White. *Height*: 5'8". *Weight*: 145 lbs. *Education*: n/a. *Prior occupation*: n/a. *County of conviction*: Harris. *Age at time of execution*: 28.

Sentenced to death for: Rape/strangulation death of a Pasadena game room manager, Ruby Mock Longsworth, whose husband a clergyman, had befriended Barney. Mrs. Longsworth was murdered in her home, strangled with a microphone cord.

Received at Death Row: June 17, 1982. Time on death row: 1,399 days, (3.83 years).

Last meal: Two boxes of Frosted Flakes and one pint of milk.

Last statement: I'm sorry for what I've done. I deserve this. Jesus forgive me.

Pronounced dead: 12:22 A.M.

13

Jay Kelly Pinkerton

Executed: May 15, 1986

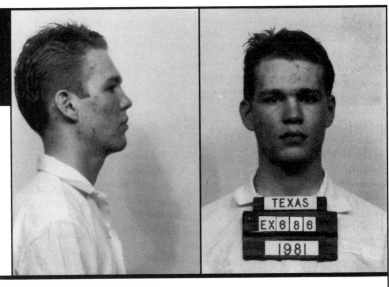

Personal Data: *Born*: February 14, 1962. *Race*: White. *Height*: 6'. *Weight*: 159 lbs. *Education*: 10 years (GED). *Prior occupation:* Truck driver. *County of conviction:* Nueces and Potter. *Age at time of execution:* 24.

Sentenced to death for: Convicted of capital murder for the death of Sarah Donn Lawrence, October 26, 1979, during a robbery (or burglary) with intent to rape. Lawrence suffered thirty stab wounds or more to her body and face. Pinkerton was also convicted of capital murder for the stabbing death of Sherry Welch, a furniture store employee in Amarillo. Ms. Welch was stabbed approximately thirty times and raped.
Note: Pinkerton was 17 years of age at time of offense.

Received at Death Row: June 29, 1981. Time on death row: 1,781 days, (4.88 years).

Last meal: Fish sandwich, french fries, milk.
Note: Pinkerton did not eat during the day in honor of Ramadan, the Muslim fasting month.

Last statement: Be strong for me. [to his father, who witnessed the execution] I want you to know I'm at peace with myself and with my God. I bear witness that there is no God but Allah. With your praise I ask for forgiveness and I return unto you. I love you, Dad.

Pronounced dead: 12:25 A.M.

14

Rudy Ramos Esquivel

Executed: June 9, 1986

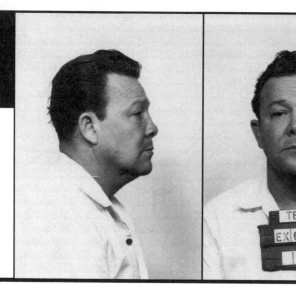

Personal Data: *Born:* n/a. *Race:* Hispanic. *Height:* n/a. *Weight:* n/a. *Education:* n/a. *Prior occupation:* n/a. *County of conviction:* Harris. *Age at time of execution:* 50.

Sentenced to death for: Convicted in the June 8, 1978, slaying of Houston narcotics officer Tim Hearn.

Received at Death Row: August 30, 1978. Time on death row: 2,840 days, (7.78 years).

Last meal: Fried breast of chicken, corn on the cob, french fries, jalapeno pepper, and pecan pie.

Last statement: Goodbye to all my friends. Be cool. Thank you for being my friends. Give my love to everybody.

Pronounced dead: 12:21 A.M.

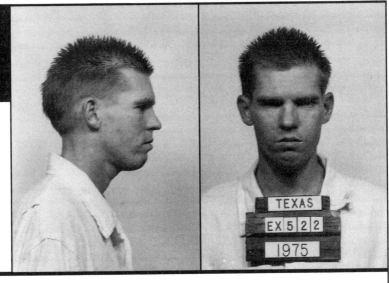

15

Kenneth Brock

Executed: June 19, 1986

Personal Data: *Born:* n/a. *Race:* White. *Height:* n/a. *Weight:* n/a. *Education:* n/a. *Prior occupation:* n/a. *County of conviction:* Harris. *Age at time of execution:* 37.

Sentenced to death for: Convicted in the 1974 robbery and shooting death of 7-Eleven store manager Michael Sedita.

Received at Death Row: March 27, 1975. Time on death row: 4,102 days, (11.24 years).

Last meal: Large double-meat cheeseburger with mustard and Dr Pepper.

Last statement: I have no last words. I am ready.

Pronounced dead: 12:18 A.M.

16

Randy Lynn Woolls

Executed:
August 20, 1986

Personal Data: *Born*: November 21, 1949. *Race*: White. *Height*: 5'11".
Weight: 182 lbs. *Education:* 10 years. *Prior occupation:* Carpenter.
County of conviction: Tom Green. *Age at time of execution:* 36.

Sentenced to death for: Convicted of capital murder in the death of Betty Stotts, age 43, a ticket teller at the Bolero Drive-In in Kerrville. On June 16, 1979, Woolls entered the ticket booth of the drive-in, hit Ms. Stotts in the head with a blunt instrument, stabbed her repeatedly, and then set her on fire. Woolls took $600 from the cash register, stole Ms. Stotts' car, and drove it into the Drive-In. Stotts' car was recognized, and Woolls was arrested on site, the stolen cash was in his pocket. Woolls was said to be under the influence of Valium and beer.

Received at Death Row: November 15, 1979. Time on death row: 2,470 days, (6.77 years).

Last meal: Two cheeseburgers, fries, and iced tea. Later requested chocolate cake.

Last statement: Goodbye to my family. I love all of you. I'm sorry for the victim's family. I wish I could make it up to them. I want those out there to keep fighting the death penalty.

Pronounced dead: 12:23 A.M.

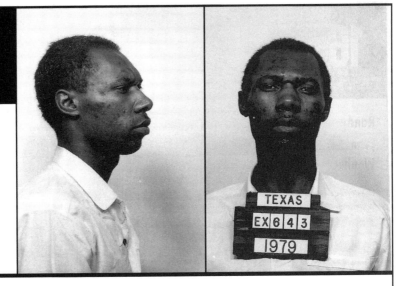

17

Larry Smith

Executed:
August 22, 1986

Personal Data: *Born*: August 26, 1955. *Race*: Black. *Height:* n/a. *Weight:* n/a. *Education:* n/a. *Prior occupation:* Laborer. *County of conviction:* Dallas. *Age at time of execution:* 30.

Sentenced to death for: Convicted of killing the night manager (Mike Mason) of a 7-Eleven store in Dallas on February 3, 1978. Mason and Fred Norris were working the midnight shift when Larry Smith and Gloster Ray Smith entered the store at 3:15 A.M. and demanded the safe be opened. Mason did not have the two keys needed to open the safe. Smith then took the cash drawer and shot Mason once in the back of the head as he lay face down on the floor.

Received at Death Row: September 19, 1979. Time on death row: 2,529 days, (6.93 years).

Last meal: Smothered steak and gravy, french fries, lemon pie, and Coke.

Last statement: Tell my mother I love her and continue on without me. Tell the guys on death row to continue their struggle to get off death row. That's about it.

Pronounced dead: 12:24 A.M.

18

Chester Le Wicker

Executed:
August 26,
1986

| PHOTOGRAPHS NOT AVAILABLE |

Personal Data: *Born*: August 28, 1948. *Race*: White. *Height*: 6'1". *Weight*: n/a. *Education*: 10 years. *Prior occupation:* Shrimper. *County of conviction:* Galveston. *Age at time of execution:* 37.

Sentenced to death for: Convicted in the April 1980 slaying of Suzanne C. Kruth, 22. Kruth was abducted from a Beaumont shopping center and taken to an isolated location near Galveston Beach. Wicker choked her, then buried her alive. Wicker confessed to the crime and led officials to the location of the body.

Received at Death Row: March 5, 1981. Time on death row: 1,999 days, (5.48 years).

Last meal: Lettuce and tomatoes.

Last statement: I love you.

Pronounced dead: 12:20 A.M.

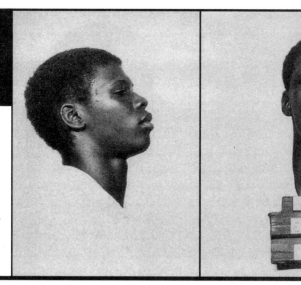

19

Michael Wayne Evans

Executed:
December 4, 1986

Personal Data: *Born*: November 13, 1986. *Race*: Black. *Height:* n/a. *Weight:* n/a. *Education:* n/a. *Prior Occupation:* Auto mechanic. *County of conviction:* Harris. *Age at time of execution:* 30.

Sentenced to death for: Evans was convicted of capital murder in the June 1977 shooting death of 36-year-old Elvira Guerrero during a robbery in the Oak Cliff area of Dallas. Guerrero, a pianist with the Second Mexican Baptist Church in Oak Cliff, was leaving church with friend Mario Garza when they were abducted by Evans and his co-defendant, Earl Stanley Smith. In a statement to police, Evans admitted robbing Guerrero of $40, shooting her twice, and then cutting her face with a carpet knife as she prayed to God to forgive her attacker. Garza was also found shot to death. Earl Stanley Smith received a life sentence for murder.

Received at Death Row: September 8, 1987. Time on death row: 3,009 days, (8.24 years).

Last meal: Declined last meal.

Last statement: I want to say I'm sorry for the things I've done and I hope I'm forgiven. I don't hold nothing against no one. Everyone has treated me well and I know it's not easy for them. That's all, I'm sorry.

Pronounced dead: 12:21 A.M.

20

Richard Andrade

Executed:
December 18, 1986

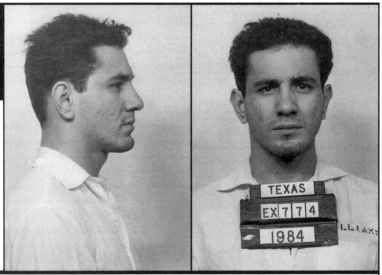

Personal Data: *Born*: April 4, 1961. *Race*: Hispanic. *Height*: 5'10". *Weight*: 169 lbs. *Education*: 7 years. *Prior occupation:* House leveller, forklift operator. *County of conviction:* Nueces. *Age at time of execution:* 25.

Sentenced to death for: Convicted of stabbing Cordelia Mae Guevara more than 14 times in the course of sexually assaulting her in Corpus Christi on March 20, 1984.

Received at Death Row: November 9, 1984. Time on death row: 769 days, (2.10 years).

Last meal: Pizza, pinto beans, Spanish rice, and cake.

Last statement: None.

Pronounced dead: 12:32 AM.

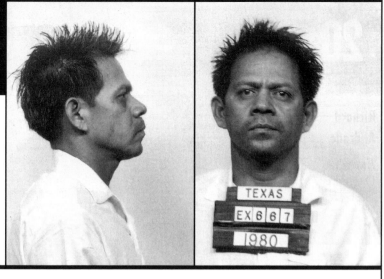

21

Ramon Hernandez

Executed: January 30, 1987

Personal Data: *Born*: March 2, 1942. *Race*: Hispanic. *Height*: 5'3". *Weight*: 130 lbs. *Education:* 9 years. *Prior Occupation*: Welder. *County of conviction:* El Paso. *Age at time of execution:* 44.

Sentenced to death for: Convicted of capital murder in the June 20, 1980, shooting death of Oscar Martin Frayre, a mechanic at a gas station in El Paso. Frayre, who was staying overnight at the station, was shot three times after Hernandez broke in and robbed the station.

Received at Death Row: September 30, 1980. Time on death row: 2,313 days, (6.34 years).

Last meal: Beef tacos, beef enchiladas, jalapeno peppers, salad, onion, hot sauce, shredded cheese, and coffee.

Last statement: Only to my wife: I love her. Only to my kids: I love my kids. [Looking at his wife] I will always love you. You know that.

Pronounced dead: 1:13 AM.

22

Eliseo Hernandez Moreno

Executed:
March 4,
1987

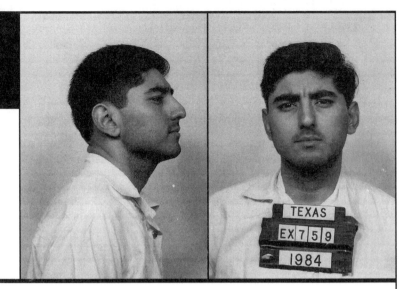

TEXAS
EX 7 5 9
1984

Personal Data: *Born*: September 15, 1959. *Race*: Hispanic. *Height*: 5'9". *Weight*: 155 lbs. *Education*: 10 years. *Prior occupation:* Mechanic. *County of conviction:* Fort Bend. *Age at time of execution:* 27.

Sentenced to death for: Moreno was convicted of capital murder in the October 11, 1983, shooting death of Texas Department of Public Safety Trooper Russell Lynn Boyd near Hempstead, Texas. Boyd, 25, was one of six people prosecutors said Moreno killed during a 160-mile crime spree that started in College Station with the slaying of his brother-in-law, Juan Garza, and Garza's wife, Esther Garza. Boyd was shot to death after stopping Moreno on Texas 6 north of Hempstead for a traffic violation. Moreno was also charged in the shooting deaths of James Bennatte, 62, Allie Wilkins, 79, and Ann Bennatt, 70, in Hempstead. Moreno later kidnapped a family of five and forced them to drive him to Pasadena. He then abducted a Friendswood man, who at gunpoint, drove Moreno south on U.S. 59 toward the Rio Grande Valley. DPS officers stopped the car at a roadblock in Wharton County and arrested Moreno. In October 1985, Moreno pleaded guilty to murder in the Garza killings and was given a 45-year sentence. Prosecutors said Moreno killed the Garzas because they wouldn't help him find his estranged wife.

Received at Death Row: February 14, 1984. Time on death row: 1,114 days, (3.05 years).

Last meal: Four cheese enchiladas, two fish patties, french fries, milk, catsup, and lemon pie.

Last statement: I'm here because I'm guilty. I have no grudges against anyone. I am paying according to the laws of the State of Texas.

Pronounced dead: 12:19 A.M.

23

Anthony Charles Williams

Executed:
May 28, 1987

Personal Data: *Born*: November 8, 1959. *Race:* Black. *Height*: 5'9". *Weight*: 169 lbs. *Education*: 11 years. *Prior occupation:* Carpenter. *County of conviction:* Harris. *Age at time of execution:* 27.

Sentenced to death for: June 1978 death of Vickie Lynn Wright, 13, who was abducted from a bowling alley, sexually assaulted, and then beaten to death with a board.

Received at Death Row: November 8, 1978. Time on death row: 3,123 days, (8.56 years).

Last meal: Fish, tartar sauce, french fries, catsup, white bread, and milk.

Last statement: Mother, I am sorry for all the pain I've caused you. Please forgive me. Take good care of yourself. Ernest & Otis: watch out for the family. Thank all of you who have helped me.

Pronounced dead: 12:22 A.M.

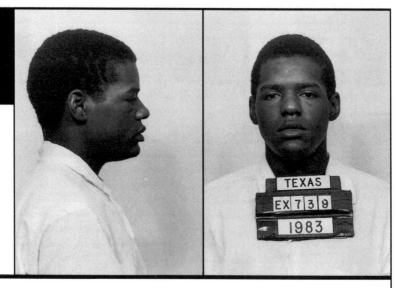

24

Elliot Rod Johnson

Executed: June 24, 1987

Personal Data: *Born*: August 17, 1958. *Race*: Black. *Height*: 5'7". *Weight*: 164 lbs. *Education*: n/a. *Prior occupation*: n/a. *County of conviction*: Jefferson. *Age at time of execution*: 38.

Sentenced to death for: Johnson was convicted of capital murder in the April 1982 execution-style shooting death of 67-year-old Joseph Granado during a robbery at Granado's Jewelry store. Store clerk Arturo Melendez, 45, was also killed in the robbery. Both victims were shot in the head at close range after being ordered to lay on the floor. A quantity of jewelry taken in the robbery was later found at the home of Johnson's co-defendant, Maurice Andrews of Port Arthur.

Received at Death Row: May 27, 1983. Time on death row: 1,489 days, (4.08 years).

Last meal: Cheeseburger and fries.

Last statement: I am very sorry for bringing all the pain and hurt to the family. I hope you find it in your heart to forgive me. Try not to worry too much about me. Remember one thing, Mother, I love you.

Pronounced dead: 12:55 A.M.

25

John R. Thompson

Executed:
July 8,
1987

Personal Data: *Born*: January 27, 1955. *Race*: White. *Height:* n/a. *Weight:* n/a. *Education:* n/a. *Prior occupation:* Laborer. *County of conviction:* Bexar. *Age at time of execution:* 32.

Sentenced to death for: Thompson was convicted of capital murder in the May 1977 shooting death of 70-year-old Mary Kneupper during a robbery attempt at her mini-storage business in San Antonio. Kneupper was shot in the neck with a .45-caliber pistol and later died at a San Antonio hospital.

Received at Death Row: September 25, 1978. Time on death row: 3,208 days, (8.79 years).

Last meal: Freshly squeezed orange juice.

Last statement: None.

Pronounced dead: 12:20 A.M.

Joseph Starvaggi

Executed:
September 10, 1987

Personal Data: *Born*: November 1, 1952. *Race*: White. *Height*: 5'9". *Weight*: 154 lbs. *Education:* n/a. *Prior occupation:* n/a. *County of conviction:* Montgomery. *Age at time of execution*: 34.

Sentenced to death for: Starvaggi was convicted in the November 19, 1976, shooting death of 43-year-old John Denson, a Montgomery County juvenile probation officer and reserve deputy sheriff, during a burglary at the officer's home in Magnolia. Starvaggi admitted during his trial that he went to Denson's home with two accomplices to steal his gun collection. Starvaggi shot Denson when the officer struggled with one of the intruders and wrestled his gun away. Starvaggi said he then shot Denson two more times to "keep him from suffering." Denson's 13-year-old daughter, who was taken upstairs with her mother, testified that she heard her father beg for mercy after he was shot once, saying, "I beg of you, don't do this." The accomplices reportedly urged Starvaggi to kill Denson's wife and daughter, but he refused, saying he only killed "dopers and pigs." Both co-defendants, Glenn Earl Martin and G. W. Green, were convicted of capital murder in Montgomery County. Martin was sentenced to life in prison, and Green was given the death penalty and was executed November 12, 1992 (See Entry 42, G. W. Green).

Received at Death Row: March 17, 1978. Time on death row: 3,426 days, (9.39 years).

Last meal: Declined last meal.

Last statement: None.

Pronounced dead: 12:30 A.M.

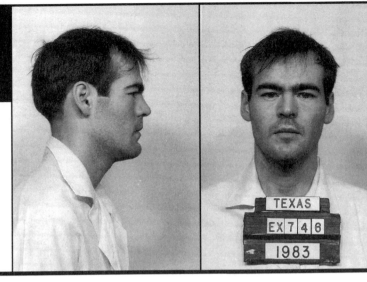

27

Robert Streetman

Executed:
January 7, 1988

TEXAS
EX 7 4 6
1983

Personal Data: *Born:* n/a. *Race:* White. *Height:* 5'11". *Weight:* 150 lbs. *Education:* 9 years. *Prior occupation:* Derrick hand. *County of conviction:* Hardin. *Age at time of execution:* 27.

Sentenced to death for: Convicted in the December 1982 robbery-slaying of 44-year-old Christine Baker of Kountez. Baker was shot in the head with a .22-caliber rifle while she sat knitting and watching television in the living room of her home, four miles south of Kountze. The fatal shot was fired through a window from outside the residence. Streetman and three other men had planned to rob Baker and her husband, Nyle, of $180,000 they believed the couple had in the home. Court records indicate the couple kept about $50,000 in cash and cashier's checks in the residence, but only Mrs. Baker's purse, and the $1 in change inside, was taken. Streetman, who began a life of crime upon becoming involved with drugs at age 8, reportedly told an accomplice on the way to the Baker home that he was "going to do something I've always wanted to do – kill another human being." Streetman's accomplice Gary Wayne Holden pleaded guilty to theft and was given 10-years probation for testimony against Streetman. Accomplice David Kirkindoll was given 45 years for burglary of a habitation. Johnny Johnson, Kirkindoll's step-father, who helped plan the robbery, was given immunity in the case.

Received at Death Row: August 11, 1983. Time on death row: 1,610 days, (4.41 years).

Last meal: ½ dozen scrambled eggs, flour tortillas, french fries, and catsup.

Last statement: None.

Pronounced dead: 3:26 A.M.

28

Donald Gene Franklin

Executed: November 3, 1988

TEXAS
EX 5 4 6
1976

Personal Data: *Born*: September 21, 1951. *Race*: Black. *Height*: 6'0". *Weight*: 198 lbs. *Education:* n/a. *Prior occupation:* n/a. *County of conviction:* Nueces. *Age at time of execution:* 37.

Sentenced to death for: Franklin was convicted of capital murder in connection with the death of Mary Margaret Moran of San Antonio on July 25, 1975. Moran was kidnapped as she approached her car in the parking lot of the Audie L. Murphy Memorial Veteran's Administration Hospital following her shift. Franklin was seen by two witnesses driving his car at a high rate of speed from the parking lot, where Moran's car was later found. Franklin was found at his home several hours later, after police traced the license number of his car. Police found his pants soaking in a pail of bloody water, found several of the nurse's personal items in a trash can. Five days later, Moran was found, nude and barely alive in a field near the hospital. She suffered from irreversible shock and died the next morning.

Received at Death Row: May 5, 1976. Time on death row: 4,565 days, (12.51 years).

Last meal: Hamburger, french fries, and catsup.

Last statement: None.

Pronounced dead: 12:30 A.M.

29

Raymond Landry

Executed:
December 13, 1988

TEXAS
EX 7 3 8
1983

Personal Data: *Born:* n/a. *Race:* Black. *Height:* 6'10". *Weight:* 198 lbs. *Education:* n/a. *Prior occupation:* n/a. *County of conviction:* Harris. *Age at time of execution:* 39.

Sentenced to death for: Convicted of capital murder in the August 6, 1982, shooting death of 33-year-old Kosmas Prittis, owner of the Dairy Maid restaurant in the 7100 block of East Bellfort in Houston. Prittis was robbed of more than $2,300 and then shot in the head while he and his family were closing up the restaurant. Witnesses testified that Landry slapped Prittis' wife and pointed a gun at the children before fleeing. Landry was arrested three days after the shooting at his home in the 7300 block of Eisenhower. Police found a bank bag from the restaurant at the house.

Received at Death Row: May 24, 1983. Time on death row: 2,030 days, (5.56 years).

Last meal: Declined last meal.

Last statement: None.

Pronounced dead: 12:45 A.M.

Note: Two minutes into the procedure, the tube attached to his right arm sprang a leak, spraying solution into the air and halting the execution. It took 14 minutes to reinsert the lethal injection needle and restart the execution. Officials blamed the delay on a mechanical problem caused by Landry's muscular arms and previous drug use.

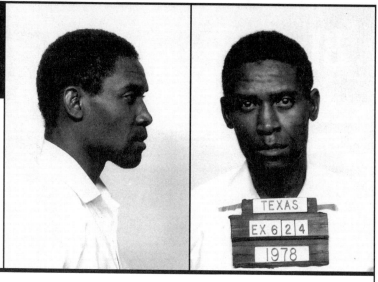

30

Leon Rutherford King

Executed:
March 22, 1989

TEXAS
EX 6 2 4
1978

Personal Data: *Born*: May 22, 1944. *Race*: Black. *Height*: 6'2". *Weight*: 176 lbs. *Education level:* 10 years. *Prior occupation:* bricklayer. *County of conviction:* Harris. *Age at time of execution:* 44.

Sentenced to death for: King and Allan Ray Carter abducted Michael Clayton Underwood, 26, and his 19-year-old girlfriend at gunpoint from a Houston night club on April 10, 1976. King and Carter took Underwood and his girlfriend to a remote area where Underwood was beaten to death with the butt of a shotgun as the young girl was forced to watch. The woman was raped and sodomized and later identified King and Carter as her attackers.
Co-defendant: Allan Ray Carter was sentenced to life in prison because he was 16 years old at the time of the crime.

Received at Death Row: December 5, 1978. Time on death row: 3,760 days, (10.30 years).

Last meal: Declined last meal.

Last statement: I would like to tell Mr. Richard [Richard Wells, a witness] I appreciate what you've done for me. I love you.

Pronounced dead: 12:27 A.M.

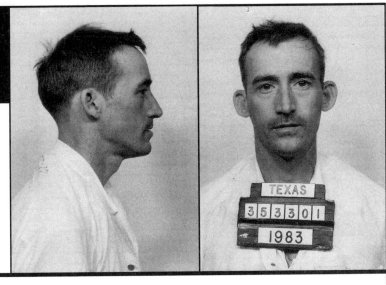

31.

Stephen A. McCoy

Executed: May 24, 1989

Personal Data: *Born*: December 17, 1948. *Race*: White. *Height*: 6'. *Weight*: 175 lbs. *Education level:* 7 years (GED). *Prior occupation:* Electrician. *County of conviction:* Harris. *Age at time of execution:* 40.

Sentenced to death for: McCoy was convicted of capital murder in the rape/strangulation death of 18-year-old Cynthia Johnson in Houston on January 1, 1981. Johnson was abducted by McCoy and co-defendants James Emery Paster and Gary Louis LeBlanc after her car broke down while returning from a New Year's Eve party. Evidence showed that McCoy raped the woman and then held her legs while Paster and LeBlanc strangled her with electrical wire. The three men were tied to the October 1980 murder for hire of Robert Edward Howard and the November 1980 rape and stabbing of Diane Trevino Oliver. Paster was sentenced to death for the shooting of Howard and life in prison for Johnson's murder. LeBlanc testified for the state and was given a 35-year sentence for murder. McCoy, who was in prison on a five-year sentence for burglary when charged in the Johnson murder, was also charged with accessory to murder and given a concurrent 30-year prison term. Courtroom testimony indicated that Johnson was killed because McCoy and his co-defendants agreed that they would each kill someone in front of each other and thus seal their mutual trust in blood.
Note: Paster was executed September 20, 1989. (See Entry 32, James Emery Paster).

Received at Death Row: August 2, 1984. Time on death row: 1,756 days, (4.81 years).

Last meal: Cheeseburger, french fries, and strawberry milkshake.

Last statement: None.

Pronounced dead: 12:25 A.M.

32

James Emery Paster

Executed:
September 20, 1989

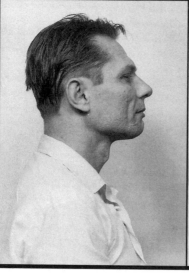

Personal Data: *Born*: January 30, 1945. *Race*: White. *Height*: 5'8". *Weight*: 156 lbs. *Education level:* 12 years. *Prior occupation:* Cook. *County of conviction:* Harris. *Age at time of execution:* 44.

Sentenced to death for: Paster was convicted of capital murder in the shooting death of 38-year-old Robert Edward Howard in Houston on October 25, 1980. Howard was shot in the head outside a southeast Houston lounge where Paster worked. Testimony supported allegations that Howard's ex-wife, Trudy, hired Paster to kill her former husband for $1,000. She was convicted of murder with a deadly weapon and sentenced to life in prison. Along with Paster, 40-year-old Gary L. LeBlanc and 38-year-old Stephen McCoy were implicated in the contract slaying of Howard as well as the January 1981 rape/strangulation death of 18-year-old Cynthia Johnson of Conroe and the November 1980 rape/stabbing death of 27-year-old Diane Trevino Oliver near Channelview.

Received at Death Row: November 22, 1983. Time on death row: 2,129 days, (5.83 years).

Last meal: T-bone steak, kinner salad, french fries, and watermelon.

Last statement: I hope Mrs. Howard can find peace in this.

Pronounced dead: 12:17 A.M.

33

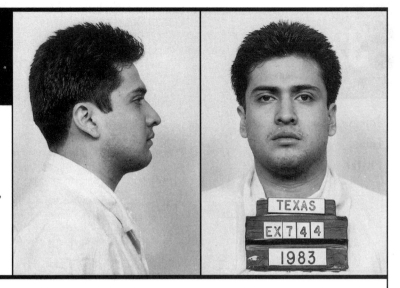

Carlos De Luna

Executed:
December 7, 1989

Personal Data: *Born:* March 15, 1962 *Race:* Hispanic. *Height:* 5'8". *Weight:* 185 lbs. *Education:* 9 years. *Prior occupation:* Electrician. *County of conviction:* Nueces. *Age at time of execution:* 27.

Sentenced to death for: Convicted in the February 2, 1983, robbery-slaying of 24-year-old Wanda Jean Lopez, a Corpus Christi service station clerk. Police said Lopez was stabbed to death minutes after she phoned police and attempted to describe her assailant to the dispatcher. Her final words recorded by police were: "You want it (money). I'll give it to you. I'll give it to you. I'm not going to do nothing to you. Please." De Luna took an undeteremined amount of money and fled on foot. Police found him hiding under a truck parked in the area. De Luna contended that another person killed Lopez and that he ran so he would not be implicated.

Received at Death Row: July 6, 1983. Time on death row: 2,326 days, (6.37 years).

Last meal: Declined last meal.

Last statement: I want to say that I hold no grudges. I hate no one. I love my family. Tell everyone on death row to keep the faith and don't give up.

Pronounced dead: 12:24 A.M.

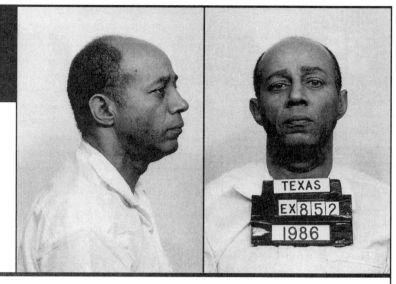

34

Jerome Butler

Executed:
April 21, 1990

TEXAS
EX852
1986

Personal Data: *Born*: April 7, 1936 *Race*: Black. *Height*: 5'6". *Weight*: 141 lbs. *Education*: 9 years (GED). *Prior occupation:* Delivery driver. *County of conviction:* Harris. *Age at time of execution:* 54.

Sentenced to death for: Butler was convicted of capital murder in the shooting death of 67-year-old Nathan Oakley, a Houston cab driver, on June 17, 1986. Butler hailed Oakley's cab at the intersection of Blodgett and Scott at 4 P.M. After riding a short distance, Butler pulled out a pistol and shot Oakley three times in the back of the head. The prosecutor said Oakley's pockets were turned inside out and all his money was missing. Oakley, who drove a Skyjack cab, was believed to have been carrying more than $300. Prosecutors said Butler may have killed Oakley because the cab driver recognized him as the man who killed his good friend, A.C. Johnson, in 1973. Ironically, State District Judge Wallace Moore presided over both the Johnson murder case and the Oakley capital murder case.

Received at Death Row: November 26, 1986. Time on death row: 1,242 days, (3.40 years).

Last meal: T-bone steak, four pieces of chicken (two breasts and two legs), fresh corn, and iced tea.

Last statement: I wish everybody a good life. Everything is O.K.

Pronounced dead: 12:26 A.M.

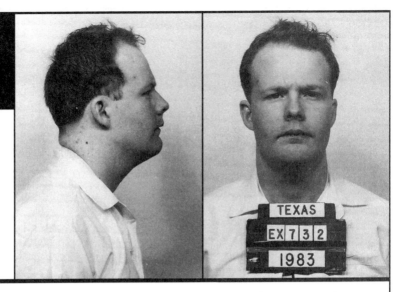

35

Johnny R. Anderson

Executed:
May 17, 1990

Personal Data: *Born*: December 28, 1959. *Race*: White. *Height*: 5'9". *Weight*: 185 lbs. *Education level*: 6 years. *Prior occupation:* Mechanic. *County of conviction:* Jefferson. *Age at time of execution:* 30.

Sentenced to death for: Shot to death his brother-in-law, Ronald Gene Goode, 22, of Kountze, in a scheme to collect insurance money. Anderson, his sister, the victim's wife, and her mother conspired to kill Goode to collect $67,000. The victim's widow and Anderson's sister were both convicted of capital murder and sentenced to life in prison.
Note: Anderson was named as a suspect in a December 1984 stabbing incident on death row. Death row inmate Kenneth D. Dunn was stabbed seven times in a dayroom after he and Anderson allegedly argued over a television program. Dunn, stabbed with a fanguard, was treated at the unit and released back to his cell.

Received at Death Row: February 15, 1983. Time on death row: 2,648 days, (7.25 years).

Last meal: Three hamburgers, french fries, chocolate ice cream with nuts, and iced tea.

Last statement: I would like to point out that I have written a statement and the warden will give you a copy. I still proclaim I am innocent, and that's all I have to say. [See Appendix 1.]

Pronounced dead: 12:30 A.M.

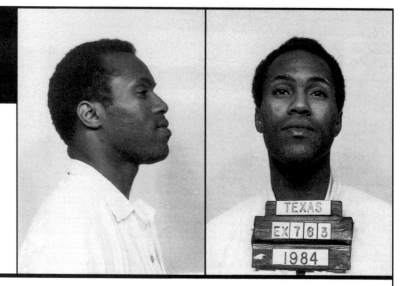

36

James Smith

Executed:
June 26, 1990

Personal Data: *Born*: October 19, 1952. *Race*: Black. *Height*: 5'10". *Weight*: 158 lbs. *Education level*: 14 years. *Prior occupation*: Retail merchant. *County of conviction*: Harris. *Age at time of execution*: 37.

Sentenced to death for: Convicted in the March 1983 shooting death of Larry Don Rohus during a robbery of offices inside the International Trade Center Building in Houston. Rohus, district manager for the Union Life Insurance Company, and another employee were in the company's cashier's office when Smith approached with a pistol and demanded money. When the second employee fled behind a filing cabinet, Rohus complied with Smith's instructions and placed an undetermined amount of money inside a small trash can and placed it on a table near the robber. As Rohus began to walk away, Smith called him back and fired a shot as Rohus pleaded for his life. Rohus ran, but was shot through the heart and died. Smith was arrested a short time later in a nearby apartment complex after being pursued on foot by one of Rohus' co-workers, a businessman on the street, and a crew of workers at the apartment comples.
Note: At one point during the jury selection of his trial, Smith ran from the courthouse. He was captured several blocks away by a police officer.

Received at Death Row: April 1984. Time on death row: 2,273 days, (6.23 years).

Last meal: Yogurt.

Last statement: See Appendix 1.

Pronounced dead: 12:31 A.M.
Note: The U.S. Supreme Court voted in the case. The court had enough votes to support review of the inmate's case (4) but not enough votes to grant a stay (5). Court rules allowed the execution to proceed.

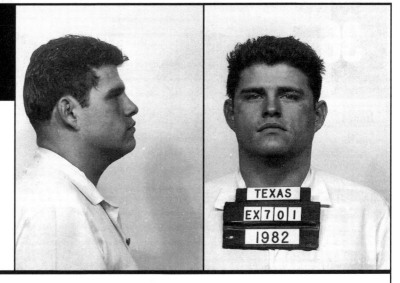

37

Mikel James Derrick

Executed: July 18, 1990

Personal Data: *Born*: February 10, 1957. *Race*: White. *Height*: 5'11". *Weight*: 201 lbs. *Education level:* 8 years. *Prior occupation:* Laborer. *County of conviction:* Harris. *Age at time of execution:* 33.

Sentenced to death for: Convicted in the October 1980 robbery-slaying of 32-year-old Edward Sonnier of Houston. Sonnier reportedly took Derrick home with him to his Montrose apartment, where the two smoked marijuana. Derrick told authorities he stabbed Sonnier 15 times when the victim allegedly made an unwelcome homosexual advance toward him. Derrick stole Sonnier's car, which he later stripped down with the help of friends. Police had no suspect in the killing until Derrick wrote to Harris County District Attorney John Holmes saying, "I killed a man to get his car." Derrick wrote from prison, where he was serving time for robbery. He said in the letter that he had heard his brother might be wrongly charged in the theft of Sonnier's car.

Received at Death Row: January 19, 1982. Time on death row: 3,102 days, (8.50 years).

Last meal: Ribeye steak, tossed green salad with blue cheese dressing, and baked potato with sour cream.

Last statement: I just ask everybody I ever hurt or done anything wrong to, to just forgive me for whatever wrongs I done to them.

Pronounced dead: 12:17 A.M.

38

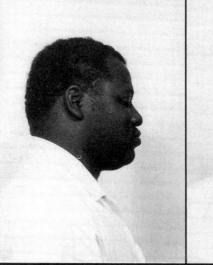

Lawrence Lee Buxton

Executed: February 26, 1991

Personal Data: *Born*: September 16, 1952. *Race*: Black. *Height*: 5'10".
Weight: 230 lbs. *Education level*: 10 years. *Prior occupation:* Truck driver/meat-cutter. *County of conviction:* Harris. *Age at time of execution:* 38.

Sentenced to death for: Buxton was convicted of capital murder in the September 19, 1980, shooting death of Joel Slotnik during a grocery store robbery in Houston. Buxton and two unknown co-defendants robbed the Safeway store at Fry Road and I-10 West. After the robbers had taken money from a cash register and left for the getaway car, Buxton shot Slotnik, a customer, because his five-year-old son, Aaron, would not get down on the floor as ordered. Slotnik died on September 23, 1980 from a neck wound.

Received at Death Row: July 5, 1983. Time on death row: 2,791 days, (7.65 years).

Last meal: Steak (filet mignon), pineapple upside-down cake, tea, punch, and coffee.

Last statement: I'm ready, Warden.

Pronounced dead: 12:21 A.M.

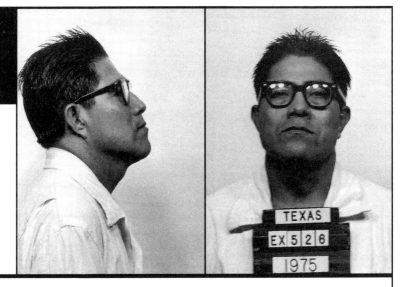

39

Ignacio Cuevas

Executed:
May 23,
1991

Personal data: *Born* July 31, 1931. *Race*: Hispanic. *Height*: 5'2". *Weight*: 140 lbs. *Education:* None. *Prior occupation:* House mover. *County of conviction:* Harris. *Age at time of execution:* 59.

Sentenced to death for: Cuevas and his two co-defendants (Fred Carasco and Rudy Dominquez) shot and killed two hostages, Julia Standley & Elizabeth Beseda in an escape attempt from the Huntsville Unit Library. Cuevas admits that he helped Carrasco in the escape attempt, but denies that he was armed at the time the murders occurred. Cuevas was convicted for the murder of Julia Standley. Cuevas escaped injury of any type during the last moments of the siege (reportedly, he fainted). Cuevas had been convicted twice of capital murder and twice sentenced to death.
Note: To make their escape, Cuevas and his co-defendants rigged a four-sided shield made of rolling chalkboards, lined with thick library books, and handcuffed eight hostages to the outside. Officials at first turned fire hoses on the shield, then gunfire erupted. Carrasco was said to have shot Elizabeth Beseda, and then himself.

Received at Death Row: May 30, 1975, at age 44. Time on death row: 2,629 days, (7.2 years).

Last meal: Chicken and dumplings, steamed rice, black-eyed peas, sliced bread, and iced tea.

Last statement: I am going to a beautiful place. Okay, Warden, roll 'em.

Pronounced dead: 12:18 A.M.

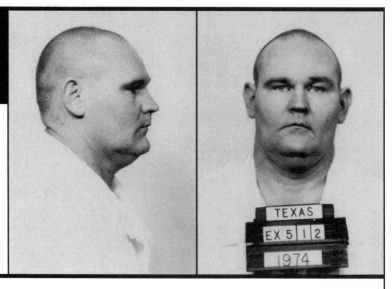

40

Jerry Joe Bird

Executed: June 17, 1991

TEXAS
EX 5 1 2
1974

Personal Data: *Born*: April 2, 1937. *Race*: White. *Height*: 5'11". *Weight*: 214 lbs. *Education level:* 14 years. *Prior occupation:* Machinist. *County of conviction:* Cameron. *Age at time of execution:* 54.

Sentenced to death for: Convicted of capital murder in the January 1974 slaying of Victor Trammel in Corpus Christi. Trammel and his wife, Jo Ellen, were robbed of a valuable antique gun collection by Bird and accomplice Emmett L. Korges. The two men, who gained entrance to the Trammels' house with claims they had guns to sell, handcuffed and bound the husband and wife and placed them in separate bedrooms. Mrs. Trammel testified she heard a muffled gunshot before she managed to slip from her constraints and flee the house through a rear window. She hid in a drainage ditch until realizing her home had been set afire. Her husband's badly burned body was found inside the house. He had been shot twice with a .22-caliber pistol fitted with a silencer.

Received at Death Row: September 16, 1974. Time on death row: 6,113 days, (16.75 years).

Last meal: Double cheeseburger with mustard, mayonnaise, pickles, onions, tomatoes, and iced tea.

Last statement: I don't think so. That's all. Go ahead. Start things rolling. [Mouthed "Hi Mom" to his mother.]

Pronounced dead: 12:21 A.M.

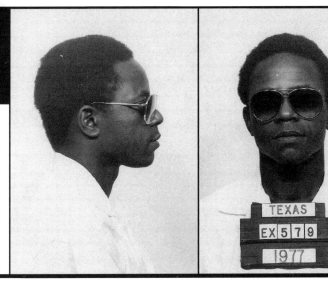

41

James Russell

Executed:
September 19, 1991

TEXAS
EX 5 7 9
1977

Personal Data: *Born*: March 5, 1949. *Race*: Black. *Height*: 5'9". *Weight*: 150 lbs. *Education level:* 10 years. *Prior occupation:* Musician. *County of conviction:* Fort Bend. *Age at time of execution:* 42.

Sentenced to death for: Convicted in the March 1974 abduction and shooting death of 24-year-old Thomas Robert Stearns of Houston. Stearns, manager of a Radio Shack store at 10810 W. Bellfort, was abducted after leaving his home and driven to a wooded area near Arcola, where he was shot twice in the head. Trial testimony indicated Russell killed Stearns because Stearns was a witness to an April 1972 robbery of the same Radio Shack store by Russell. Russell was out of jail on bond when Stearns was killed. He had been convicted in March 1977 of robbery and given a 50-year prison sentence based on testimony given by Stearns during a 1972 examining trial.

Received at Death Row: November 30, 1977. Time on death row: 5,053 days, (13.84 years).

Last meal: Apple.

Last statement: His exact final statement was not recorded, but it lasted three minutes. He thanked everybody who fought against his sentence. He spoke to his family and said he would carry their love with him.

Pronounced dead: 12:20 A.M.

42

G. W. Green

Executed:
November 12, 1991

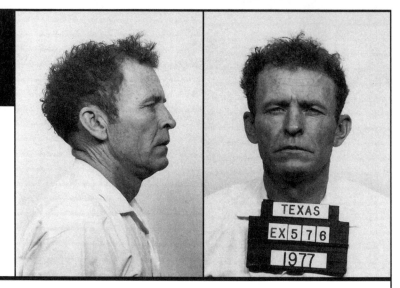

TEXAS
EX 5 7 6
1977

Personal Data: *Born*: November 21, 1936. *Race*: White. *Height*: 5'5".
Weight: 130 lbs. *Education level:* 14 years. *Prior occupation:* Cement mason.
County of conviction: Montgomery. *Age at time of execution:* 49.

Sentenced to death for: Convicted in the November 1976 shooting death of 43-year-old John Denson, a Montgomery County juvenile probation officer and reserve deputy sheriff, during a burglary at the officer's home in Magnolia. Green and accomplices Joseph Starvaggi and Glenn Earl Martin went to Denson's home to steal his gun collection. Starvaggi shot Denson when the officer struggled with one of the intruders and wrestled his gun away. Starvaggi then shot Denson two more times, but declined Green's alleged urgings to kill the officer's wife and 13-year-old daughter.
Note: Starvaggi was executed September 10, 1987. (See Entry 26, Joseph Starvaggi.)

Received at Death Row: October 13, 1977. Time on death row: 5,140 days, (14.08 years).

Last meal: Pizza, coffee, and tea.

Last statement: Let's do it, man. Lock and load. Ain't life a [expletive deleted]?

Pronounced dead: 12:17 A.M.

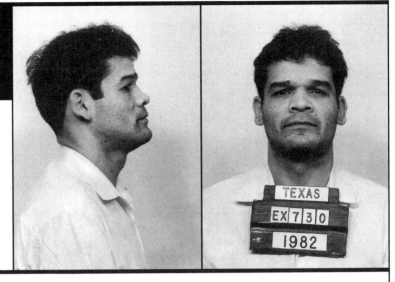

43

Joe Angel Cordova

Executed:
January 22, 1992

Personal Data: *Born*: March 29, 1952. *Race*: Hispanic. *Height*: 5'7". *Weight*: 143 lbs. *Education level*: 14 years. *Prior occupation:* Carpenter. *County of conviction:* Harris. *Age at time of execution:* 39.

Sentenced to death for: Cordova was sentenced to death for the February 27, 1982, murder/robbery of Masel Williams, 32. Williams was abducted from a phone booth on Little York near the Eastex Freeway and taken to a wooded area, where he was stripped and shot in the chest at close range with a shotgun. *Co-defendant*: Paul Guillory was convicted of aggravated robbery, sentenced to 15 years and paroled in March 1987.

Received at Death Row: December 30, 1982. Time on death row: 3,309 days, (9.07 years).

Last meal: Fried chicken, french fries, hot sauce, rolls, salad with thousand island dressing, and ice cream.

Last statement: None.

Pronounced dead: 12:18 A.M.

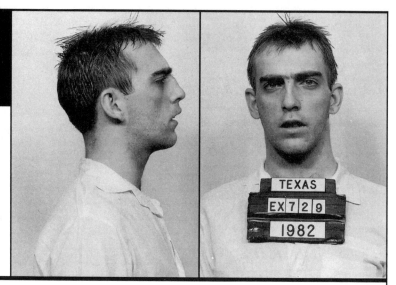

44

Johnny Frank Garrett

Executed: February 11, 1992

Personal Data: *Born*: December 24, 1963. *Race*: White. *Height*: 5'11". *Weight*: 152 lbs. *Education level:* 7 years. *Prior occupation:* Laborer. *County of conviction:* Potter. *Age at time of execution:* 28.

Sentenced to death for: Convicted in the October 1981 murder of Sister Tadea Benz, a 76-year-old nun of the St. Francis Convent in Amarillo. Sister Benz was raped, strangled, beaten, and stabbed in her second-floor room at the convent. Garrett's fingerprints were found at the convent located across the street from his home. In a statement to police, Garrett admitted breaking into the convent and said he strangled and raped the nun after she awoke and found him in her room.
Note: Garrett was 17 years of age at time of offense.

Received at Death Row: December 15, 1982. Time on death row: 3,343 days, (9.16 years).

Last meal: Ice cream.

Last statement: None.

Pronounced dead: 12:18 A.M.

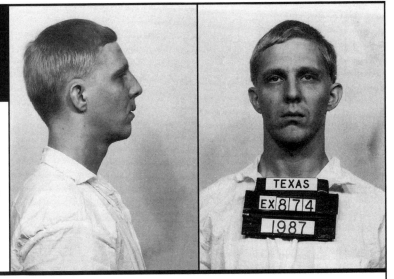

45

David M. Clark

Executed:
February 28, 1992

Personal Data: *Born*: March 5, 1959. *Race*: White. *Height*: 5'8". *Weight*: 145 lbs. *Education level*: 10 years (GED). *Prior occupation*: Construction. *County of conviction*: Brazos. *Age at time of execution*: 32.

Sentenced to death for: Clark was convicted and sentenced to die for the murders of Beverly Benninghoff and Charles Gears at their residence on February 18, 1987. Investigative reports indicate that the victims were shot, stabbed, and clubbed to death. A .25-caliber weaon, a club, and a knife were used in the slayings. Clark and three co-defendants were arrested for the murders on February 20, 1987.
Co-defendants: Mary Copeland was convicted of murder and sentenced to life. Gary Penuel was convicted of burglary and sentenced to 30 years.

Received at Death Row: June 30, 1987. Time on death row: 1,666 days, (4.56 years).

Last meal: Told officials he wanted to fast.

Last statement: None. But as he lay there he did say, "Praise the Lord," and seemed to be praying.

Pronounced dead: 1:38 A.M.

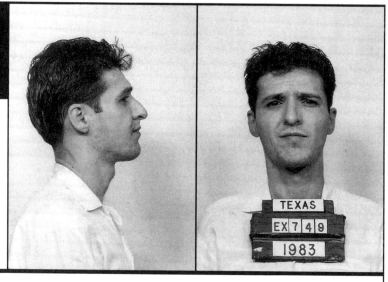

46

Edward Ellis

Executed:
March 3, 1992

Personal Data: *Born*: June 15, 1953. *Race*: White. *Height*: 5'8". *Weight*: 133 lbs. *Education level*: 10 years. *Prior occupation*: Welder/maintenance man. *County of conviction*: Harris. *Age at time of execution*: 38.

Sentenced to death for: Ellis was convicted of capital murder in the February 27, 1983, death of 74-year-old Bertie Elizabeth Eakens of Houston. Eakens' body was found March 1, 1983, in the bathtub of her apartment in the 2200 block of 18th Street. Her hands were handcuffed, and a pillow case had been tied around her neck so she suffocated. Her jewelry, checks, furs, and car were taken from the residence. Ellis had formerly worked as a maintenance man at Eakens' apartment complex and reportedly used a pass key to gain entrance to her apartment. The killing of Eakens and two other Houston women found in bathtubs came to be called the "bathtub slayings."

Received at Death Row: September 12, 1983. Time on death row: 3,093 days, (8.47 years).

Last meal: Steak, baked potato with butter, salad, biscuits, pineapple pie, and iced tea.

Last statement: I just want everyone to know that the prosecutor and Bill Scott are some sorry sons of bitches. [To his family he added that he loved them all.]
Note: Bill Scott was an inmate who testified against Ellis. Exact last statement was not recorded.

Pronounced dead: 3:39 A.M.
Note: Execution was delayed until U.S. Supreme Court refused a stay at approximately 3 A.M.

47

Billy Wayne White

Executed: April 23, 1992

Personal Data: *Born*: October 13, 1957. *Race*: Black. *Height*: 5'11". *Weight*: 167 lbs. *Education level:* 10 years. *Prior occupation:* Dump truck driver. *County of conviction:* Harris. *Age at time of execution:* 34.

Sentenced to death for: Convicted in the August 1976 robbery-slaying of 65-year-old Martha Spinks, co-owner of a Houston furniture store. Spinks and her husband, Alge, were closing their store when White entered, pulled a pistol and demanded money. Without provocation, he then shot Mrs. Spinks once in the face at point-blank range. White ordered Mr. Spinks to open the safe and then lie on the floor. When White dropped his pistol while attempting to steal rings and a watch from Mrs. Spinks' body, her husband grabbed the pistol and managed to fire two shots, striking White in the groin. White ran from the store, but was captured by police a quarter mile away after a car lot attendant who heard the shots flagged down a patrol car. Police found $269 in stolen money in White's pants pocket.

Received at Death Row: February 24, 1978. Time on death row: 5,170 days, (14.16 years).

Last meal: T-bone steak, french fries, and ice cream.

Last statement: None.

Pronounced dead: 12:58 A.M.

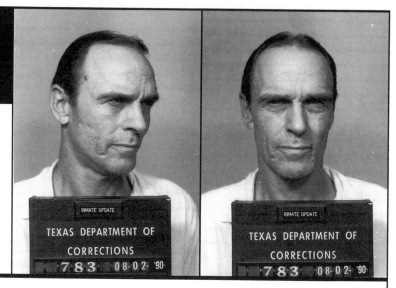

48

Justin Lee May

Executed: May 7, 1992

Personal Data: *Born:* April 26, 1946. *Race:* White. *Height:* 6'1". *Weight:* 185 lbs. *Education level:* 11 years. *Prior occupation:* Welder. *County of conviction:* Brazoria. *Age at time of execution:* 46.

Sentenced to death for: Convicted in the shooting death of 43-year-old Jeanetta Murdaugh during a robbery of the Western Auto Store she and her husband, Frank, owned and operated in Freeport. Mrs. Murdaugh died from two gunshot wounds to the head. Her husband was killed by four gunshots to the neck, chest, and back. Police believed the Murdaughs were two of five people robbed and killed by May during a two-week crime spree.
Co-defendant: Richard Allen Miles was convicted of robbery and murder, sentenced to 42 years and paroled on December 5, 1990.

Received at Death Row: February 20, 1985. Time on death row: 2,632 days, (7.21 years).

Last meal: Two cheeseburgers, catsup, french fries, and shake.

Last statement: Thanked his family.

Pronounced dead: 12:18 A.M.

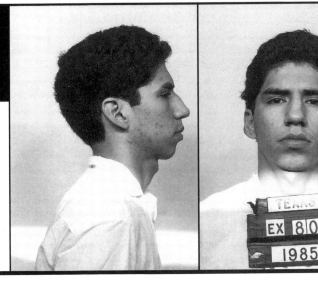

49

Jesus Romero, Jr.

Executed:
May 20, 1992

Personal Data: *Born*: February 3, 1965. *Race*: Hispanic. *Height*: 5'6".
Weight: 128 lbs. *Education level:* 11 years. *Prior occupation:* Laborer. *County of conviction*: Cameron. *Age at time of execution:* 27.

Sentenced to death for: Convicted in the December 1984 rape-slaying of 15-year-old Olga Perales near near San Benito. Romero and three co-defendants drove Perales to a remote location 1.3 miles west of State Highway 2520, where she was raped repeatedly and then beaten around the head with a pipe and stabbed twice in the chest with a knife. Her nude body was found the same day in a brushy area off Kilgore Road.
Co-defendants: Davis Losado was convicted of capital murdered, received the death penalty and was executed on June 4, 1997 (See Entry 127, Davis Losada). Jose F. Cardenas was convicted of capital murder and received a life sentence. Rafael Leyva, Jr., was convicted of sexual assault and given a 20-year sentence.

Received at Death Row: July 24, 1985. Time on death row: 2,555 days, (7.00 years).

Last meal: T-bone steak, baked potato, salad, vanilla shake, and chocolate ice cream.

Last statement: None.

Pronounced dead: 1:40 A.M.

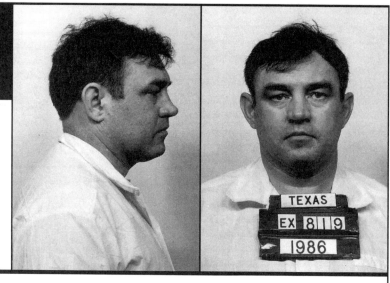

50

Robert Black, Jr.

Executed:
May 22,
1992

Personal Data: *Born*: January 31, 1947. *Race*: White. *Height*: 5'9". *Weight*: 200 lbs. *Education level:* 14 years. *Prior occupation:* Insurance salesman/electrician. *County of conviction:* Brazos. *Age at time of execution:* 45.

Sentenced to death for: Hired John Wayne Hearn to murder his wife, Sandra Black, for insurance money. The victim was found dead with two bullet wounds to the head. The house appeared to have been burglarized. During the investigation, evidence came into being that Robert Black had increased his wife's life insurance by $100,000 shortly before her death.
Co-defendant: John Wayne Hearn received life in prison concurrent with two life sentences in Florida.
Note: Black hired Hearn after Hearn responded to an ad Black placed in *Soldier of Fortune* magazine. The magazine was later ordered to pay $1.5 million in actual damages to Mrs. Black's son Gary W. Black and $400,000 to her mother.

Received at Death Row: February 26, 1986. Time on death row: 2,276 days, (6.24 years).

Last meal: T-bone steak, baked potato, bowl of lettuce, corn, roll, chocolate milkshake, and tea.

Last statement: None. Black began to recite the poem "High Flight" as the lethal injection began. After Black recited the line "And done a hundred things you have not thought of...," he gasped and stopped breathing.

Pronounced dead: 12:20 A.M.

51

Curtis L. Johnson

Executed: August 11, 1992

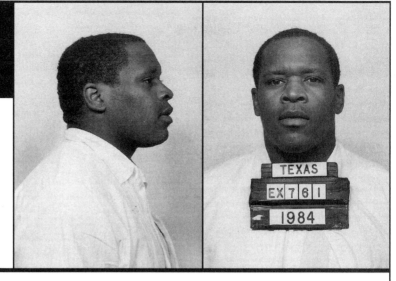

TEXAS
EX 7 6 1
1984

Personal Data: *Born*: April 22, 1954. *Race*: Black. *Height*: 5'9 ". *Weight*: 230 lbs. *Education level:* 10 years. *Prior occupation:* Laborer. *County of conviction:* Harris. *Age at time of execution:* 38.

Sentenced to death for: Shot to death Murray Dale Sweat, 25, in Houston. Sweat was shot once in the chest with a .38-caliber revolver when he returned to his apartment at 603 W. Saulnier and found Johnson and an accomplice in the kitchen. The two intruders were arrested six days later while committing aggravated robbery.
Co-defendant: Roy Junior Jones was convicted of burglary of a habitation with intent to commit theft and aggravated robbery and sentenced to 45 years.

Received at Death Row: March 21, 1984. Time on death row: 3,064 days, (8.39 years).

Last meal: Scrambled eggs, bacon, toast, jelly, butter, and strawberry milkshake.

Last statement: I want to thank my mother and my aunt for sticking by me and to tell that I love them very much. Everybody who participated in this is forgiven.

Pronounced dead: 12:16 A.M.

52

James Demouchette

Executed:
September 22, 1992

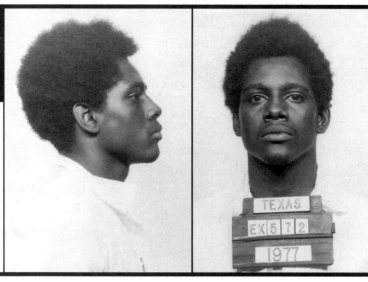

Personal Data: *Born:* n/a. *Race:* Black. *Height:* 5'10". *Weight:* 150 lbs. *Education level:* 9 years. *Prior occupation:* Painter. *County of conviction:* Harris. *Age at time of execution:* 37.

Sentenced to death for: Convicted in October 17, 1976 shooting deaths of Scott Sorrell, 19, Asst. Manager and his roommate Robert White, 20, at a Pizza Hut restaurant on Antoine Rd. in Northwest Houston. Both Sorrell and White were shot in the head with a .38-caliber revolver as they and restaurant manger Geoff Hambrick, 18, sat at a table with Demouchette and his brother, Christopher, after closing. Hambrick was also shot in the head by James Demouchette but survived his wound. Hambrick who slumped over the table and played dead, testified that the Demouchette brothers ransacked the back office, taking a sack of change and a piece of stereo equipment. Before leaving the restaurant, James Demouchette heard Sorrell choking on his own blood and shot him a second time. James then turned the gun on Hambrick a second time, but found it empty when he pulled the trigger. Christopher Demouchette surrendered to police the next morning and gave a written statement implicating himself and his brother in the shootings. James was arrested at his home that afternoon.
Note: James' capital murder and death sentence were overturned in 1981 by the Texas Court of Criminal Appeals on grounds that he had not been warned of his right to remain silent by the court-appointed psychologist prior to his competency examination in 1977. He was again convicted of capital murder in April 1983 and given the death penalty.
Co-defendant: Christopher Demouchette was convicted of capital murder and sentenced to life in prison.

Received at Death Row: August 3, 1977. Time on death row: 5,525 days, (15.14 years).

Last meal: Grilled steak, baked potato, any vegetable except squash or okra, and dessert and anything to drink except punch or milk.

Last statement: None.

Pronounced dead: 12:22 A.M.

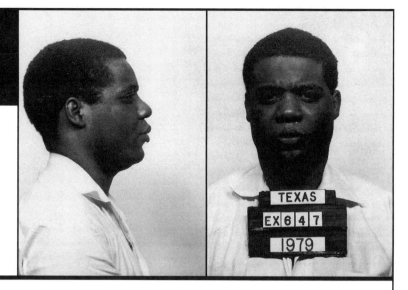

53

Jeffery Griffin

Executed: November 19, 1992

Personal Data: *Born:* January 3, 1955. *Race:* Black. *Height:* 5'6". *Weight:* 165 lbs. *Education level:* 4 years. *Prior occupation:* Laborer. *County of conviction:* Harris. *Age at time of execution:* 37.

Sentenced to death for: Convicted in the March 1979 abduction and stabbing death of 19-year-old David Sobotik, night manager at the One Stop Drive-In grocery at 3814 Fulton in Houston. Sobotik and 7-year-old Horatio DeLeon, who worked as an errand boy at the store, were abducted and led to an area about 10 blocks from the store, where both were repeatedly stabbed in a concise pattern around the heart. Sobotik was also robbed of personal items. The bodies of the two victims were found inside Sobotik's car the next morning. Griffin, himself, alerted the store's owner of the incident, saying he had seen the two victims abducted. When discrepancies were found in his story, he confessed to the murders. He was never tried in the death of DeLeon. Nor was he ever tried after being charged in the murder of 20-year-old Silvia Mendoza, whose slashed body was found inside a dumpster in Houston in July 1978.

Received at Death Row: November 30, 1979. Time on death row: 4,725 days, (12.95 years).

Last meal: T-bone (medium to well-done), french fries and catsup, whole kernel corn, sweet peas, lettuce and tomato salad with egg and French dressing, iced tea (sweet), saltines, ice cream, Boston cream pie, and rolls.

Last statement: n/a

Pronounced dead: 12:48 A.M.

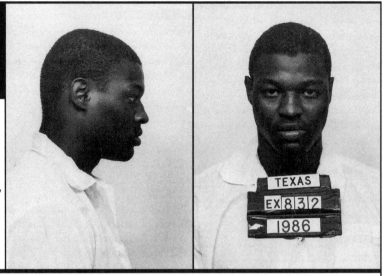

54

Kavin Lincecum

Executed: December 10, 1992

Personal Data: *Born:* June 17, 1963. *Race:* Black. *Height:* 5'10". *Weight:* 178 lbs. *Education level:* 10 years. *Prior occupation:* Laborer. *County of conviction:* Brazoria. *Age at time of execution:* 29.

Sentenced to death for: Convicted in the August 1985 abduction, attempted rape, and strangulation of Kathy Coppedge, a 35-year-old Brenham schoolteacher. Coppedge and her 11-year-old son, Casey, were abducted from a Brenham church parking lot and driven in their car to an isolated area about 13 miles west of Brenham. There, Lincecum attempted to rape Mrs. Coppedge, and then strangled her with a cord or rope when she resisted. At some point, he bound her hands behind her back with her purse strap. Her son's hands were also bound behind his back before he was placed in the trunk of the car, where he suffocated. Both bodies were found in the trunk of the car, which Lincecum abandoned. He took jewelry pieces from Mrs. Coppedge and gave them to his girlfriend. He also took the boy's shoes and later sold them to a friend for $7.

Received at Death Row: June 5, 1986. Time on death row: 2.378 days, (6.52 years).

Last meal: Declined last meal.

Last statement: None.

Pronounced dead: 12:18 A.M.

55

Carlos Santana

Executed:
March 23, 1993

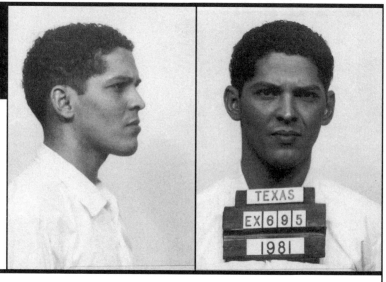

Personal Data: *Born:* October 10, 1952. *Race:* Hispanic. *Height:* 5'9". *Weight:* 147 lbs. *Education level:* 11 years. *Prior occupation:* Electrician. *County of conviction:* Harris. *Age at time of execution:* 40.

Sentenced to death for: Convicted in connection with the failed $1.1 million robbery of a Purolator Armored, Inc., van and the killing of 29-year-old security guard Oliver Flores in Houston on April 21, 1981. Testimony showed that Santana and accomplice James Ronald Meanes wore matching green military-like uniforms for a noon attack on the van in a department store parking lot in the 8500 block of the Gulf Freeway. A second security guard who survived the attack said Flores was shot even though he had not gone for his gun. Santana and Meanes were arrested shortly after the robbery in the 8900 block of Winkler. Police found a getaway car parked nearby and recovered two weapons, two green jumpsuits and the money from the van.
Co-defendant: James Ronald Meanes was convicted of capital murder, sentenced to death, and executed on December 15, 1998. (See Entry 164, James Ronald Meanes.)

Received at Death Row: November 9, 1981. Time on death row: 4,149 days, (11.37 years).

Last meal: Requested, "Justice, Temperance, with Mercy."

Last statement: Love is the answer, not hatred. I love all of you guys. I will see some of you in the state of heaven. Bye.

Pronounced dead: 2:54 A.M.

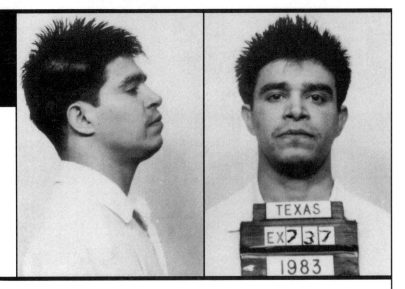

56

Ramon Montoya

Executed: March 25, 1993

Personal Data: *Born:* January 15, 1954. *Race:* Hispanic. *Height:* 5'3". *Weight:* 125 lbs. *Education level:* 7 years. *Prior occupation:* Laborer. *County of conviction:* Dallas. *Age at time of execution:* 38.

Sentenced to death for: Montoya was convicted of capital murder in the shooting death of Dallas police officer John R. Pasco. Pasco was shot once in the head after chasing Montoya in the vicinity of the Spanish Villa Apartments at 1818 Park Ave. He had gone to the apartments to check out residents' complaints about an armed man. Police said Montoya fired at Pasco's squad car as it pulled into the complex but did not hit the officer. Pasco called for help on the car radio and then gave chase on foot. Montoya said he ran from the patrolman to avoid being arrested for carrying a weapon. He said he fell during the chase and the gun fired while he was attempting to throw the weapon away.
Note: U.S. immigration officials said Montoya had earlier been deported on a weapons charge but had re-entered the country illegally.

Received at Death Row: May 19, 1983. Time on death row: 3,595 days, (9.85 years).

Last meal: Cheeseburger, french fries, ice cream, and Coke.

Last statement: None.

Pronounced dead: 12:18 A.M.

57

Darryl Elroy Stewart

Executed:
May 4,
1993

Personal Data: *Born:* April 2, 1955. *Race:* Black. *Height:* 5'7". *Weight:* 148 lbs. *Education level:* 12 years. *Prior occupation:* Auto mechanic. *County of conviction:* Harris. *Age at time of execution:* 38.

Sentenced to death for: Convicted in the February 1980 shooting death of 22-year-old Donna Kate Thomas inside her south Houston apartment. Stewart and Kelvin Kelly, who lived in the same apartment complex as the victim at 11710 Algonquin, were walking through the complex when they noticed Thomas' door open. Stewart asked Kelly for his .25-caliber pistol because he wanted to go in and see what he could steal. Kelly heard Thomas scream, "Oh, my God" and rushed in to see what was happening. Kelly said Stewart and Thomas were in a bedroom and that Stewart told her to undress. After she complied, Stewart placed her in a closet, where she was joined by her 4-year-old daughter when she entered the apartment. Stewart eventually removed the two from the closet and demanded sex from Thomas. When she refused and started crying, he became upset, put his pistol to her head, covered it with a pillow, and shot her twice. Stewart reportedly left the apartment with $50.

Received at Death Row: August 20, 1980. Time on death row: 4,626 days, (12.66 years).

Last meal: Steak, baked potato, garden salad, and tea.

Last statement: None.

Pronounced dead: 12:25 A.M.

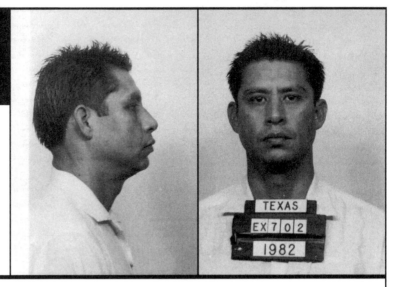

58

**Leonel
Torres
Herrera**

Executed:
May 12,
1993

Personal Data: *Born:* September 17, 1947. *Race:* Hispanic. *Height:* 5'11". *Weight:* 188 lbs. *Education level:* 11 years (GED). *Prior occupation:* Roofer. *County of conviction:* Cameron. *Age at time of execution:* 45.

Sentenced to death for: Convicted in the September 1981 shooting death of Enrique Carrisalez, a Los Fresnos police officer. Carrisalez was shot after stopping Herrera for speeding. Before the police officer died, he identified a police mug shot of Herrera as the man who shot him.

Received at Death Row: January 22, 1982. Time on death row: 4,126 days, (11.30 years).

Last meal: Declined last meal.

Last statement: I am innocent, innocent, innocent. Make no mistake about this, I owe society nothing. Continue the struggle for human rights, helping those who are innocent, especially Mr. Graham [death row inmate Gary Lee Graham, executed June 22, 2000]. I am an innocent man, and something very wrong is taking place tonight. May God bless you all. I am ready.

Pronounced dead: 4:49 A.M.

59

John Sawyers

Executed:
May 18, 1993

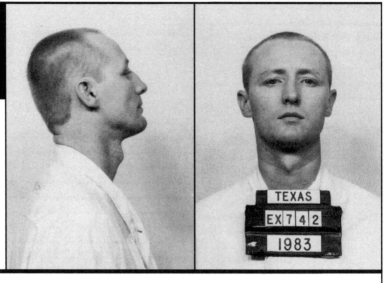

TEXAS
EX 7 4 2
1983

Personal Data: *Born:* July 30, 1955. *Race:* White. *Height:* 5'10". *Weight:* 165 lbs. *Education level:* 12 years. *Prior occupation:* Millwright. *County of conviction:* Harris. *Age at time of execution:* 38.

Sentenced to death for: Convicted in the February 1983 robbery-slaying of 67-year-old Ethyl Delaney at her Houston home. Delaney, who lived alone at 1834 Ojeman and worked as a notary public and property manager, was beaten to death with a cast-iron frying pan and robbed of her cash, jewelry (three rings), and car. Sawyers, a neighbor of Delaney's who had been to her home previously to have her notarize his personal papers, told police he ripped off the woman's pants, slapped her, put her on her bed, and hit her four times over the head with the skillet. He said the fourth blow broke the handle of the skillet. Testimony showed Sawyers later showed the stolen car and jewelry to friends and then pawned the jewelry for about $200. The pawn ticket and an accident Sawyers was involved in while driving Delaney's car led to his arrest.

Received at Death Row: June 21, 1983. Time on death row: 3,527 days, (9.66 years).

Last meal: Cheeseburger, french fries, and strawberry shake.

Last statement: None.

Pronounced dead: 12:23 A.M.

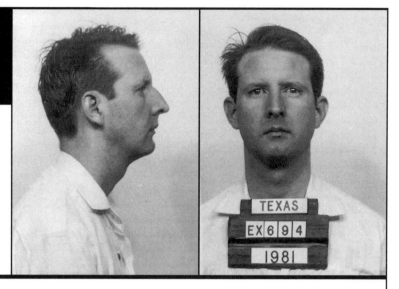

60

Markum Duff-Smith

Executed: June 29, 1993

TEXAS
EX694
1981

Personal Data: *Born:* January 14, 1947. *Race:* White. *Height:* 5'9". *Weight:* 146 lbs. *Education level:* 14 years. *Prior occupation:* Insurance investor. *County of conviction:* Harris. *Age at time of execution:* 46.

Sentenced to death for: The October 15, 1975, strangulation death of his wealthy adoptive mother, Getrude Duff-Smith Zabolio, at her home in the River Oaks neighborhood of Houston. Through two accomplices, Duff-Smith hired Allen Wayne Janecka to kill his mother so he could collect his inheritance. Duff-Smith promised to pay Janecka and co-conspirator Paul MacDonald a total of $10,000 for the murder. Court records show that Duff-Smith also wanted his stepfather, Dow Zabolio, killed at the same time, but he had traveled to Austria on business. Mrs. Zabolio's death was originally ruled a suicide based on two suicide notes found in her bedroom. Duff-Smith was not arrested in the case until 1979, when he was suspected of masterminding the murders of his sister and brother-in-law, Diana and John Wanstrath, and their 14-month-old son, Kevin, to gain control of their estate. The probe into Gertrude Zabolio's death was reopened and police learned that Duff-Smith had bragged to a friend about having his mother killed. *Co-defendants:* Paul MacDonald testified against Duff-Smith in his mother's murder trial, served a 16-year sentence for murder, and was paroled in November 1984.

Received at Death Row: October 20, 1981. Time on death row: 4,196 days, (11.50 years).

Last meal: None.

Last statement: I am the sinner of all sinners. I was responsible for the '75 and '79 cases. My trial was not just; it was not fair; they lied against me. I love all those on death row, and I will always hold them in my hands. Those who stood by me, I will always love you. Jim and Judy Peterson and Chaplain Lopez, I thank you for staying by my side.

Pronounced dead: 12:16 A.M.

61

Curtis Paul Harris

Executed:
July 1, 1993

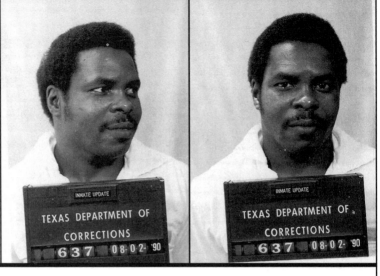

Personal Data: *Born:* August 31, 1961. *Race:* Black. *Height:* 5'5". *Weight:* 144 lbs. *Education level:* 8 years. *Prior occupation:* Laborer. *County of conviction:* Brazos. *Age at time of execution:* 31.

Sentenced to death for: Convicted of capital murder in the December 11, 1978, killing of Timmothy Michael Merka, 27, who was beaten to death with a tire iron and robbed after rendering assistance to Harris and three companions in rural Brazos County.
Note: Harris was 17 years of age at time of offense.
Co-defendants: Danny Ray Harris, Harris' brother, was convicted of capital murder, sentenced to death, and executed July 30, 1993 (See Entry 62, Danny Harris). James Charles Manuel was convicted of burglary and murder with a deadly weapon, sentenced to 25 years and released on October 27, 1989. Valarie Denise Rencher, turned state's evidence and was not sentenced to prison. She was 16 years old at the time of the crime.

Received at Death Row: June 7, 1979. Time on death row: 5,313 days, (14.56 years).

Last meal: Cheeseburger, ice cream, and water.

Last statement: None.

Pronounced dead: 12:27 A.M.

62

Danny Ray Harris

Executed:
July 30, 1993

Personal Data: *Born:* July 31, 1960. *Race:* Black. *Height:* 5'10". *Weight:* 156 lbs. *Education level:* 9 years. *Prior occupation:* Laborer. *County of conviction:* Brazos. *Age at time of execution:* 32.

Sentenced to death for: Convicted of capital murder in the December 11, 1978 killing of Timmothy Michael Merka, 27, who was beaten to death with a tire iron and robbed after rendering assistance to Harris and three companions in rural Brazos County.
Note: Harris was 17 years of age at time of offense.
Co-defendants: Curtis Harris, Harris' brother, was convicted of capital murder, sentenced to death, and executed July 1, 1993 (See Entry 61, Curtis Paul Harris). James Charles Manuel was convicted of burglary and murder with a deadly weapon, sentenced to 25 years, and released on October 27, 1989. Valarie Denise Rencher, 16, turned state's evidence and was not sentenced to prison.

Received at Death Row: February 25, 1980. Time on death row: 5,055 days, (13.85 years).

Last meal: God's saving grace, love, truth, peace and freedom.

Last statement: I would like to tell my family I love them very dearly, and I know they love me. I love all of the people who supported me all of these years. I would like to tell the Merka family I love them, too. I plead with all the teenagers to stop the violence and accept Jesus Christ and find victory. Today I have victory in Christ and I thank Jesus for taking my spirit into His precious hands. Thank you, Jesus.

Pronounced dead: 12:18 A.M.

63

Joseph Paul Jernigan

Executed: August 5, 1993

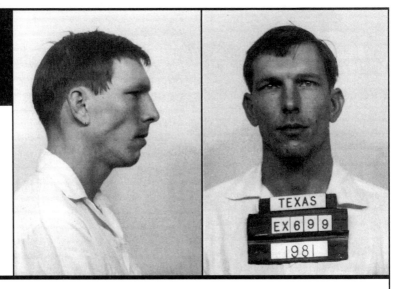

TEXAS
EX 6 9 9
1981

Personal Data: *Born:* January 31, 1954. *Race:* White. *Height:* 5'10". *Weight:* 152 lbs. *Education level:* 13 years. *Prior occupation:* Mechanic. *County of conviction:* Navarro. *Age at time of execution:* 39.

Sentenced to death for: Jernigan was convicted and sentenced to death for the July 3, 1981, murder of Edward Hale, 75, of Dawson, a community near Corsicana. Authorities said Hale was stabbed several times, then shot three times with his single-shot .410-gauge shotgun. Jernigan said that he killed Hale with a knife and a shotgun after the robbery because he feared that man would be able to identify him.
Co-defendant: Roy Dean Lamb was convicted of murder with a deadly weapon and sentenced to 30 years.

Received at Death Row: November 20, 1981. Time on death row: 4,422 days, (12.12 years).

Last meal: Two cheeseburgers, french fries, tossed salad with thousand island dressing, and iced tea.

Last statement: None.

Pronounced dead: 12:31 A.M.

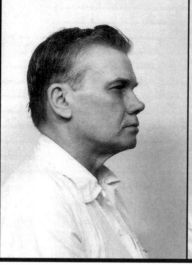 

David Holland

Executed: August 12, 1993

Personal Data: *Born:* July 7, 1935. *Race:* White. *Height:*5'11". *Weight:* 190 lbs. *Education level:* 13 years. *Prior occupation:* Dispatcher for trucking company. *County of conviction:* Jefferson. *Age at time of execution:* 58.

Sentenced to death for: Holland was sentenced to death for the July 16, 1985 robbery/slaying of Helen Jean Barnard, 29, a branch manager at Jefferson Savings and Loan in Beaumont. A teller at the office, Dianna Joy Jackson, 23, also was slain in the robbery.

Received at Death Row: February 26, 1986. Time on death row: 2,865 days, (7.85 years).

Last meal: Cheeseburger, french fries, and coffee.

Last statement: None.

Pronounced dead: 12:16 A.M.

65

Carl E. Kelly

Executed:
August 20,
1993

Personal Data: *Born:* March 27, 1959. *Race:* Black. *Height*: 6'2". *Weight:* 186 lbs. *Education level:* 11 years. *Prior occupation:* Laborer. *County of conviction*: McLennan. *Age at time of execution:* 34.

Sentenced to death for: Kelly was convicted of capital murder for his role in the September 1980 overnight robbery, abduction, and murder spree in Waco. Victims were Steven Pryon (convenience store clerk) and David Wade Riley (transient). Kelly allegedly shot both men, then threw their bodies over a cliff. *Co-defendant*: Thomas Graves was convicted of murder with a deadly weapon and sentenced to life in prison.

Received at Death Row: July 22, 1981. Time on death row: 4,543 days, (12.45 years).

Last meal: "Wild game or whatever is on the menu and cold lemonade." Served cheeseburger and french fries.

Last statement: I am an African warrior, born to breathe, and born to die.

Pronounced dead: 12:22 A.M.

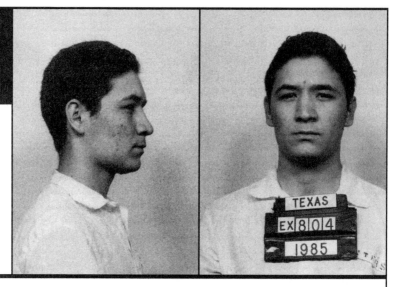

66

Ruben Montoya Cantu

Executed: August 24, 1993

Personal Data: *Born:* December 5, 1966. *Race:* Hispanic. *Height:* 5'10". *Weight:* 142 lbs. *Education level:* 9 years. *Prior occupation:* Laborer. *County of conviction:* Bexar. *Age at time of execution:* 26.

Sentenced to death for: Convicted of capital murder for the shooting/robbery of Pedro Gomez and Juan Moreno. Moreno survived the gunshot wounds and testified in the case. Gomez, 35, died as a result of multiple rimfire rifle wounds. Approximately $600 and a watch was taken.
Co-defendant: David Garza was 15 years old at the time of the incident. He was certified to stand trial as an adult, convicted of robbery, and sentenced to 20 years.

Received at Death Row: September 10, 1985. Time on death row: 3,022 days, (8.28 years).

Last meal: Barbecue chicken, refried beans, brown rice, sweet tea, and bubble gum (bubble gum is not permitted under TDCJ regulations).

Last statement: None.

Pronounced dead: 12:22 A.M.

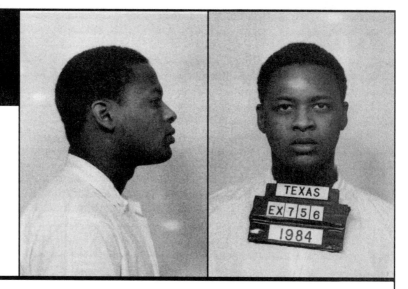

67

Richard J. Wilkerson

Executed:
March 31, 1984

Personal Data: *Born:* April 18, 1964. *Race:* Black. *Height:* 5'11". *Weight:* 191 lbs. *Education level:* 10 years. *Previous occupation:* Laborer. *County of conviction:* Harris. *Age at time of execution:* 29.

Sentenced to death for: Convicted in the July 1983 robbery-slaying of 18-year-old Anil Varughese, night manager of the Malibu Grand Prix Race Track Amusement center in Houston. Varughese, a pre-med student at Houston Baptist University, and three other amusement center employees were fatally stabbed during a robbery that netted about $2,000. Also killed were Roddy Harris, 22, and brothers, Arnold Pequeno, 19, and Joerene Pequeno, 18. All four victims died of multiple stab wounds to the upper body, neck, and head. Wilkerson had been fired from his job as a pit attendant at the raceway and amusement center in the 6100 block of the Southwest Freeway about two weeks before the murders.
Co-defendant: Kenneth Ray Ransom was convicted of capital murder, sentenced to death, and executed on October 28, 1997 (See Entry 139, Kenneth Ransom). James Edward Randall was convicted of capital murder and given a life sentence. Randall, who was Wilkerson's cousin, was 16 years old at the time of the murders.

Received at Death Row: January 17, 1984. Time on death row: 3,633 days, 9.95 years.

Last meal: Two double-meat cheeseburgers, french fries, and ice cream (chocolate or chocolate chip).

Last statement: See Appendix 1.

Pronounced dead: 12:16 A.M.

68

Johnny James

Executed:
September 3, 1993

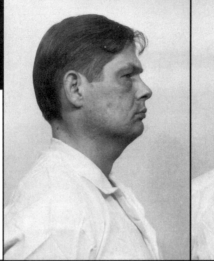

Personal Data: *Born:* January 30, 1934. *Race:* White. *Height:* 5'9". *Weight:* 185 lbs. *Education level:* 9 years. *Prior occupation:* Truck driver. *County of conviction:* Chambers. *Age at time of execution:* 39.

Sentenced to death for: Convicted in the October 1985 abduction and shooting death of 47-year-old Barbara Harrington Mayfield, owner of a High Island lounge where James once tended bar. Mayfield was abducted from BJ's Lounge and shot twice in the head with a .38-caliber pistol after being forced to drive James around three southeast Texas counties while he raped a 23-year-old convenience store clerk he had earlier robbed of $300 and kidnapped. The clerk, a black female who worked at Porter's Get It & Go store in Winnie, was shot three times in the head, but survived to identify James. Both women were found lying on Russell's Landing Road in Jefferson County.

Received at Death Row: July 17, 1984. Time on death row: 2,712 days, (7.43 years).

Last meal: Double meat cheeseburgers, double order of french fries, Dr Pepper, and a pint of banana nut ice cream.

Last statement: None.

Pronounced dead: 12:17 A.M.

69

Antonio Nathaniel Bonham

Executed: September 28, 1993

Personal Data: *Born:* February 6, 1960. *Race:* Black. *Height:* 5'6". *Weight:* 165 lbs. *Education level:* 9 years. *Prior occupation:* Laborer. *County of conviction:* Harris. *Age at time of execution:* 33.

Sentenced to death for: Bonham was convicted in the July 9, 1981, abduction and murder of 62-year-old Marie Jones McGowen, a key punch instructor at Massey Business College in Houston. McGowen was abducted outside the college, raped, and then run over by her own car. Prosecutors also said the woman had been hit over the head with a brick and was locked in the trunk of her car before being run over. Her crushed body was found underneath her car on a secluded road in southeast Houston about 11 hours after her abduction. Bonham was arrested by Houston police on July 17, 1981. He had been on parole less than two months before committing the crime.

Received at Death Row: November 25, 1981. Time on death row: 4,322 days, (11.84 years).

Last meal: Hamburgers, french fries, and water.

Last statement: None.

Pronounced dead: 12:28 A.M.

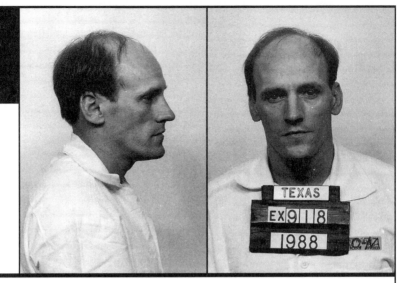

70

Anthony Quinn Cook

Executed: November 10, 1993

Personal Data: *Born:* January 4, 1959. *Race:* White. *Height:* 5'6". *Weight:* 150 lbs. *Education level:* 9 years. *Prior occupation:* Construction. *County of conviction:* Milam. *Age at time of execution:* 34.

Sentenced to death for: Convicted in the June 1988, abduction and slaying of 35-year-old David Dirck VanTassel, Jr., a University of Texas law student. Cook and co-defendant Robert Brian Moore abducted VanTassel from outside the Sheraton Crest Hotel in Austin where he had just completed a State Bar test review. Cook and Moore drove VanTassel in his car to a roadside park 14 miles west of Cameron on Hwy. 36 and tied him with his shirt and belt. After taking his watch and wallet, Cook shot VanTassel four times in the head with a .22-caliber pistol. Cook and Moore stole VanTassel's car and later sold it to a man who later identified them in a police lineup. When arrested, Cook was wearing VanTassel's watch and had the victim's wallet in his pocket.
Co-defendant: Robert Brian Moore was awaiting trial for capital murder at the time of Cook's execution.

Received at Death Row: October 28, 1988. Time on death row: 1,837 days, (5.03 years).

Last meal: Double-meat cheeseburger and strawberry shake.

Last statement: I just want to tell my family I love them; and I thank the Lord Jesus for giving me another chance and for saving me.

Pronounced dead: 12:15 A.M.

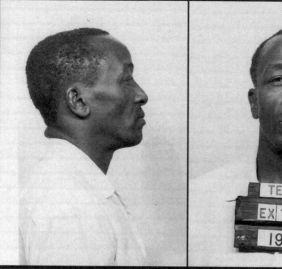

Clifford X. Phillips

Executed:
December 15, 1993

Personal Data: *Born:* December 2, 1954. *Race:* Black. *Height:* 5'7". *Weight:* 155 lbs. *Education level:* 7 years. *Prior occupation:* General contractor. *County of conviction:* Harris. *Age at time of execution:* 59.

Sentenced to death for: Convicted in the January 1982 strangulation death of 58-year-old Iris Siff, managing director of the Alley Theater in Houston. Phillips, a former security guard at the theater, said he had gone to Siff's office in January 13 to rob her, but was forced to kill her in self-defense when she allegedly attacked him. Siff was found dead in her office. She had been strangled to death with a telephone cord. Testimony showed Phillips stole Siff's television, fur coat, jewelry, tote bag, and Lincoln Continental after the killing. He was arrested in Los Angeles about three weeks after the slaying.

Received at Death Row: September 28, 1982. Time on death row: 4,094 days, (11.22 years).

Last meal: Declined last meal.

Last statement: I want to express my feelings regarding the mishap of the deceased Mrs. Iris Siff. That was a very unfortunate incident and only God knows it was an unintentional situation that took place. I want to express my remorse to the family and the discomfort and pain I caused in their lives. Only God will determine if I am truly guilty or innocent of being the type of person I have been drawn up to be by the press and the media. I have given my wife the power and energy to be a disciple of Islam. I rescued her from a wretched life in Ireland. I thank Allah for sending her to me. Certainly murder cannot be an instrument of Allah. My wife is very devoted and a very pious wife. I am very grateful Allah has chosen me to teach the greatness of Allah through her. I am grateful to Allah for allowing me to touch other people's lives through Allah. In spite of what the newspapers have said of me, my wife I love you very deeply. May Allah continue to bless you and shower you with his glory. [Prayer and chanting].

Pronounced dead: 12:53 A.M.

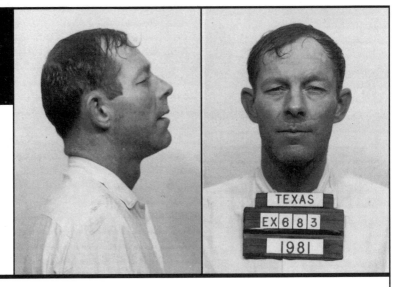

72

Harold Amos Barnard

Executed:
February 2, 1994

Personal Data: *Born:* November 1, 1942. *Race:* White. *Height:* 5'8". *Weight:* 155 lbs. *Education level:* 12 years. *Prior occupation:* Carpenter. *County of conviction:* Galveston. *Age at time of execution:* 51.

Sentenced to death for: Killed Tuan Nguyen, 16, a clerk at a Galveston 7-Eleven store managed by his family. Nguyen was shot once in the heart with a sawed-off .22-caliber rifle fired by Barnard during a robbery. Barnard and three co-defendants fled in a stolen car following the shooting and were arrested about 30 minutes later on I-45 north of Galveston. The murder weapon was found inside the car, along with a Buck knife and a 12-gauge shot gun. Although Nguyen and his father were forced to put the money from the cash register into a bag, Barnard and his co-defendants left the store empty-handed after the shooting.
Note: The three co-defendants were convicted of aggravated robbery and sentenced to prison terms of 15 years, 12 years, and 7 years.

Received at Death Row: May 14, 1981. Time on death row: 645 days, (12.73 years).

Last meal: Steak, french fries, and wine (water was substituted).

Last statement: God, please forgive me of my sins. Look after my people. Bless and protect all people. I am sorry for my sins. Lord, take me home with you. Amen. [Barnard said several other sentences which prison officials could not understand.]

Pronounced dead: 12:27 A.M.

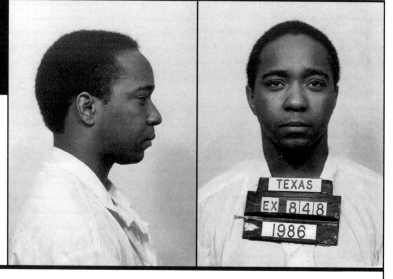

73

**Freddie
Lee
Webb**

Executed:
March 31,
1994

Personal Data: *Born:* August 17, 1960. *Race:* Black. *Height:* 5'8". *Weight:* 165 lbs. *Education level:* 11 years. *Prior occupation:* Construction worker. *County of conviction:* Nueces. *Age at time of execution:* 33.

Sentenced to death for: Convicted in the December 1985 abduction and slaying of 26-year-old Leopoldo Cantu of Corpus Christi. Cantu and his wife, Elizabeth, a supervisor at Ship Ahoy restaurant in Corpus Christi, were abducted at a car wash after closing the restaurant. They were driven back to the restaurant, where Elizabeth was forced to open the safe and turn over the day's receipts. She was tied up and left inside the restaurant. Her husband was driven to an isolated location and shot five times with a .45-caliber pistol. Webb and an accomplice were arrested in George West on March 29, 1986, following the armed robbery of a convenience store there.

Received at Death Row: October 27, 1986. Time on death row: 2,710 days, (7.42 years).

Last meal: Declined last meal.

Last statement: Peace.

Pronounced dead: 12:20 A.M.

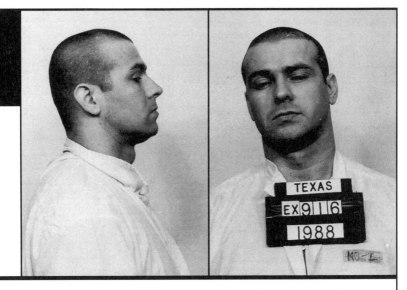

74

Richard Lee Beavers

Executed:
April 4, 1994

Personal Data: *Born:* December 9, 1955. *Race:* White. *Height:* 5'11". *Weight:* 200 lbs. *Education level:* 5 years. *Prior occupation:* Laborer. *County of conviction:* Harris. *Age at time of execution:* 39.

Sentenced to death for: Convicted in the August 1986 abduction and slaying of Douglas G. Odle, a 24-year-old Houston restaurant manager. Odle and his wife, Jenny, also 24 at the time, were abducted from their apartment at gun-point and forced to drive to several banks and withdraw money from automatic teller machines. They were then forced to drive to the restaurant Odle managed and return with the money. Beavers than forced the couple to drive to a field in Galveston County, where Doug Odle was shot through the throat after being forced to kneel before Beavers. Beavers drove away from the scene with Odle's wife, who was later raped, shot in the head, and left for dead. She survived a destroyed left eye and brain damage to testify against Beavers, who was arrested by the FBI in Virginia following the crime.

Received at Death Row: October 18, 1988 Time on death row: 1,993 days, (5.46 years).

Last meal: Six pieces of french toast with syrup, jelly, butter, six barbecued spare ribs, six pieces of well burned bacon, four scrambled eggs, five well cooked sausage patties, french fries with catsup, three slices of cheese, two pieces of yellow cake with chocolate fudge icing, and four cartons of milk.

Last statement: Jesus Christ, the way of truth and light. I thank you, Lord Jesus, for giving me the way.

Pronounced dead: 12:29 A.M.

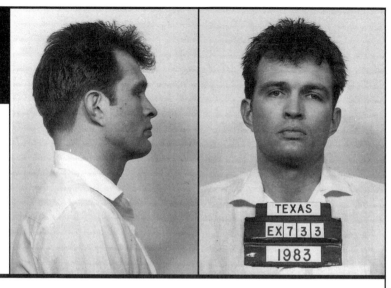

75

Larry Norman Anderson

Executed: April 26, 1994

Personal Data: *Born:* August 30, 1952. *Race:* White. *Height:* 6'4". *Weight:* 180 lbs. *Education level:* 12 years. *Prior occupation:* Electrician. *County of conviction:* Harris. *Age at time of execution:* 41.

Sentenced to death for: March 28, 1982, stabbing death of 28-year-old Zelda Webster, a northwest Houston bar manager. Webster was abducted as she was closing Shelee's Club in the 7700 block of Long Point. About $1,000 was taken from the club. Two bank bags, along with a blood-stained knife, were found in Anderson's truck when it was stopped near the Addicks reservoir that night for traveling without headlights. Anderson admitted to the killing and told police he left Webster's body in a ditch on Clay Road.

Received at Death Row: March 25, 1983. Time on death row: 4,048 days, (11.09 years).

Last meal: Barbecued ribs, chefs salad, baked potato, peach cobbler, and tea.

Last statement: None.

Pronounced dead: 12:42 A.M.

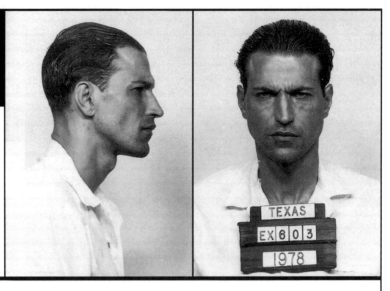

76

Paul Rougeau

Executed: May 3, 1994

Personal Data: *Born:* December 22, 1947. *Race:* Black. *Height:* 6'1". *Weight:* 160 lbs. *Education level:* 9 years. *Prior occupation:* Carpenter. *County of conviction:* Harris. *Age at time of execution:* 46.

Sentenced to death for: Convicted in the January 1978 slaying of Albert C. Wilkins, a 50-year-old Harris County deputy constable. Wilkins was killed at the Stock Exchange Lounge in the 5400 block of Griggs Road while working an off-duty security job. The murder reportedly occurred during an attempted robbery. Prosecutors said Rougeau cursed the officer as he begged for his life and then shot him in the head with a .38-caliber pistol. Rougeau's younger brother Joseph was reportedly killed at the scene of the shooting during a gun battle with police. Paul Rougeau was arrested 12 hours after the killing, reportedly after being shot while fleeing police.

Received at Death Row: August 16, 1978. Time on death row: 5,735 days, (15.71 years).

Last meal: Declined last meal.

Last statement: No last statement but greeted three of his sisters and a niece who witnessed with words "Love you all. Peace be with you all."

Pronounced dead: 12:20 A.M.

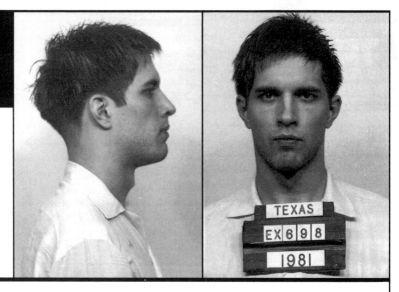

77

Stephen Ray Nethery

Executed: May 27, 1994

Personal Data: *Born:* June 2, 1960. *Race:* White. *Height:* 5'11". *Weight:* n/a. *Education level:* 12 years. *Prior occupation:* Laborer. *County of conviction:* Dallas. *Age at time of execution:* 33.

Sentenced to death for: Convicted in the February 1981 shooting death of 24-year-old John T. McCarthy, Dallas police officer. Nethery was raping a 22-year-old woman in his car parked near White Rock Lake when McCarthy and his partner Phillip Brown pulled up in their squad car. Not knowing the woman was being raped, the officers told the two to leave the area. As the officers started to walk away, Nethery stepped from the car, said, "Officers, I'm sorry," and fired three shots at McCarthy, striking him in the back of the head. Brown fired three shots at Nethery before chasing him into the lake, where Nethery swam a few yards before surrendering when Brown fired a fourth shot at him. Nethery was not hit by any of the shots. McCarthy was rushed to a Dallas hospital where he died two days later.

Received at Death Row: November 13, 1981. Time on death row: 4,544 days, (12. 45 years).

Last meal: Two cheeseburgers with lettuce, tomato, and onion, french fries, and milk.

Last statement: Well, I just wanted to ask people to pray for two families, my family and the family of Officer McCarthy. I appreciate the prayers. Lord Jesus, receive my spirit.

Pronounced dead: 12:30 A.M.

78

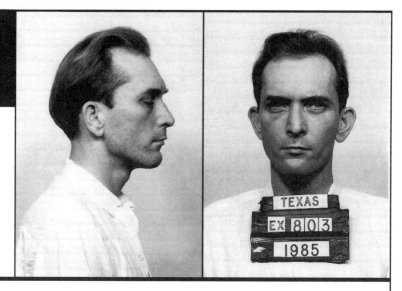

Denton Crank

Executed: June 14, 1994

Personal Data: *Born:* October 10, 1955. *Race:* White. *Height:* 5'9". *Weight:* 161 lbs. *Education level:* 12 years. *Prior occupation:* Construction worker. *County of conviction:* Harris. *Age at time of execution:* 38.

Sentenced to death for: Convicted for the murder of grocery store manager Terry Oringderff, 31. Crank and his half-brother, Truman Moffett, Jr., kidnapped Oringderff and wired him with dynamite, robbed his store, and shot him to death.
Co-defendant: Truman O. Moffett, Jr., was convicted of aggravated robbery with a deadly weapon and sentenced to life.

Received at Death Row: August 6, 1985. Time on death row: 3,232 days, (8.85 years).

Last meal: Cheeseburger (double meat, double cheese) with lettuce, pickles, tomato, onions, and mayonnaise, onion rings, and two chocolate shakes.

Last statement: To my family who has kept me strong, I give my love.

Pronounced dead: 12:22 A.M.

79

Robert Nelson Drew

Executed:
August 2, 1994

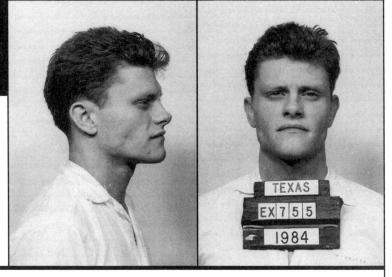

TEXAS
EX 7 5 5
1984

Personal Data: *Born:* April 8, 1959. *Race:* White. *Height:* 5'5". *Weight:* 140 lbs. *Education level:* 10 years. *Prior occupation:* Carpenter. *County of conviction:* Harris. *Age at time of execution:* 35.

Sentenced to death for: Drew was sentenced to die for the February 22, 1983, stabbing death of Jeffrey Leon Mays, a 17-year-old runaway from Alabama. According to court records, Drew stabbed Mays after a fight. Drew allegedly took Mays' watch and wallet after the slaying.
Note: Earnest Purleauski, 37, charged originally with capital murder, signed a statement after pleading guilty to murder and received a 60-year sentence. He later recanted his testimony stating, "I alone committed the murder of Jeffrey Mays. Robert Drew did not assist me in any way. Robert Drew is innocent."

Received at Death Row: January 5, 1984. Time on death row: 3,859 days, (10.57 years).

Last meal: Steak (cooked rare), ham, two hamburgers, two pieces of fish, and chocolate milk.

Last statement: [first two or three words were unintelligible] I don't know why Marta Glass wasn't allowed in here. I love you all. Keep the faith. Remember the death penalty is murder. They are taking the life of an innocent man. My attorney will read my letter at a press conference after this is over. [See Appendix 1.] That is all I have to say. I love you all.

Pronounced dead: 12:22 A.M.

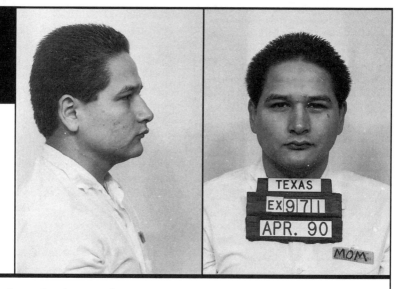

80

Jesse Gutierrez

Executed:
September 16, 1994

Personal Data: *Born:* April 30, 1065. *Race:* Hispanic. *Height:* 5'5". *Weight:* 155 lbs. *Education level:* 8 years. *Prior occupation:* Welder. *County of conviction:* Brazos. *Age at time of execution:* 29.

Sentenced to death for: Convicted in the September 1989 robbery and murder of 42-year-old Dorothy McNew, a College Station store clerk. McNew was working the counter at the Texas Coin Exchange, 404 University, when Jessie Gutierrez and his brother Jose entered shortly after 10 A.M. McNew attempted to flee inside an office when she saw one of the men pull a handgun from his coat but was shot in the head. The Gutierrez brothers fled the store with gems and jewelry worth approximately $500,000. Both were traced to Houston, where they were arrested on September 13, 1989. Approximately $375,000 worth of the stolen merchandise was recovered.
Co-defendant: Jose Gutierrez, Jesse's brother, was convicted of capital murder, sentenced to death and executed on November 18, 1999 (See Entry 195, Jose Gutierrez).

Received at Death Row: April 27, 1990. Time on death row: 1,602 days, (4.39 years).

Last meal: Declined last meal.

Last statement: I just love everybody, and that's it.

Pronounced dead: 12:20 A.M.

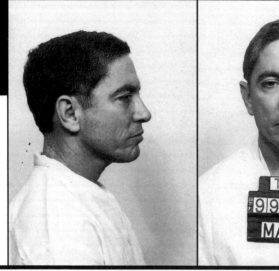

81

George Douglas Lott

Executed: September 20, 1994

Personal Data: *Born:* June 7, 1947. *Race:* White. *Height:* 5'4". *Weight:* 144 lbs. *Education level:* 16 years/4 years college. *Prior occupation:* Computer programmer. *County of conviction:* Potter. *Age at time of execution:* 47.

Sentenced to death for: Convicted in the random shooting of 41-year-old Clyde Christopher Marshall, an assistant district attorney, inside the old Tarrant County Court House at 100 W. Weatherford in Fort Worth. Lott entered a fourth-floor courtroom carrying a 9mm automatic handgun shortly before 10 A.M. and opened fire. Marshall died at the scene from multiple gun shot wounds. Another man, John Edwards, was also killed, and Judge John Hill was wounded. Lott fled from the court house to the studios of WFAA-TV in Dallas, where he confessed to the crime. Police arrested him while he was being interviewed by a reporter.

Received at Death Row: March 18, 1993. Time on death row: 552 days, (1.51 years).

Last meal: Three pieces of french toast with syrup, baked sweet potato with butter, two sausage patties, and one fried egg.

Last statement: None.

Pronounced dead: 12:19 A.M.

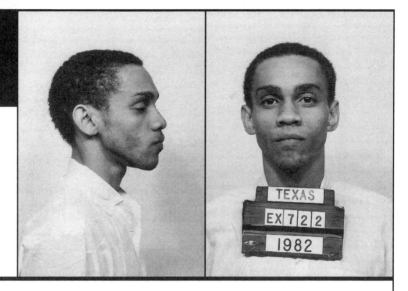

82

Walter Key Williams

Executed:
October 5, 1994

Personal Data: *Born:* January 30, 1982. *Race:* Black. *Height:* 5'5". *Weight:* 130 lbs. *Education level:* 12 years. *Prior occupation:* Laborer. *County of conviction:* Bexar. *Age at time of execution:* 32.

Sentenced to death for: The murder of a San Antonio convenience store clerk February 11, 1981. Williams was convicted of shooting Daniel Liepold in the back with a .38-caliber pistol during a robbery attempt at the Circle K Food Store, where Williams once worked. At his trial, eyewitnesses testified that they had seen Williams and his accomplice, Theodore Roosevelt Edwards, in the store at the time of the robbery, and prosecutors introduced a confession signed by Williams some eight hours after the crime. Authorities found the gun used in the store robbery at his parents' home on a nightstand next to the bed Williams was sleeping in. Williams married at 17 and was separated from his wife when the crime took place. He had worked as a clerk at the Circle K Food Store for about a year, taking home $180 a week, and knew Liepold casually, he said. Edwards was later convicted of murder in another robbery and sentenced to life in prison.

Received at Death Row: September 3, 1982. Time on death row: 4,412 days, (12.09 years).

Last meal: Hamburger (double meat, double cheese), chocolate cake, peas and corn, and tea.

Last statement: Mumbled something about wishing his whole life would have been spent as Islamic.

Pronounced dead: 12:21 A.M.

83

Warren Eugene Bridge

Executed:
November 22, 1994

Personal Data: *Born:* July 3, 1960. *Race:* White. *Height:* 5'7". *Weight:* 135 lbs. *Education level:* 11 years. *Prior occupation:* Cashier/restaurant worker. *County of conviction:* Galveston. *Age at time of execution:* 34.

Sentenced to death for: Bridge was convicted in the February 10, 1980, robbery-shooting of Walter Rose, a 62-year-old convenience store clerk, in Galveston. Rose was shot four times with a .38-caliber pistol as Bridge and co-defendant Robert Joseph Costa robbed a Stop & Go store at 710 Fourth Street of $24. Rose died of his wounds on February 24, 1980, four days following the arrest of Bridge and Costa.
Co-defendant: Robert Joseph Costa was convicted of aggravated robbery and sentenced to 13 years in prison.

Received at Death Row: October 1, 1980. Time on death row: 5,161 days, (14.14 years). *Note:* While on death row, Bridge was been implicated in the bombing of another inmate's cell in September 1984 and the non-fatal stabbing of another inmate in March 1985.

Last meal: Double-meat cheeseburger.

Last statement: I'll see you. [To stepfather Bill Mathis, a witness] I would like to tell the surviving victims here, society, my family, and friends, that I ask that they forgive me for anything I have done. I beg for your forgiveness. I would like to ask Lord Jesus Christ's forgiveness and say that in spite of my circumstances I have been blessed by him. My first thought is that Jesus Christ came down and separated the humans from God. I would like to see the wall that separates these groups here tonight brought down and that we would all have love and compassion for one another and that you all build a future for all of us. There are a lot of men on the row that need to be remembered. I love all of you all the same.

Pronounced dead: 12:25 A.M.

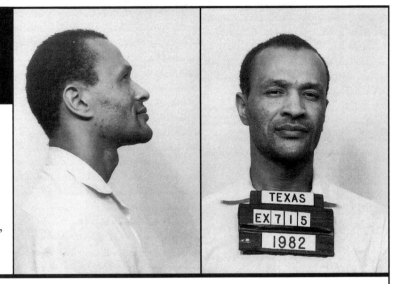

84

Herman Robert Charles Clark, Jr.

Executed: December 6, 1994

Personal Data: *Born:* July 26, 1946. *Race:* Black. *Height:* 5'11". *Weight:* 188 lbs. *Education level:* 14 years. *Prior occupation:* Manager, Houston Plastic Products. *County of conviction:* Harris. *Age at time of execution:* 48.

Sentenced to death for: Clark was sentenced to die for the April 4, 1981 murder of bartender Joseph Edward McClain. At approximately 3 A.M. Clark broke into McClain's apartment in the 3200 block of Clarewood and awoke the victim, his girlfriend, Paulette Spies, and her son. He burglarized the apartment and was attempting to rape Spies when a three-way fight over Clark's pistol ensued. During the struggle, Spies was shot in the arm and McClain was fatally shot in the chest. Court records show that approximately two weeks after this incident, Clark burglarized another apartment during which he robbed the male victim and raped the female victim. He also raped and sodomized the female victim's 10-year-old daughter. Several months later Clark again burglarized an apartment, raped and sodomized both the complainant and her 11-year-old daughter. Clark admitted terrorizing more than 100 families during late-night burglaries and often sexually assaulting the women.

Received at Death Row: June 17, 1982. Time on death row: 4,552 days, (12.47 years).

Last meal: Declined last meal.

Last statement: I told the daughter not to come. Discontinue. Be quiet please. Specifically, I want to say that the bad man I was when I came to death row 13 years ago is nowhere – by the power of God; Jesus Christ; God almighty Holy Spirit he has transformed me as a new creature of Christ. I know that I am a Christ child and that my Lord will welcome me into his arms. Jesus Christ is the Lord of Lords and the King of Kings. I love all of you, those I can and can't see, with the love of Christ. My love for you is secure and I love you purely and wholeheartedly in the name of the Almighty God [record ends here].

Pronounced dead: 12:28 A.M.

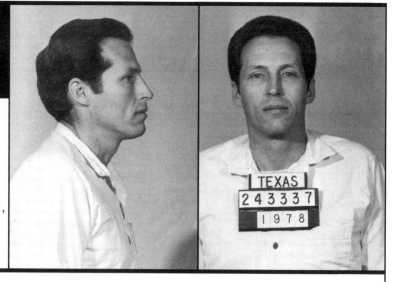

85

Raymond Kinnamon

Executed: December 11, 1994

Personal Data: *Born:* November 20, 1941. *Race:* White. *Height:* 5'10". *Weight:* 180 lbs. *Education level:* 11 years. *Prior occupation:* Mechanic. *County of conviction:* Harris. *Age at time of execution:* 53.

Sentenced to death for: Convicted in the December 1984 robbery and slaying of 41-year-old Ronald Charles Longmire at NJ's, a bar in the 3800 block of Magnum in Houston. Kinnamon was in the bar drinking when he pulled a pistol and demanded money from customers and employees. He took more than $1,500, including $250 from Longmire. Longmire was shot once in the back when he reportedly slapped Kinnamon's hand away when the robber touched his back pocket, asking what was in it. Kinnamon fled and was arrested about two weeks later as a result of a tip from a police informant.

Received at Death Row: October 10, 1985. Time on death row: 3,347 days, (9.17 years).

Last meal: Fish, salad, vanilla ice cream, and tea.

Last statement: See Appendix 1.
Note: Press reports noted that Kinnamon staged a filibuster in an attempt to talk until sunrise, because his death warrant called for the execution to occur before dawn. Among statements recorded by the press "Wherever I'm buried, I'd like it to say: 'Here lies a man who loved women.' I've always been that way." Kinnamon finally tried to slip out of his leather straps on the gurney that kept him connected to the intravenous tubes carrying the solution of lethal drugs. As he tried to free himself, he said, "I can see no reason for my death." Warden Morris Jones and prison chaplain Alex Taylor helped control the inmate and the lethal dose was begun.

Pronounced dead: 5:56 A.M.

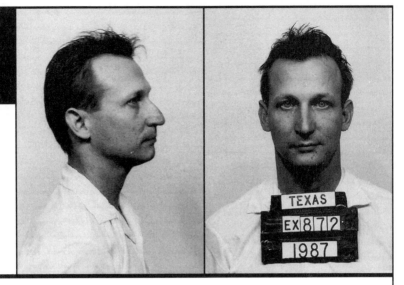

86

Jesse Dewayne Jacobs

Executed:
January 4, 1995

Personal Data: *Born:* February 12, 1950. *Race:* White. *Height:* 5'5". *Weight:* 131 lbs. *Education level:* 12 years. *Prior occupation:* Auto mechanic. *County of conviction:* Walker. *Age at time of execution:* 44.

Sentenced to death for: Convicted in the February, 1986, abduction and shooting death of Etta Ann Urdiales, the ex-wife of his sister's boyfriend. Jacobs told police his sister, Bobbie Jean Hogan, offered him $500 and a place to stay if he would kill Urdiales. He said Urdiales, 25, was supposedly pestering her ex-husband, Michael Urdiales, about child-support payments and custody. Jacobs, posing as a co-worker of Urdiales' boyfriend, abducted the victim from her Conroe apartment, drove her to an area south of Sawdust Road near The Woodlands, and shot her once in the head with a .38-caliber pistol after blindfolding her with a towel. He then wrapped her body in a sleeping bag and buried her in a wooded area. Her body was not discovered until Sept. 13, 1986. Meanwhile, Jacobs went on a six-month crime spree, during which he committed nine robberies and stole six vehicles. He was finally stopped in a stolen car at a check point near Sierra Blanco on Sept. 9, 1986, and arrested for armed robbery. He was returned to Conroe three days later and gave an oral confession to the Urdiales murder.

Received at Death Row: June 17, 1987. Time on death row: 2,756 days, (7.55 years).

Last meal: T-bone steak, french fries, catsup, and milk.

Last statement: See Appendix 1.

Pronounced dead: 12:19 A.M.

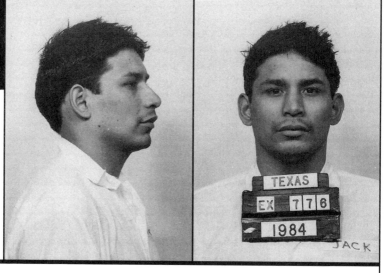

87

Mario Marquez

Executed: January 17, 1995

Personal Data: *Born:* August 22, 1958. *Race:* Hispanic. *Height:* 5'8". *Weight:* 165 lbs. *Education level:* 6 years. *Prior occupation:* Drywaller. *County of conviction:* Bexar. *Age at time of execution:* 36.

Sentenced to death for: Convicted of capital murder in the January 27, 1984, rape-strangulation death of 14-year-old Rachel Gutierrez of San Antonio. Gutierrez and Rebecca Marquez, the defendant's 18-year-old estranged wife, were both strangled to death after being sexually assaulted in their home. Gutierrez and Rebecca Marquez were sisters and lived with their mother, Rosa Gutierrez, in the Villa Veramendi Courts.

Received at Death Row: November 28, 1984. Time on death row: 3,700 days, (10.14 years).

Last meal: Fried chicken, baked potato, and cinnamon roll.

Last statement: Thank you for being my Lord Jesus and Savior and I am ready to come home. Amen.

Pronounced dead: 12:21 A.M.

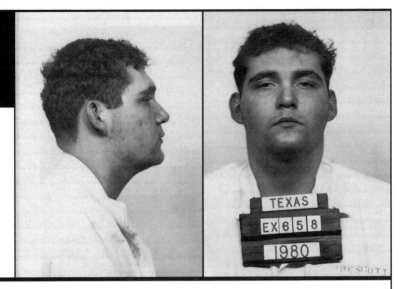

88

Clifton Charles Russell, Jr.

Executed: January 31, 1995

Personal Data: *Born:* August 5, 1961. *Race:* White. *Height:* 6'1". *Weight:* 210 lbs. *Education level:* 7 years. *Prior occupation:* Laborer. *County of conviction:* Taylor. *Age at time of execution:* 38.

Sentenced to death for: Convicted in the December 1979 robbery-slaying of 41-year-old Hubert Otha Tobey in Abilene. Tobey, an air traffic controller, was found dead outside an abandoned house. He had been stabbed repeatedly and his skull crushed with a rock. Russell and an accomplice, William Battee, Jr., stole Tobey's car and drove to Hobbs, N.M., where they were arrested. *Co-defendant:* William Battee, Jr. was convicted of burglary and murder and given a 60-year sentence.

Received at Death Row: April 30, 1980. Time on death row: 5,385 days, (14.75 years).

Last meal: No preference. Asked for whatever was on the menu (chili dogs, baked beans, corn, and peanut butter cookies).

Last statement: I would like to thank my friends and family for sticking with me through all of this. I would like to encourage my brothers to continue to run the race. I think my Father, God in Heaven, for the grace he has granted me. I am ready.

Pronounced dead: 12:19 A.M.
Note: This was the first time in almost 45 years that Texas officials executed two men in a single night. Russell was executed first because his death row number 658 was lower than the death row number of Willie Williams, 677. (See Entry 89, Willie Williams).

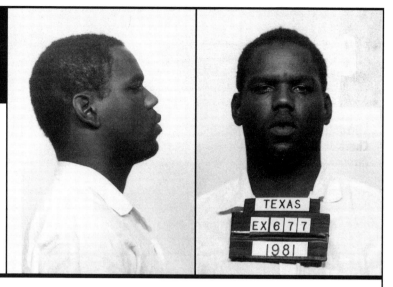

89

Willie Ray Williams

Executed: January 31, 1995

Personal Data: *Born:* February 12, 1956. *Race:* Black. *Height:* 6'0". *Weight:* 210 lbs. *Education level:* 11 years. *Prior occupation:* Laborer. *County of conviction:* Harris. Age at time of execution: 38.

Sentenced to death for: The October 1980 murder of Claude Schaffer, Jr., during the robbery of a Houston delicatessen. Williams' accomplice, Joseph Bennard Nichols, was also sentenced to death in connection with the robbery and shooting. Lawyers for Nichols claimed that Williams went back inside the store after the robbery and shot Schaffer as he crouched behind a counter.

Received at Death Row: February 27, 1981. Time on death row: 5,083 days, (13.93 years).

Last meal: Two double-meat cheeseburgers, onion rings, cheesecake, and root beer.

Last statement: There's love and peace in Islam.

Pronounced dead: 1:57 A.M.
Note: This is the first time in almost 45 years that Texas officials executed two men in a single night. Williams was executed second because his death row number, 677, was higher than the death row number of Clifton Russell, 658. (See Entry 88, Clifton Russell).

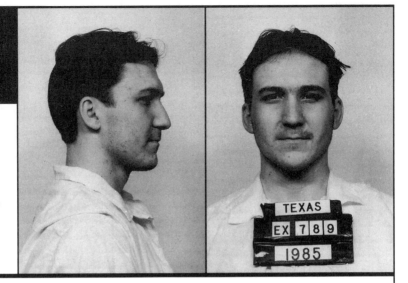

90

Jeffery Dean Motley

Executed: February 7, 1995

Personal Data: *Born:* September 17, 1965. *Race:* White. *Height:* 6'2". *Weight:* 194 lbs. *Education level:* 9 years. *Prior occupation:* Air conditioning repairman. *County of conviction:* Harris. *Age at time of execution:* 29.

Sentenced to death for: Court records reflect the fact that Motley abducted Marie Edelia Duron, 30, at gunpoint and forced her to take him to a bank, where she withdrew funds totaling $300. He either shot her immediately in the back causing her death or waited later in the day to shoot her. The exact time is unknown. Her decomposed body was found in a field in La Porte on August 1, 1984.

Received at Death Row: April 17, 1985. Time on death row: 3,947 days, (10.81 years).

Last meal: Declined last meal.

Last statement: I love you, Mom, goodbye.

Pronounced dead: 12:20 A.M.

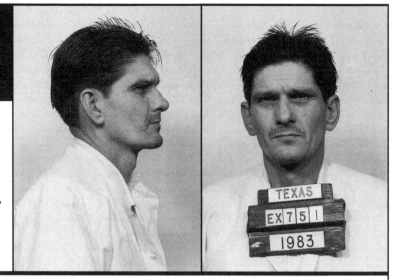

91

Billy Conn Gardner

Executed: February 16, 1995

Personal Data: *Born:* July 28, 1943. *Race:* White. *Height:* 5'11". *Weight:* 157 lbs. *Education level:* 12 years. *Prior occupation:* Welder. *County of conviction:* Dallas. *Age at time of execution:* 52.

Sentenced to death for: Convicted in the May 1983 shooting death of Thelma Catherine Row, cafeteria supervisor at Lake Highlands High School in the Richardson Independent School District. Row was shot twice in the chest with a .357-caliber pistol during a robbery of the cafeteria office that netted $1,600. She died nine days later. Gardner was arrested in his home on July 26, 1984, and was later picked out of a lineup by witnesses who saw him at the school the day of the murder.

Received at Death Row: November 3, 1983. Time on death row: 4,490 days, (12.30 years).

Last meal: Hamburger, french fries, tea, and any dessert (no preference).

Last statement: I forgive all of you and hope God forgives all of you too.

Pronounced dead: 12:30 A.M.

92

Samuel Hawkins

Executed:
February 21, 1995

Personal Data: *Born:* September 1, 1943. *Race:* Black. *Height:* 5'10". *Weight:* 140 lbs. *Education level:* 12 years. *Prior occupation:* Meat trimmer. *County of conviction:* Lubbock. *Age at time of execution:* 52.

Sentenced to death for: Sentenced to death for the slaying of Abbe Rogus Hamilton, 19, of Borger. She was six months pregnant when she was allegedly raped and stabbed to death with a hunting knife.

Received at Death Row: April 8, 1978. Time on death row: 6,159 days, (16.87 years).

Last meal: Double-meat cheeseburger, french fries, and tea.

Last statement: None.

Pronounced dead: 12:21 A.M.

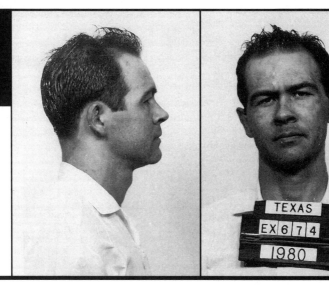

93

Noble Mays

Executed: April 6, 1995

Personal Data: *Born:* August 15, 1953. *Race:* White. *Height:* 6'1". *Weight:* 185 lbs. *Education level:* 15 years. *Prior occupation:* Roughneck. *County of conviction:* Denton. *Age at time of execution:* 42.

Sentenced to death for: Convicted in the April 7, 1979, stabbing death and robbery of Jerry Lamb in Wichita Falls. Lamb was stabbed three times with a knife after being robbed of his money and chased from his car by Mays and co-defendant James Thomas Moore, 27.
Co-defendant: Moore was convicted of murder and sentenced to 45 years.

Received at Death Row: November 7, 1980. Time on death row: 5,260 days, (14.41 years).

Last meal: Four to five fried eggs (sunny side up), three sausage links, three biscuits, and coffee.

Last statement: None.

Pronounced dead: 1:42 A.M.
Note: Mays offered to stop his appeals in exchange for a payment of $10,000 for his family.

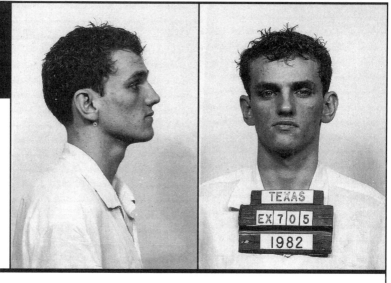

94

Fletcher Thomas Mann

Executed: June 1, 1995

Personal Data: Born*: April 7, 1961. *Race:* White. *Height:* 5'6". *Weight:* 135 lbs. *Education level:* 8 years. *Prior occupation:* Laborer. *County of conviction:* Dallas. *Age at time of execution:* 34.

Sentenced to death for: Mann was convicted of capital murder in the Sept. 11, 1980, shooting death of Christopher Lee Bates in Dallas County. Mann and a companion entered an apartment where Bates, his roommate Robert Matzig, and a woman, Barbara Hoppe, were watching a football game. Both Bates and Matzig were robbed and Hoppe was raped before being strangled and stabbed to death. Bates and Matzig were driven to grocery stores where they cashed two checks and gave the money to the intruders. They were then driven to a secluded area where Bates was shot in the head. Matzig was shot in the neck, but survived. Mann said he and his accomplice went to the victims' apartment because he and his accomplice "needed the money and knew they had cocaine." *Co-defendant*: Martin David Verbrugge was convicted of attempted murder and sentenced to life in prison.

Received at Death Row: February 22, 1982. Time on death row: 4,845 days, (13.27 years).

Last meal: Two hamburger steaks, sliced onions, four pieces of toast, french fries, mustard and catsup, fruit cocktail, and Coke.

Last statement: I would like to tell my family I love them. My attorneys did their best. All of my brothers on death row – those who died and those who are still there – to hang in there – and that's all I have to say.

Pronounced dead: 12:20 A.M.

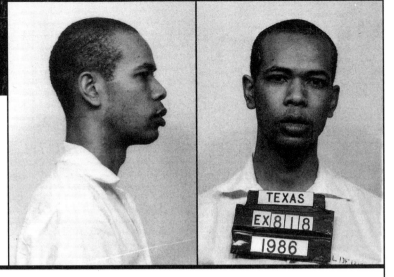

95

Ronald Keith Allridge

Executed: June 8, 1995

Personal Data: *Born:* September 27, 1960. *Race:* Black. *Height:* 6'4". *Weight:* n/a. *Education level:* 10 years (GED). *Prior occupation:* Unemployed. *County of conviction:* Tarrant. *Age at time of execution:* 35.

Sentenced to death for: Shot and killed customer Carla McMillen during a robbery of a What-a-Burger restaurant in Fort Worth on March 25, 1985.

Received at Death Row: February 20, 1986. Time on death row: 2,663 days, (7.30 years).

Last meal: Declined last meal.

Last statement: None.

Pronounced dead: 12:21 A.M.
Note: Officials had trouble finding a vein in Allridge's left arm. They went ahead with only one IV in the right arm.

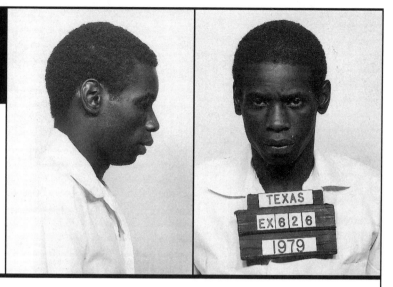

96

John W. Fearance

Executed:
June 20, 1995

Personal Data: *Born:* October 27, 1954. *Race:* Black. *Height:* 5'8". *Weight:* 157 lbs. *Education level:* 8 years. *Prior occupation:* Auto body repairman. *County of conviction:* Dallas. *Age at time of execution:* 41.

Sentenced to death for: Convicted in the December 1977 stabbing death of Larry Faircloth in Dallas. Faircloth was stabbed repeatedly after Fearance broke in to burglarize his north Dallas home. The victim's wife identified Fearance as the intruder, and he was arrested about three hours later. In 1980, the Texas Court of Criminal Appeals ruled that a prospective juror was improperly excluded from the jury and granted a new trial. Fearance was again convicted of capital murder in October 1981 and sentenced to death a second time.

Received at Death Row: January 5, 1979. Time on death row: 5,651 days, (15.48 years).

Last meal: Double-meat cheeseburger, french fries, vanilla ice cream, and milk.

Last statement: I would like to say that I have no animosity towards anyone. I made a mistake 18 years ago. I lost control of my mind but I didn't mean to hurt anyone. I have no hate towards humanity. I hope He will forgive me for what I done. I didn't mean to.

Pronounced dead: 12:22 A.M.

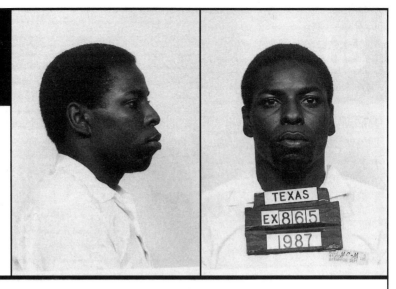

97

Karl Hammond

Executed:
June 21, 1995

Personal Data: *Born:* July 4, 1964. *Race:* Black. *Height:* 5'10". *Weight:* 170 lbs. *Education level:* 9 years. *Prior occupation:* Construction worker. *County of conviction:* Bexar. *Age at time of execution:* 31.

Sentenced to death for: Hammond was convicted of capital murder in the death of 21-year-old Donna Lynn Vetter in San Antonio on September 4, 1986. Vetter, an FBI secretary, was raped and stabbed to death after Hammond broke into her apartment at 4848 Goldfield sometime between 9:30 and 10:55 P.M. Police said Hammond pulled the screen from the front window and surprised Vetter. She was stabbed once in the chest with a knife from her kitchen and sexually assaulted. Hammond's prints were found on an end table and on the murder weapon. *Note:* A few hours after he was convicted of capital murder on March 30, Hammond escaped from the Bexar County Jail when a jailer left open a door separating a second-floor holding area and a visitation area. He was recaptured the following evening when police spotted him running across a street. Two jailers and two sergeants were fired for allowing Hammond to escape.

Received at Death Row: April 7, 1987. Time on death row: 2,995 days, (8.21 years).

Last meal: Double-meat cheeseburger, french fries, chocolate milk, and cake or pie.

Last statement: n/a.

Pronounced dead: 12:23 A.M.

98

Vernon Lamar Sattiewhite

Executed: August 15, 1995

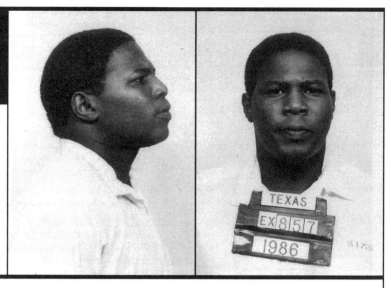

Personal Data: *Born:* September 1, 1955. *Race:* Black. *Height:* 5'7". *Weight:* 209 lbs. *Education level:* 10 years. *Prior occupation:* Forklift operator. *County of conviction:* Bexar. *Age at time of execution:* 40.

Sentenced to death for: Convicted in the June 1986 abduction and shooting death of his ex-girlfriend, Sandra Sorrell, in San Antonio. Sorrell was walking to nursing school near downtown San Antonio when Sattiewhite grabbed her in a headlock, dragged her several hundred feet across a parking lot, and then shot her twice in the head with a .22-caliber pistol. Sattiewhite then turned the gun on himself and attempted to commit suicide. The gun misfired. For more than a month before the murder, Sorrell had been calling police and the Bexar County District Attorney's Office in an effort to keep Sattiewhite away from her.

Received at Death Row: December 16, 1986. Time on death row: 3,892 days, (10.56 years).

Last meal: Six scrambled eggs with cheese, seven pieces of buttered white toast, fifteen pieces of bacon, three hash browns, a bowl of grits with butter, jelly, and orange juice.

Last statement: I would like to say – I just hope Ms. Tielden is happy now. I would like to thank my lawyer Nancy for her help on my case and for being with me now.

Pronounced dead: 12:25 A.M.

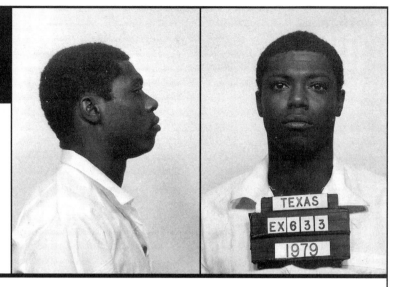

99

Carl Johnson

Executed: September 19, 1995

Personal Data: *Born:* March 5, 1955. *Race:* Black. *Height:* 5'8". *Weight:* 150 lbs. *Education level:* 8 years. *Prior occupation:* Iron worker. *County of conviction:* Harris. *Age at time of execution:* 40.

Sentenced to death for: Johnson was convicted of murdering 75-year-old Ed Thompson, a security guard, during an armed robbery at Wayne's Food Store at 9210 W. Montgomery in Houston on October 6, 1978. Baltimore allegedly held a gun to the storeowner's head, and Johnson shot Thompson five times with a .38-caliber revolver.
Co-defendant: Carl Baltimore was convicted of murder, sentenced to 40 years, and paroled August 17, 1987.

Received at Death Row: May 4, 1979. Time on death row: 5,976 days, (16.37 years).

Last meal: T-bone steak, green salad, baked potato, banana nut ice cream, and Coke.

Last statement: I want the world to know I'm innocent and that I've found peace. Let's ride.

Pronounced dead: 12:24 A.M.

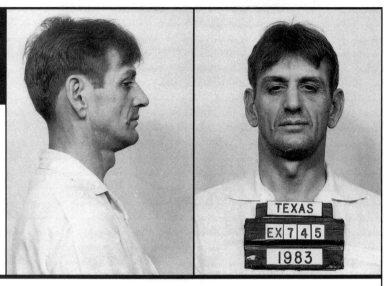

100

Harold Lane

Executed: October 4, 1995

TEXAS
EX 7 4 5
1983

Personal Data: *Born:* August 30, 1945. *Race:* White. *Height:* 5'10". *Weight:* 160 lbs. *Education level:* 9 years (GED). *Prior occupation:* Electrician. *County of conviction:* Dallas. *Age at time of execution:* 50.

Sentenced to death for: Lane was sentenced to death for the November 20, 1982, shooting death of Tammy Davis, 17, a high school senior who was employed at a Dallas Winn-Dixie store. According to testimony, Lane robbed the store's cashier's office of $3,300, then tried to flee through the "entrance" side of the store's electronic doors. Tammy, apparently unaware that a robbery had taken place, tried to explain that Lane was going through the wrong doors when he raised his gun and shot her in the head.

Received at Death Row: July 28, 1983. Time on death row: 4,448 days, (12.19 years).

Last meal: Two double-meat cheeseburgers, french fries, and strawberry shake.

Last statement: I wish you eternal happiness and everlasting peace. I have found everlasting peace with God. I wish the guys on the row peace. I have everlasting peace now and I am ready.

Pronounced dead: 6:28 P.M.

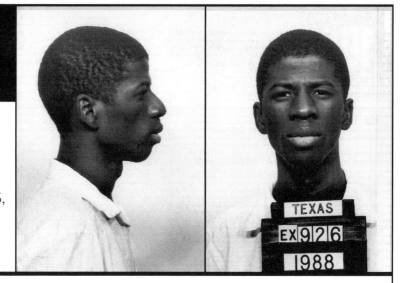

101

Bernard Eugene Amos

Executed: December 6, 1995

Personal Data: *Born:* December 22, 1961. *Race:* Black. *Height:* 6'0". *Weight:* 150 lbs. *Education level:* 11 years. *Prior occupation:* Mechanic. *County of conviction:* Dallas. *Age at time of execution:* 33.

Sentenced to death for: Convicted in the shooting death of 34-year-old James Joe at a Dallas apartment complex. Joe was investigating a burglary in progress in an apartment near his home when he confronted Amos and an unknown accomplice. Shots were exchanged before Joe fell with a fatal chest wound. Amos, wounded in the arm and leg, fled with his accomplice in a car that was later spotted by a police helicopter. Amos was arrested while attempting to crawl from the vehicle after it had been stopped. His accomplice apparently escaped.

Received at Death Row: December 15, 1988. Time on death row: 2,546 days, (6.98 years).

Last meal: Two turkey sandwiches.

Last statement: The State of Texas is making a mistake tonight. It does not do any good to have lawyers; they hold you to procedural law, 50 percent of the cases before the CCA. They only hear the white ones. The State of Texas will take my life with 11 unanswered claims. May the grace of God have mercy on them.

Pronounced dead: 6:31 P.M.

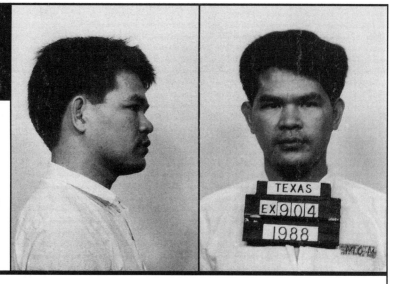

102

**Hai
Hai
Vuong**

Executed:
December 7,
1995

Personal Data: *Born:* September 12, 1955. *Race:* Other. *Height:* 5'5". *Weight:* 154 lbs. *Education level:* 7 years. *Prior occupation:* Shrimper. *County of conviction:* Jefferson. *Age at time of execution:* 40.

Sentenced to death for: Convicted in the December 1986 shooting deaths of 16-year-old Hien Quang Tran and 27-year-old Tien Van Nguyen at a Port Arthur game room. The two victims were shot with a rifle inside the Tam Game Room at 648 9th Ave. Three other men were wounded during the shooting, which reportedly stemmed from a prior argument.
Note: Court records indicate a capital murder indictment returned against Thien Huu Nguyen, but TDC has no record of incarceration as of July 1988.

Received at Death Row: May 27, 1988. Time on death row: 2,749 days, (7.53 years).

Last meal: Steak, french fries, beans, and water.

Last statement: I thank God that he died for my sins on the cross. And I thank Him for saving my soul so I will know when my body lays back in the grave my soul goes to be with the Lord. Praise God. I hope whoever hears my voice tonight will turn to the Lord. I give my spirit to Him. Praise the Lord. Praise Jesus. Hallelujah.

Pronounced dead: 6:22 P.M.

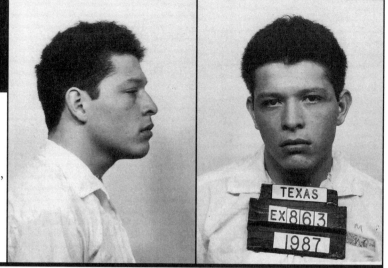

103

Esequel Banda

Executed:
December 11, 1995

Personal Data: *Born:* December 19, 1963. *Race:* Hispanic. *Height:* 5'5". *Weight:* 140 lbs. *Education level:* 9 years. *Prior occupation:* Laborer. *County of conviction:* Hamilton. *Age at time of execution:* 31.

Sentenced to death for: Convicted of capital murder in the stabbing death of Merle Laird, a Hamilton housewife, on August 3, 1986. Laird was sexually assaulted and then stabbed several times inside her home at 620 South Bell Street. Banda reportedly told friends that he stabbed a woman and sucked the blood that was coming from her mouth.

Received at Death Row: March 25, 1987. Time on death row: 3,265 days, (8.95 years).

Last meal: Declined last meal.

Last statement: None.

Pronounced dead: 6:21 P.M.

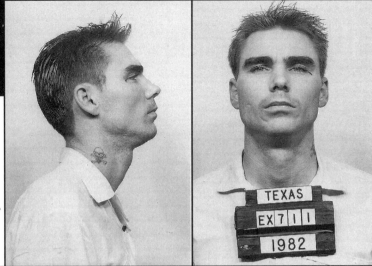

104

James Michael Briddle

Executed: December 12, 1995

Personal Data: *Born:* April 7, 1955. *Race:* White. *Height:* 5'11". *Weight:* 160 lbs. *Education level:* 7 years. *Prior occupation:* Laborer. *County of conviction:* Harris. *Age at time of execution:* 40.

Sentenced to death for: Convicted of capital murder in the February 24, 1980, slaying of Robert Banks, a 30-year-old oil company worker in Houston. Banks and a friend, 26-year-old Bob Skeens, were found strangled in Bank's home in the 2900 block of Hepburn. Missing from the home was $800 cash, credit cards, a car, a camera, and several weapons. Testimony showed that Briddle, his ex-wife, Linda Briddle Fletcher, and companion Pamela Lynn Perillo, were picked up by banks while they were hitchhiking near the Houston Astrodome and offered a ride and a place to spend the night. Banks and Skeens, who was visiting at Banks' home from Louisiana, were both strangled with a rope after returning with coffee and donuts for their guests. The three suspects drove Skeens' car to Dallas and then took a bus to Colorado, where they were arrested in early March 1980 after Perillo gave a statement to authorities in Denver.
Co-defendants: Linda Briddle Fletcher was convicted of robbery and placed on five years probation. Pamela Lynn Perillo was convicted of capital murder in Skeens' death and sentenced to die by injection.

Received at Death Row: April 15, 1982. Time on death row: 4,986 days, (13.66 years).

Last meal: T-bone steak (rare), six fried eggs, hash browns, buttered toast, milk, and orange juice.

Last statement: I love you. You all take care of mom and dad. I'm ready. [when needle reinserted] I'm leaving you. I can taste it. I'll see you later on.
Note: Officials removed needle from the left arm because of poor flow. At 6:15, the left arm blew out, and officials had to start over. At 6:23, officials set the needle in the left forearm.

Pronounced dead: 6:35 P.M.

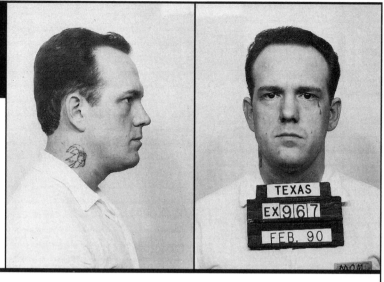

105

Leo Ernest Jenkins, Jr.

Executed:
February 9,
1996

Personal Data: *Born:* October 12, 1957. *Race:* White. *Height:* 5'10" *Weight:* 182 lbs. *Education level:* 10 years. *Prior occupation:* Mechanic. *County of conviction:* Harris. *Age at time of execution:* 38.

Sentenced to death for: Convicted in the August 1988 shooting deaths of Kara Denise Voss and her brother Mark Brandon Kelley during the robbery of a Houston pawnshop. The brother and sister were working at the Golden Nugget at 9822 Airline Dr. when Jenkins and co-defendant Eugene Hart entered around 2 pm. Jenkins approached the counter and told Voss he was interested in placing a rifle in layaway. As Voss was preparing the layaway slip, Jenkins pulled out a .22-caliber pistol and shot her in the head. Jenkins then shot Kelley in the face and head. The co-defendants took several trays of jewelry before fleeing. Jenkins confessed the crime to police following his and Hart's arrest on September 1, 1988. Co-defendant Hart was convicted of murder (2) and credit card abuse and sentenced to life in prison.
Note: Jenkins was identified in part because of his extensive tattoos. Each tear tattooed on his face denoted a trip to prison for burglary.

Received at Death Row: March 1, 1990. Time on death row: 2,170 days, (5.95 years).

Last meal: Two bacon cheeseburgers, french fries, and Coke.

Last statement: I would like to say that I believe that Jesus Christ is my Lord and Saviour. I am sorry for the loss of the Kelly but my death won't bring them back. I believe that the state of Texas is making a mistake tonight. Tell my family I love them. I'm ready.

Pronounced dead: 6:29 P.M.

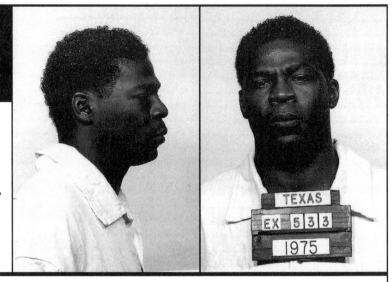

106

Kenneth Granviel

Executed:
February 27, 1996

TEXAS
EX 533
1975

Personal Data: *Born:* August 4, 1950. *Race:* Black. *Height:* 6'2". *Weight:* 190 lbs. *Education level:* 12 years. *Prior occupation:* Machinist. *County of conviction:* Tarrant. *Age at time of execution:* 45.

Sentenced to death for: Granviel was convicted of capital murder in the October 1974 stabbing death of two-year-old Natasha McClendon in Fort Worth. The young girl was one of seven people Granviel killed during two separate murdering sprees. Also killed on October 7 inside a Fort Worth apartment complex were Martha McClendon, the young girl's mother, Linda McClendon, and Laura McClendon and her three-year-old son, Steven. All of the victims were murdered with a butcher knife. All were friends of Granviel's. Granviel surrendered to police of February 8, 1975. He later admitted to the killings of two other personal friends, Betty Williams and Vera Hill. Both women were raped and stabbed to death with a knife. Granviel led authorities to their bodies.
Note: The 5th U.S. Circuit Court of Appeals in New Orleans set aside the death penalty in Granviel's case because at least one prospective juror was improperly disqualified after members of the jury panel were questioned about their views on the death penalty. Granviel was again tried in May 1983 and sentenced to death upon conviction.

Received at Death Row: : November 21, 1975. Time on death row: 7399 days, (20.27 years).

Last meal: Double-meat cheeseburger, french fries, chocolate cake, and punch.

Last statement: None.

Pronounced dead: 6:20 P.M.

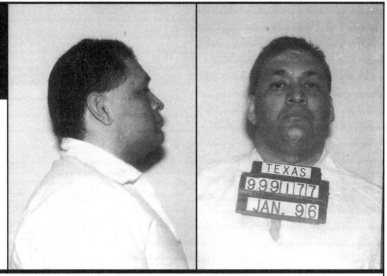

107

Joe Fedelfido Gonzales, Jr.

Executed: September 18, 1996

Personal Data: *Born:* November 17, 1960. *Race:* Hispanic. *Height:* 5'10". *Weight:* 253 lbs. *Education level:* 11 years (GED). *Prior occupation:* General contracting. *County of conviction:* Potter. *Age at time of execution:* 36.

Sentenced to death for: Convicted in the October 19, 1992, shooting death of 50-year-old William J. Veader in Amarillo. Veader died from a single gunshot wound to the head, which initially appeared to have been self-inflicted. A subsequent investigation revealed that Gonzales killed Veader and then arranged the crime scene to make it look like a suicide. Police also discovered that Gonzales had stolen a number of items, including cash, from the rental home Veader owned at 1001 S. Hodges.

Received at Death Row: January 10, 1996. Time on death row: 252 days, (.69 years).

Last meal: Strawberry shake and cheesecake.

Last statement: There are people all over the world who face things worse than death on a daily basis; and in that sense I consider myself lucky. I cannot find the words to express the sadness I feel for bringing this hurt and pain on my loved ones. I will not ask forgiveness for the decisions I have made in this judicial process, only acceptance. God bless you all.

Pronounced dead: 6:19 P.M.

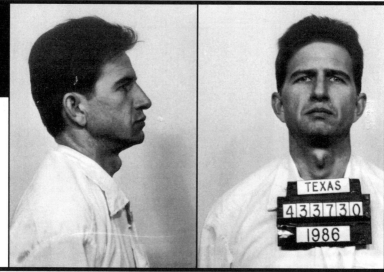

108

Richard Brimage, Jr.

Executed: February 10, 1997

Personal Data: *Born:* December 5, 1955. *Race:* White. *Height:* 5'8". *Weight:* 153 lbs. *Education level:* 12 years. *Prior occupation:* Electrician. *County of conviction:* Kleberg. *Age at time of execution:* 42.

Sentenced to death for: Convicted in the October 1987 abduction and slaying of Mary Beth Kunkel of Kingsville. Kunkel was reportedly lured to Brimage's residence where she was sexually assaulted, strangled, and suffocated with a sock.
Co-defendant: Leonel Molina was convicted of murder and sentenced to 50 years in prison.

Received at Death Row: April 20, 1988. Time on death row: 3,216 days, (8.81 years).

Last meal: Pepperoni pizza (medium) and Dr Pepper.

Last statement: Not from me but I have a message to you from God. Save the children. Find one who needs help and make a small sacrifice of your own wealth and save the innocent ones. They are the key for making the world a better place.

Pronounced dead: 6:20 P.M.

109

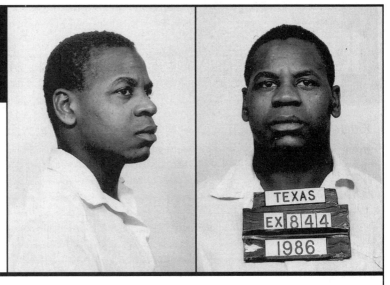

John Kennedy Barefield

Executed: March 12, 1997

Personal Data: *Born:* March 30, 1964. *Race:* Black. *Height:* 5'8". *Weight:* 168 lbs. *Education level:* 8 years. *Prior occupation:* Carpenter. *County of conviction:* Harris. *Age at time of execution:* 32.

Sentenced to death for: Convicted in the April 1986 rape and execution-style slaying of Cindy Rounsaville, a 25-year-old Rice University student. Rounsaville was abducted by Barefield and two other men as she was walking to her car in the parking lot of her southwest Houston apartment complex. She was forced into her car and driven to her bank, where she was forced to withdraw $70 from an automatic teller machine. Rounsaville was then taken to a remote field in far southwest Houston, where she was sexually assaulted by all three men and finally shot twice in the back of the head by Barefield after she tried to run. After the shooting, the suspects reportedly drove the victim's car to the other side of Houston and robbed another woman at gunpoint. They then drove back to near where Rounsville was killed and set her car afire. *Note:* Co-defendant Perry J. Barefield was convicted of aggravated robbery and sentenced to 45 years in prison. Earnest Lee Sonnier is serving a life sentence for an unrelated aggravated kidnapping of a 24-year-old Houston woman.

Received at Death Row: September 26, 1986. Time on death row: 3,817 days, (10.46 years).

Last meal: Double-meat cheeseburger, and french fries.

Last statement: [mumbled] Tell Mama I love her.

Pronounced dead: 6:18 P.M.

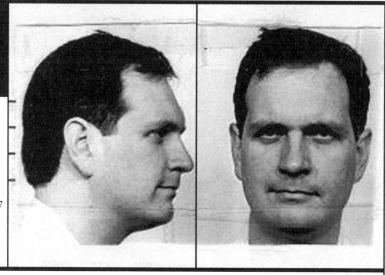

110

David Lee Herman

Executed:
April 2, 1997

Personal Data: *Born:* November 7, 1957. *Race:* White. *Height:* 6'4". *Weight:* 235 lbs. *Education level:* 14 years. *Prior occupation:* Stockbroker. *County of conviction:* Tarrant. *Age at time of execution:* 39.

Sentenced to death for: Convicted in the December 1989 shooting death of 21-year-old Jennifer E. Burns during the robbery of the LACE topless nightclub in Arlington. Burns, a club employee, was shot three times after fighting off an attempted sexual assault by Herman. She and club manager Harold "Clay" Griffin and club hostess Sally Fogle were forced to the club office where Herman stole $20,000 from a safe and then shot all three employees. Griffin and Fogle survived. Approximately $8,500 of the stolen money was recovered following Herman's arrest in Kennedale on December 30, 1989. Herman had been employed as manager of the LACE nightclub in 1987.

Received at Death Row: June 21, 1991. Time on death row: 2,658 days, (7.28 years).

Last meal: Hamburger, pizza, root beer, and vanilla ice cream.

Last statement: It was horrible and inexcusable for me to take the life of your loved one and to hurt so many mentally and physically. I am here because I took a life and killing is wrong by an individual and by the state and I am sorry we are here but if my death gives you peace and closure then this is all worthwhile. To all of my friends and family I love you and I am going home.

Pronounced dead: 7:09 P.M.

111

David Wayne Spence

Executed:
April 3, 1997

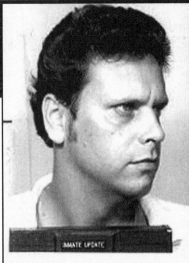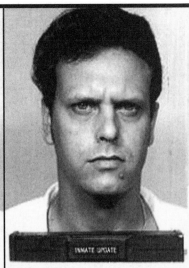

Personal Data: *Born:* July 18, 1956. *Race:* White. *Height:* 5'9". *Weight:* 176 lbs. *Education level:* 9 years (GED). *Prior occupation:* Roofer. *County of conviction:* McLennan. *Age at time of execution:* 40.

Sentenced to death for: Twice convicted of capital murder in the July 1982 mistaken identity killings of three teenagers in a botched murder-for-hire scheme. Accomplice Muneer Mohammed Deeb reportedly hired Spence and two other co-defendants to kill his girlfriend, Gayle Kelley, for a share of the benefits to be paid on a life insurance policy he had taken out on her. However, Spence and his accomplices apparently mistook 17-year-old Jill Montgomery of Waxahachie for Kelley, who friends said closely resembled Montgomery. Montgomery and friends Raylene Rice, 17, and Kenneth Franks, 18, were stabbed to death at a Waco lakeside park. Both women were sexually assaulted before being killed. Spence was convicted of capital murder and given the death penalty for the slaying of Montgomery and Franks.
Co-defendants: Muneer Mohammad Deeb was convicted of capital murder and sentenced to death. His case was retried and dismissed in 1996. Anthony Melendez was convicted of murder (2) and sentenced to 99 years in prison. Gilbert Melendez was convicted of murder and sentenced to life in prison.

Received at Death Row: October 11, 1984. Time on death row: 4,554 days, (12.48 years).

Last meal: Fried chicken, french fries, chocolate ice cream, Coke, tea, and coffee.

Last statement: Yes, I do. First of all, I want you to understand I speak the truth when I say I didn't kill your kids, anyone – honestly, I have not killed anyone – I wish you could get the rage from your hearts and you could see the truth and get rid of the hatred. I love you all {names of children, other names garbled}. This is very important. I love you and I miss you. OK. Now I'm finished.

Pronounced dead: 6:32 P.M.

112

Billy Joe Woods

Executed: April 14, 1997

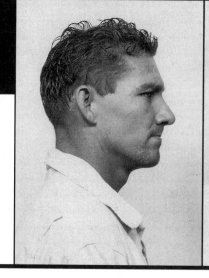 

TEXAS
EX 552
1976

Personal Data: *Born:* December 20, 1946. *Race:* White. *Height:* 5'11". *Weight:* 150 lbs. *Education level:* 10 years. *Prior occupation:* Laborer. *County of conviction:* Harris. *Age at time of execution:* 50.

Sentenced to death for: Convicted in the beating and strangulation death of Mabel E. Ehatt, a 62-year-old disabled woman. Woods broke into Ehatt's second-story apartment in the 2000 block of Fairmont in Houston and brutally beat her before raping her. Woods then ransacked the apartment and was in the process of stealing her television set when police arrived. Woods was a suspect in a similar attack on a Louisiana woman who survived.

Received at Death Row: July 30, 1976. Time on death row: 7,560 days, (20.71 years).

Last meal: Hamburger, french fries, banana pudding, and coffee.

Last statement: None.

Pronounced dead: 6:30 P.M.

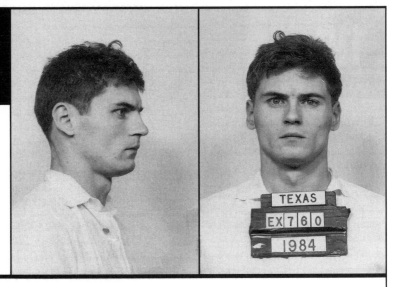

113

Kenneth Edward Gentry

Executed: April 16, 1997

TEXAS
EX 7 6 0
1984

Personal Data: *Born:* January 28, 1961. *Race:* White. *Height:* 6'2". *Weight:* 157 lbs. *Education level:* 9 years (GED). *Prior occupation:* Mechanic. *County of conviction:* Denton. *Age at time of execution:* 36.

Sentenced to death for: Convicted in the September 1983 capital murder of 23-year-old Jimmy Don Ham, whose body was found in a park on the shore of Lake Lewisville. Ham had been shot once in the chest and once in the head. Prosecutors said Gentry, who escaped from a Georgia prison in 1982, killed Ham in a scheme to assume Ham's identity because Gentry was wanted. He was arrested in Austin, Minnesota, on September 15, 1983, two days after Ham's body was found.
Note: In November 1984 Gentry and fellow death row inmate Jewel McGee attempted to escape from the Ellis Unit by jumping a security fence. Correctional Officer Minnie Houston, armed with a shotgun, stopped the pair at the front gate and held them until assistance arrived. Gentry broke his ankle in the escape attempt.

Received at Death Row: March 5, 1984. Time on death row: 4,787 days, (13.12 years).

Last meal: Bowl of butterbeans, mashed potatoes, onions, tomatoes, biscuits, chocolate cake, and Dr Pepper with ice.

Last statement: Thank you Lord for the past 14 years that have allowed me to grow as a man. To JD's family, I am sorry for the suffering you have gone through the past 14 years. I hope you can get some peace tonight. To my family, I am happy to be going home to Jesus. Sweet Jesus, here I come. Take me home. I am going your way.

Pronounced dead: 6:24 P.M.

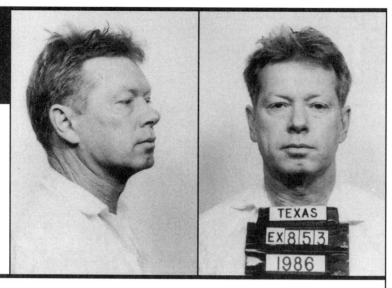

114

Benjamin H. Boyle

Executed: April 21, 1997

TEXAS
EX 8 5 3
1986

Personal Data: *Born:* July 22, 1943. *Race:* White. *Height:* 5'5". *Weight:* 192 lbs. *Education level:* 10 years. *Prior occupation:* Truck driver. *County of conviction:* Potter. *Age at time of execution:* 53.

Sentenced to death for: Convicted in the October 1985 murder of 20-year-old Gail Lenore Smith near Amarillo. Smith, who worked as a cocktail waitress in Fort Worth and often hitched rides with truckers, was raped and strangled to death with a necktie by Boyle, a driver for Jewett Scott Trucking of Magnum, Oklahoma. Her nude body was found north of Amarillo near the Canadian River bridge on Highway 287. Both her hands and feet had been bound by duct tape. Boyle's fingerprints were lifted from the adhesive side of some duct tape found in a trash can not far from the victim's body. Smith's mother told police that her daughter often hitchhiked and preferred to ride with truckers because she trusted them. She had accepted a ride with Boyle in Fort Worth on October 14. The truck was reportedly traveling to Canon City, Colorado with a load of lumber when the murder occurred.

Received at Death Row: December 5, 1986. Time on death row: 3,787 day, (13.38 years).

Last meal: Double-meat cheeseburger, french fries with catsup, and Coke.

Last statement: None.

Pronounced dead: 6:21 P.M.

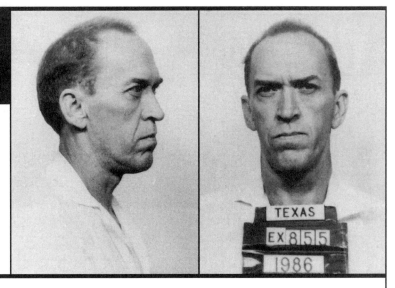

115

Ernest Orville Baldree

Executed: April 29, 1997

Personal Data: *Born:* March 27, 1942. *Race:* White. *Height:* 5'9". *Weight:* 174 lbs. *Education level:* 7 years. *Prior occupation:* Construction worker. *County of conviction:* Navarro. *Age at time of execution:* 55.

Sentenced to death for: Convicted in the August 1986 deaths of Homer and Nancy Howard at their residence in Coolidge. Baldree was last paroled to the care of a Coolidge man who was a friend of the Howards. He said that on August 20, 1986, the Howards had come to his home and convinced Baldree to return with them so he could help Mr. Howard fix his fence. The bodies of the husband and wife were found seven days later. Mrs. Howard was found lying on the kitchen floor with knife and gunshot wounds. Her husband's body was found inside his pickup parked in a field adjacent to their house trailer. He had been shot once in the head. Baldree fled in the victim's car, taking cash and jewelry worth approximately $1,500. He was arrested in Arlington on October 31, 1986.

Received at Death Row: December 10, 1986. Time on death row: 3,790 days, (10.38 years).

Last meal: Double-meat cheeseburger, french fries, pack of cigarettes (not permitted by policy).

Last statement: None.

Pronounced dead: 6:25 P.M.

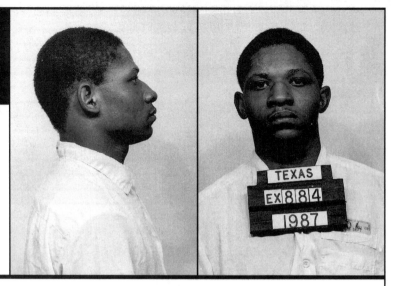

116

Terry Washington

Executed:
May 6,
1997

Personal Data: *Born:* September 12, 1963. *Race:* Black. *Height:* 5'6". *Weight:* 150 lbs. *Education level:* 9 years. *Prior occupation:* Dishwasher. *County of conviction:* Brazos. *Age at time of execution:* 33.

Sentenced to death for: Convicted in the January 1987 robbery-slaying of 29-year-old Beatrice Louise Huling, manager of Julie's Place restaurant at 607 Texas Avenue in College Station. Washington, a dishwasher at the restaurant, stabbed Huling 85 times after closing and then stole $628 from the restaurant safe and cash register. Witnesses reported seeing Washington with several $100 bills days after the murder. Police also discovered Huling's blood on the pants and boots Washington wore to work the day of the murder. He was arrested at his aunt's home in Bryan on February 25, 1987.

Received at Death Row: : September 15, 1987. Time on death row: 3,505 days, (9.60 years).

Last meal: Steak, mashed potatoes, green beans, buttered rolls, chocolate ice cream, and punch.

Last statement: None.

Pronounced dead: 6:18 P.M.

117

Anthony Ray Westley

Executed: May 13, 1997

Personal Data: *Born:* July 18, 1960. *Race:* Black. *Height:* 6'3". *Weight:* 225 lbs. *Education level:* 8 years. *Prior occupation:* Laborer. *County of conviction:* Harris. *Age at time of execution:* 36.

Sentenced to death for: Convicted in the April 1984 robbery and murder of 39-year-old Chester Frank Hall, owner of Eileen's Bait and Tackle Shop on C. E. King Parkway in northeast Harris County. Westley and two accomplices were robbing a female clerk of approximately $75 from the cash register when Hall entered with a pistol. Shots were exchanged, with one fatally wounding accomplice Lee Edward Dunbar. He died at the scene. When Hall retreated from the store, Westley pursued him and shot him once in the back with a .22-caliber pistol after a struggle.

Received at Death Row: May 23, 1985. Time on death row: 4,375 days, (11.99 years).

Last meal: Fried chicken, french fries, bread, and cigarettes (prohibited by policy).

Last statement: I want you to know that I did not kill anyone. I love you all. [Inmate's words were not clear – he was choked up.]

Pronounced dead: 6:30 P.M.

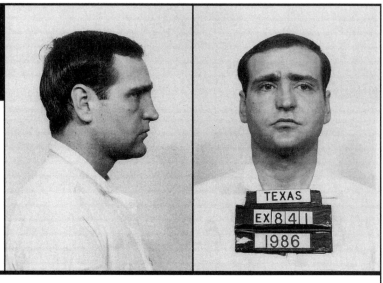

118

Clifton Eugene Belyeu

Executed: May 16, 1997

Personal Data: *Born:* June 30, 1958. *Race:* White. *Height:* 5'8". *Weight:* 165 lbs. *Education level:* 7 years. *Prior occupation:* Painter. *County of conviction:* McLennan. *Age at time of execution:* 38.

Sentenced to death for: Convicted of the December 10, 1985, murder of 36-year-old Melodie Lundgren Bolton of West, about 15 miles north of Waco, during a robbery of her home.

Received at Death Row: September 3, 1986. Time on death row: 4,270 days, (11.70 years).

Last meal: Cheeseburger, french fries, Coke, and a pack of cigarettes (prohibited by policy).

Last statement: See Appendix 1.

Pronounced dead: 6:22 P.M.

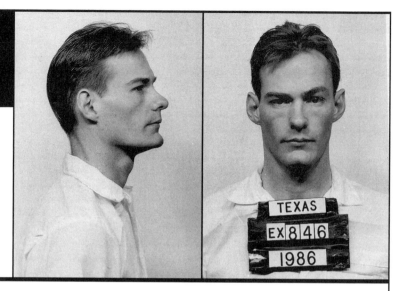

119

Richard G. Drinkard

Executed:
May 19, 1997

TEXAS
EX 8 4 6
1986

Personal Data: *Born:* July 11, 1957. *Race:* White. *Height:* 5'11". *Weight:* 150 lbs. *Education level:* 12 years. *Prior occupation:* Carpenter. *County of conviction:* Harris. *Age at time of execution:* 39.

Sentenced to death for: Drinkard was convicted of capital murder in connection with the stabbing/bludgeoning slayings of three persons in a Houston town-home in November 1985. Killed were Lou Ann Anthony, 44, owner of the townhome; her sister, LaDean Hendrix, 47, and Hendrix's friend, Jerry Mullens, 43. The three were stabbed and beaten with a claw hammer. Drinkard had been introduced to Anthony the day of the murder and had several drinks in her northwest Houston townhome that night. Drinkard returned to the townhome hours later, broke in by prying open a window and dismantling a deadbolt lock, and began beating the victims. He took $350 from the house. Police arrested Drinkard November 20, 1985.

Received at Death Row: October 16, 1986. Time on death row: 3,865 days, (10.59 years).

Last meal: Double cheeseburger, french fries, Coke, and strawberry ice cream.

Last statement: None.

Pronounced dead: 6:17 P.M.

120

Clarence Allen Lackey

Executed:
May 20, 1997

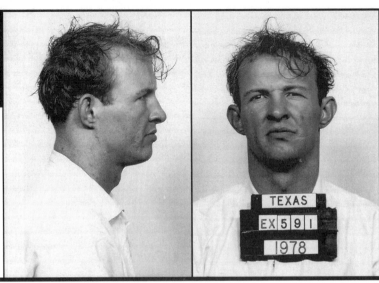

Personal Data: *Born:* August 3, 1954. *Race:* White. *Height:* 6'1". *Weight:* 190 lbs. *Education level:* 9 years. *Prior occupation:* Laborer. *County of conviction:* Tom Green. *Age at time of execution:* 42.

Sentenced to death for: Convicted in the July 1977 abduction and slashing death of 20-year-old Diane Kumph in Lubbock. Kumph was raped, beaten, and had her throat slashed by Lackey, who also burglarized her apartment. Her partially nude body was discovered beside a dirt road near Lackey's house outside of Lubbock. Kumph's apartment door had been kicked open, and there were indications of a violent struggle inside her apartment. In September 1982, the Texas Court of Criminal Appeals ruled that a juror was improperly dismissed at Lackey's trial and reversed the case. He was tried a second time in Midland County in May 1983 and sentenced to death upon conviction.

Received at Death Row: April 18, 1978. Time on death row: 6,967 days, (19.09 years).

Last meal: T-bone steak, large salad, french fries, chocolate ice cream, pack of Camel cigarettes (cigarettes prohibited by policy).

Last statement: I would like to thank my Lord Jesus Christ for keeping me strong all these years. I would also like to thank my mother for standing by me all these years. I would also like to thank my pen pals Joe and Camille Nelling and Jo Ann for helping me stay strong all these years. I also thank my two lawyers Rita and Brent for fighting to keep me alive.

Pronounced dead: 6:17 P.M.

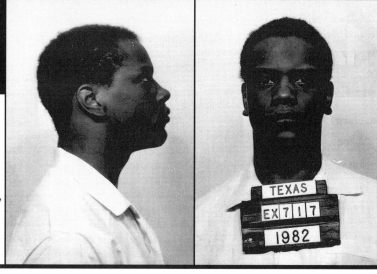

121

Bruce Edwin Callins

Executed:
May 21, 1997

TEXAS
EX 7 1 7
1982

Personal Data: *Born:* February 22, 1960. *Race:* Black. *Height:* 5'11". *Weight:* 190 lbs. *Education level:* 10 years. *Prior occupation:* Cement finisher. *County of conviction:* Tarrant. *Age at time of execution:* 37.

Sentenced to death for: At approximately 4 pm on June 27, 1980, Callins, armed with a gun, entered a Dallas bar and announced he would "shoot anyone who held anything back." Callins apparently thought bar customer Allen Huckleberry was responding too slowly and shot him once in the neck. Callins was sentenced to die for the murder of Huckleberry and was given two life sentences and fined $20,000 for the aggravated robberies of George Torrez nd Kathy Harmon.
Note: On April 15, 1985, Callins threw a caustic liquid in the face and eyes of TDCJ officer Deryl W. Robertson and cut officer Charles B. Anderson with a handmade spear. He was sentenced to five years for aggravated assault.

Received at Death Row: July 5, 1982. Time on death row: 5,428 days, (14.87 years).

Last meal: Steak, french fries, salad, pecan pie, and pack of cigarettes (cigarettes prohibited by policy).

Last statement: I want to let all of my people know and everybody who is here and supported me that I love them and wish them all the best.

Pronounced dead: 6:29 P.M.

122

Larry Wayne White

Executed: May 22, 1997

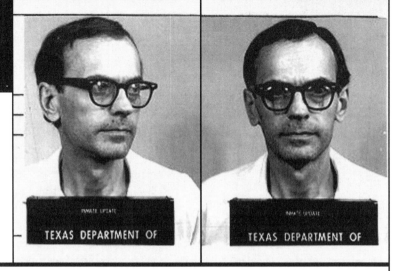

TEXAS DEPARTMENT OF   TEXAS DEPARTMENT OF

Personal Data: *Born:* March 10, 1950. *Race:* White. *Height:* 5'8". *Weight:* 140 lbs. *Education level:* 12 years. *Prior occupation:* Produce manager. *County of conviction:* Harris. *Age at time of execution:* 47.

Sentenced to death for: Convicted in the March 1977 robbery/slaying of Elizabeth St. John at the Airline Apartments in Houston. St. John (court records list her age as 72 while newspaper accounts list her age as 92) was strangled and stabbed in the back with a screwdriver. White, who at the time of the murder worked as a maintenance man at the apartment complex in the 4300 block of Airline, stole St. John's car and drove to Myrtle Beach, South Carolina, where he was arrested while burglarizing a restaurant.

Received at Death Row: August 6, 1979. Time on death row: 2,840 days, (7.79 years).

Last meal: Liver and onions, cottage cheese, red tomatoes, and a single cigarette (cigarettes prohibited by policy).

Last statement: I would like to apologize for all of the hurt and pain and disappointment I caused to my family, the victim's family, and all my friends. I hope all the veterans and teenagers out there who have a drug problem will get help. I hope the Lord will forgive me of all of my sins. I thank Jack and Kathy for being with me. I hope those who support the death row inmates will continue to work and maybe we can get this resolved and do away with the death penalty. I hope that this is a lot better place where I am going.

Pronounced dead: 6:16 P.M.
Note: First executed offender in Texas to be given a military burial. White was a veteran of the Vietnam war.

123

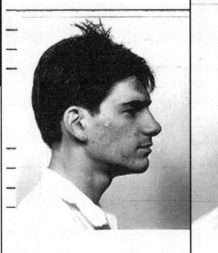 

Robert Anthony Madden

Executed: May 28, 1997

Personal Data: *Born:* 27, 1963. *Race:* White. *Height:* 5'9". *Weight:* 138 lbs. *Education level:* 12 years. *Prior occupation:* Cook. *County of conviction:* Leon. *Age at time of execution:* 33.

Sentenced to death for: Convicted in the September 1985 shooting/stabbing deaths of Herbert Elbert Megason, 56, and his son Don Gary Lynn Megason, 22. The bodies of the victims had been bound and placed in a small creek with brush piled on top of them. One man's throat was cut.

Received at Death Row: February 28, 1986. Time on death row: 3,739 days, (10.24 years).

Last meal: Asked that final meal be provided to a homeless person.

Last statement: Yessir I do. Well, here we are. I apologize for your loss and your pain but I didn't kill those people. Hopefully we will all learn something about ourselves and about each other and we will learn enough to stop the circle of hate and vengeance and come to value what is really going on in this world. We can't look back. I forgive everyone for this process which seems to be wrong. We all end up doing experiences which we create. That is all I have to say about that. [There were a couple of sentences that could not be understood.]

Pronounced dead: 6:42 P.M.

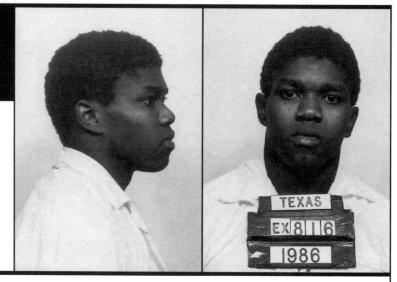

124

Patrick F. Rogers

Executed: June 2, 1997

Personal Data: *Born:* January 6, 1964. *Race:* Black. *Height:* 5'5". *Weight:* 150 lbs. *Education level:* 10 years. *Prior occupation:* Waiter. *County of conviction:* Collin. *Age at time of execution:* 33.

Sentenced to death for: Convicted in the September 1985 shooting death of 23-year-old David Wilburn Roberts, a Paris police officer. Rogers and co-defendant Willis Deron Cooper had robbed a Paris store of approximately $685 when their car was spotted and stopped by Officer Roberts at the entrance of the Ramada Inn in Paris. Before Officer Roberts could get out of his patrol car, Rogers reportedly got out of his vehicle and fired shots through the patrol car windshield. He then stepped to the driver's side window and fired four to six more times through the window. Officer Roberts died at the scene. Rogers and Cooper were arrested after robbing a Paris woman of her car and wedding ring and kidnapping another man.
Co-defendant: Willis Deron Cooper was convicted of aggravated robbery with a deadly weapon and sentenced to life in prison.

Received at Death Row: January 20, 1986. Time on death row: 4,148 days, (11.36 years).

Last meal: A Coke.

Last statement: Yes. I would like to praise Allah and I am praying to Allah. Allah is most gracious. I will ask Allah for forgiveness because he created me and he will forgive me. All for the brothers on the row stay strong. [Some words about Allah that were not intelligible]. I love my family. My mother I will see you sooner or later. Life goes on. Don't let these people break you. Keep true to nature. You do not have to act like them. Rise above it [garbled]. Praise Allah [garbled].

Pronounced dead: 6:17 P.M.

125

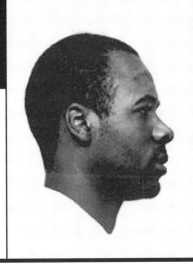

Kenneth Bernard Harris

Executed: June 3, 1997

Personal Data: *Born:* August 8, 1962. *Race:* Black. *Height:* 5'11". *Weight:* 184 lbs. *Education level:* 11 years. *Prior occupation:* Truck driver. *County of conviction:* Harris. *Age at time of execution:* 34.

Sentenced to death for: Convicted in the July 1986 rape and slaying of 28-year-old Lisa Ann Stonestreet in Houston. Stonestreet was raped inside her apartment at 5402 Renwick then strangled and drowned. Prosecutors contend Harris committed at least seven other rapes and robberies in Houston between December 1985 and July 1986.

Received at Death Row: May 13, 1988. Time on death row: 3,306 days, (9.06 years).

Last meal: Barbecue, french fries, ice cream, punch, and cigarettes (cigarettes prohibited by policy).

Last statement: I would like to thank all of you for coming. I am sorry for all of the pain I have caused both the families – my family and yours. I would like for you to know that I am sorry for all the pain I caused for all these years. I have had time to understand the pain I have caused you. I am ready, Warden.

Pronounced dead: 6:17 P.M.

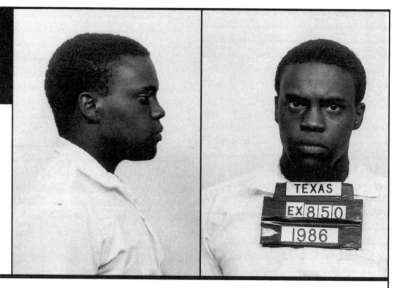

126

Dorsie Johnson, Jr.

Executed:
June 4,
1997

Personal Data: *Born:* March 10, 1967. *Race:* Black. *Height:* 5'2". *Weight:* 158 lbs. *Education level:* 11 years. *Prior occupation:* Janitor. *County of conviction:* Scurry. *Age at time of execution:* 30.

Sentenced to death for: Convicted in the March 1986 shooting death of 53-year-old Jack Huddleston, a clerk at Allsup's Convenience store in Snyder. Huddleston was shot once in the head with a .25-caliber pistol after being told to lie down on the floor during a robbery that netted $161.92.
Co-defendant: Amanda Lynn Miles was convicted of aggravated robbery and sentenced to 60 years in prison.

Received at Death Row: November 20, 1986. Time on death row: 3,846 days, (10.54 years).

Last meal: Fried chicken, french fries, chocolate cake, and Coke.

Last statement: I would like to tell my family that I love them and always be strong and keep their heads up and keep faith in Jesus. That's it.

Pronounced dead: 6:18 P.M.
Note: Executed same day as Davis Losada (See Entry 127, Davis Losada).

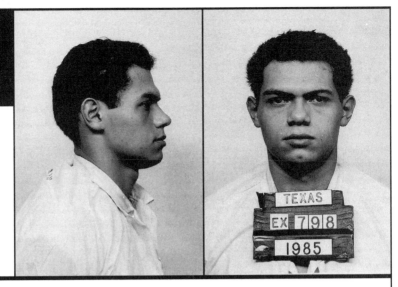

127

Davis Losada

Executed: June 4, 1997

Personal Data: *Born:* April 28, 1965. *Race:* Hispanic. *Height:* 5'9". *Weight:* 166 lbs. *Education level:* 11 years. *Prior occupation:* Cook. *County of conviction:* Cameron. *Age at time of execution:* 32.

Sentenced to death for: Convicted along with three co-defendants in the rape and murder of 15-year-old Olga Perales near San Benito. Perales was stabbed twice in the chest and abdomen and beaten around the head with a pipe. She had been raped repeatedly before her death.
Co-defendants: Jesus Romero, Jr., was convicted of capital murder, sentenced to death by lethal injection, and executed May 20, 1992 (See Entry 49, Jesus Romero, Jr.). Jose F. Cardenas was convicted of murder and sentenced to life in prison. Rafael Layva, Jr., was convicted of sexual assault, sentenced to 20 years, and released under mandatory supervision on July 1, 1996.

Received at Death Row: June 20, 1985. Time on death row: 4,364 days, (11.96 years).

Last meal: Declined last meal.

Last statement: If it matters to anyone, I didn't kill Olga. Brian, thank you for caring. Dee Dee you have been a good sister to all of us. Ana and Chico [not sure of name] trust in God. I will always love you, Lynn. I will always love you. OK, Warden.

Pronounced dead: 7:30 P.M.
Note: Executed same day as Dorsie Johnson (See entry 126, Dorsie Johnson).

128

Earl Russell Behringer

Executed:
June 11, 1997

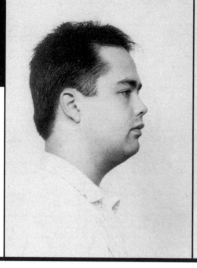 

Personal Data: *Born:* January 3, 1964. *Race:* White. Height: 5'11". *Weight:* 186 lbs. *Education level:* 14 years. *Prior occupation:* Student/sales. *County of conviction:* Tarrant. *Age at time of execution:* 33.

Sentenced to death for: Convicted in the September 1986 slayings of 22-year-old Daniel B. Meyer, Jr., and his 21-year-old fiancée Janet Louise Hancock. Meyer, a Texas A&M student, and Hancock, who attended the University of Texas at Arlington, were shot to death after Behringer and co-defendant Lawrence Scott Rouse saw the couple parked in a field near Mansfield. Both were shot repeatedly in the head with a 9mm pistol police later recovered from Behringer. Meyer's wallet and Hancock's purse were taken. Rouse surrendered to police and confessed that Behringer wanted to go to the area so he could harass parkers. *Co-defendant:* Lawrence Scott Rouse was convicted of murder and sentenced to 40 years in prison.

Received at Death Row: September 27, 1988. Time on death row: 3,177 days, (8.70 years).

Last meal: Large portion of scrambled eggs, two tablespoons of picante sauce on side, hash browns, two pieces of toast, gravy, two pieces of sausage, and grape juice.

Last statement: It's a good day to die. I walked in here like a man and I am leaving here a man. I've had a good life. I have known the love of a good woman, my wife. I have a good family. My grandmother is the pillar of the community. I love and cherish my friends and family. Thank you for your love. To the Hancock family I am sorry for the pain I caused you. If my death gives you any peace, so be it. I want my friends to know it is not the way to die, but I belong to Jesus Christ. I confess my sins. I have been baptized. I am going home with Him. I thank my friends for their support, and I thank the Dallas Cowboys for bringing me lots of joy these past years. Tell my wife and family I love them.

Pronounced dead: 6:17 P.M.

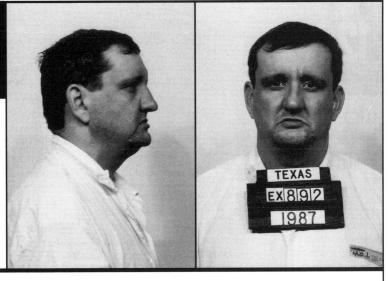

129

David Stoker

Executed: June 16, 1997

Personal Data: *Born:* January 25, 1959. *Race:* White. *Height:* 5'11". *Weight:* 223 lbs. *Education level:* 8 years. *Prior occupation:* Heavy equipment operator/carpenter. *County of conviction:* Hale. *Age at time of execution:* 38.

Sentenced to death for: Convicted in the November 1986 robbery-slaying of 50-year-old David Manrrique, a clerk at Allsup's convenience store in Hale Center. Manrrique was shot with a .22-caliber pistol during an early morning robbery that netted $60. Stoker also served a 30-year sentence for delivery of methamphetamine. That sentence was assessed in Swisher County in August 1988.

Received at Death Row: December 7, 1987. Time on death row: 3,476 days, (9.52 years).

Last meal: Two double-meat cheeseburgers, french fries, ice cream, and cigarettes (cigarettes prohibited by policy).

Last statement: I have a statement prepared that I have given to the Chaplain that I want released to the media. I am ready, Warden. [Statement n/a.]

Pronounced dead: 6:15 P.M.

130

Eddie James Johnson

Executed: June 17, 1997

Personal Data: *Born:* July 31, 1952. *Race:* Black. *Height:* 6'2". *Weight:* 225 lbs. *Education level:* 11 years. *Prior occupation:* Welder. *County of conviction:* Aransas. *Age at time of execution:* 44.

Sentenced to death for: Convicted in the September 1987 abduction and slaying of three people in Aransas County. Victims David Magee, Virginia Cadena, and Cadena's 10-year-old daughter Elizabeth Galvan were abducted from the Jackson Square Apartments in Aransas Pass and driven to a remote location near the intersection of FM 1069 and Johnson Road where they were shot to death with a .25-caliber pistol. Magee's hands and feet were bound by telephone and electrical cords, as were Cadena's hands. Her young daughter died from four bullet wounds to the abdomen. Johnson, who once worked for the same company as Magee, had recently been fired from his job and reportedly blamed Magee for his termination. The victims' bloodstained car was found parked at a nursing home close to Johnson's residence. Police also found Johnson's fingerprints at Magee's apartment and on a can inside the car. A pair of bloodsoaked blue jeans worn by Johnson were also recovered from a dumpster near his home.

Received at Death Row: April 19, 1988. Time on death row: 3,344 days, (9.16 years).

Last meal: Double-meat cheeseburger, french fries, and broccoli with cheese.

Last statement: I would like to say to the Magee family and to the Cadena family that I was friends with David and Virginia and I did not commit this offense. I have tried to do something to compensate the families by writing a book. I would like for the proceeds to go to the Magee family and the Cadena family. There is someone who will be contacting them or they can get in touch with my attorney. I would like to thank you for standing by me and Canney [spelling?]. My best to my "sun," my butterfly. Goodbye sun, I love you.

Pronounced dead: 6:34 P.M.

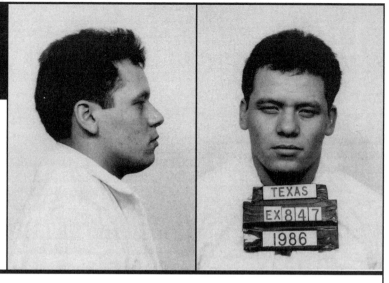

131

Irineo Montoya

Executed: June 18, 1997

Personal Data: : *Born:* June 3, 1938. *Race:* Hispanic. *Height:* 5'8". *Weight:* 140 lbs. *Education level:* 5 years. *Prior occupation:* Laborer. *County of conviction:* Cameron. *Age at time of execution:* 29.

Sentenced to death for: Convicted in the November 1985 robbery and murder of 46-year-old John Edgar Kilheffer in Brownsville. Kilheffer, a resident of South Padre Island, was stabbed to death after offering Montoya and accomplice Juan Villavicencio a ride as they were hitchhiking. Kilheffer suffered 21 stab wounds to the neck, torso, and legs. His body was stripped of its clothing and dumped in a grapefruit orchard where it was discovered a week later. The victim's bloodstained 1984 Chevrolet Blazer was recovered by Mexican state police in Matamoros on Thanksgiving Day. Records indicate that Montoya was also suspected in the abduction, rape, and robbery of two Brownsville women. He reportedly told the court following his conviction for capital murder that he would have the prosecutors and the trial judge killed.
Co-defendant: Juan Villavicencio was arrested and charged with capital murder on December 3, 1985. It is unclear whether he was acquitted of the charge or won a dismissal.

Received at Death Row: October 20, 1986. Time on death row: 3,891 days, (10.66 years).

Last meal: Fish, french fries, jalapenos, carrots, and ice cream.

Last statement: Goodbye. I wait for you in heaven. I will be waiting for you. I love my parents. I am at peace with God. Fight for the good.

Pronounced dead: 6:16 P.M.

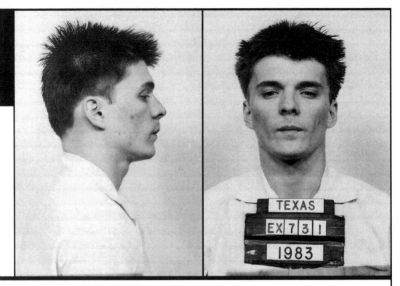

132

Robert Wallace West, Jr.

Executed: July 29, 1997

TEXAS
EX 7 3 1
1983

Personal Data: *Born:* December 12, 1961. *Race:* White. *Height:* 5'10". *Weight:* 139 lbs. *Education level:* 8 years (GED). *Prior occupation:* Student. *County of conviction:* Harris. *Age at time of execution:* 35.

Sentenced to death for: Convicted in the slaying of 22-year-old DeAnn Klaus at the Memorial Park Hotel on Waugh Drive in Houston. Klaus, who lived and worked as a waitress at the hotel, was strangled with a belt and a pillowcase and then beaten and stabbed with a wooden club after West broke into her room, stripped her of her clothes, and tied her up. West, who was also staying at the motel, told police he killed the woman because he believed she was indirectly responsible for the death of one of his friends. Other guests of the hotel saw West leaving the woman's room covered with blood. He was arrested at the scene about 30 minutes after Klaus' body was found with the splintered piece of wood still embedded in her back.

Received at Death Row: February 3, 1983. Time on death row: 5,286 days, (14.48 years).

Last meal: Cheeseburger, french fries, Coke, and Camel cigarettes (cigarettes prohibited by policy)

Last statement: I would like to apologize for all of the pain and suffering I put you all through. I hope this will give you closure now and later on down the line. Bob, I appreciate you coming. Stacy and Jess, I will wait for you.

Pronounced dead: 6:41 P.M.

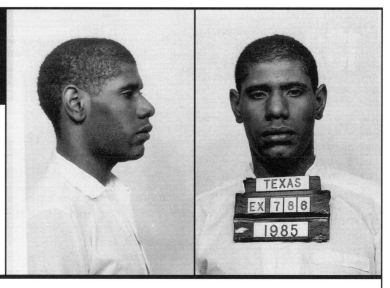

133

**James
Carl Lee
Davis**

Executed:
September 9,
1997

Personal Data: *Born:* February 8, 1963. *Race:* Black. *Height:* 5'9". *Weight:* 156 lbs. *Education level:* 8 years. *Prior occupation:* Roofer. *County of conviction:* Travis. *Age at time of execution:* 34.

Sentenced to death for: Convicted of beating to death three children, Even Johnson, 15, Tyron Johnson, 6, and Tom Johnson, 4, with a lead pipe during a burglary of their home. The Johnsons lived next door to Davis. Even Johnson was raped and sodomized.

Received at Death Row: March 22, 1985. Time on death row: 4,551 days, (12.47 years).

Last meal: Steak and eggs (eggs over easy), toast, punch, and package of Marlboro cigarettes (cigarettes prohibited by policy).

Last statement: All my friends in my heart I'm ready. [Officials could not understand him, but this is what it sounded like.]

Pronounced dead: 6:17 P.M.

134

Jessel Turner

Executed: September 22, 1997

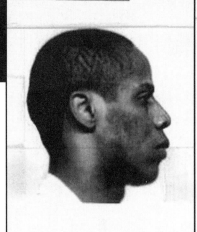

ry 1986 robbery-sl̲g of Charles Hur

Personal Data: *Born:* June 7, 1960. *Race:* Black. *Height:* 6'1". *Weight:* 180 lbs. *Education level:* 11 years. *Prior occupation:* Truck driver. *County of conviction:* Harris. *Age at time of execution:* 37.

Sentenced to death for: Convicted in the February 1986 robbery-slaying of Charles Hunter, a Houston cab driver. Hunter was robbed and shot in the chest with a .22-caliber pistol after picking Turner up in Houston's Fifth Ward. Hunter's body was found in the street about half a mile from where he picked Turner up. Turner stole Hunter's cab and drove it to his apartment complex. The cab was found ransacked. Turner was arrested a short time later while driving another car near the murder scene. The murder weapon was found in the car Turner was driving.

Received at Death Row: November 12, 1988. Time on death row: 3,568 days, (9.78 years).

Last meal: None.

Last statement: First I would like to give praise to God for the love and grace that He has allowed for all of this to come together. I would like to thank and ask blessings for all of the men who are in prison and have shared in my struggle and have allowed me to help them. I would like to thank my family for their blessings and for sharing my struggle and having been there for me and endured this with me. I would like to thank the Chaplain and all the rest who have offered their prayers. I would also like to thank Mrs. Hunter's brother and family who have offered their forgiveness and all of their prayers. I pray that God's praise be upon all of you and that you will be touched by the grace of God. Til we meet again, may all of God's blessings be upon you.

Pronounced dead: 6:18 P.M.

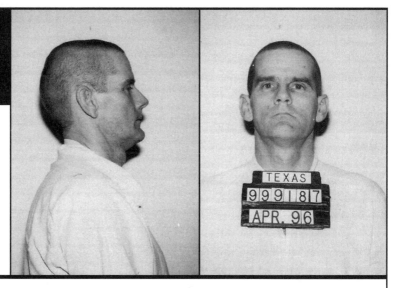

135

Benjamin C. Stone

Executed: September 25, 1997

Personal Data: *Born:* June 3, 1952. *Race:* White. *Height:* 6'0". *Weight:* 175 lbs. *Education level:* 12 years. *Prior occupation:* Plumber. *County of conviction:* Nueces. *Age at time of execution:* 45.

Sentenced to death for: Convicted in the strangling death of his 34-year-old ex-wife Patsy Lynn Stone and his 12-year-old step-daughter Keith Lynn Van Coney at their Corpus Christi home. Stone used his hands to strangle the two victims following a verbal and physical altercation between himself and his ex-wife. The victims were also sexually assaulted by Stone. Stone was arrested the next day after he called 911 from a highway rest area and confessed to killing the two women.

Received at Death Row: April 25, 1996. Time on death row: 518 days, (1.42 years).

Last meal: Coke.

Last statement: None.

Pronounced dead: 6:16 P.M.

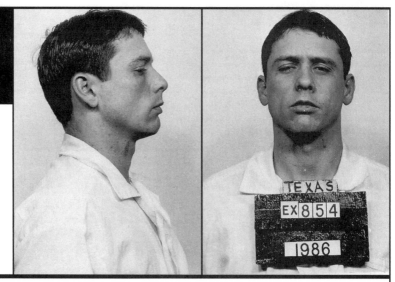

136

John William Cockrum

Executed: September 30, 1997

Personal Data: *Born:* December 20, 1958. *Race:* White. *Height:* 5'9". *Weight:* 175 lbs. *Education level:* 9 years. *Prior occupation:* Bricklayer. *County of conviction:* Bowie. *Age at time of execution:* 38.

Sentenced to death for: Convicted in the May 1986 death of 69-year-old Eva May near DeKalb. May was shot once in the head during a robbery of the L.A. May Grocery located approximately six miles east of DeKalb. Cockrum was arrested the next day. Co-defendant Jerry Morgan reportedly led police to the .22-caliber pistol used in the shooting and later testified against Cockrum in exchange for a reduced charge.
Co-defendant: Jerry Morgan was convicted of burglary of a habitation and sentenced to 99 years in prison.

Received at Death Row: December 9, 1986. Time on death row: 3,945 days, (10.81 years).

Last meal: Cheeseburger, onion rings, banana pudding, and iced tea.

Last statement: I would like to apologize to the victim's family for all of the pain I have caused them. I would like to tell my family I love them and I hope to see them again soon. Lord Jesus, thank you for giving me the strength and the time in my life to find Jesus Christ and to be forgiven for all of my sins. Thank you for the changes in my life you have given me. The love and closeness of my family and my beautiful daughter. Thank you for using me.

Pronounced dead: 6:17 P.M.

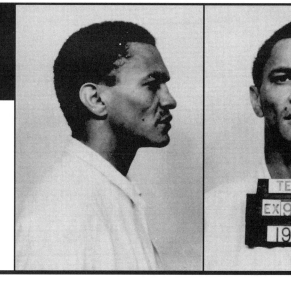

137

Dwight Dwayne Adanandus

Executed: October 1, 1997

Personal Data: *Born:* February 19, 1956. *Race:* Black. *Height:* 5'10". *Weight:* 148 lbs. *Education level:* 11 years. *Prior occupation:* Auto mechanic. *County of conviction:* Bexar. *Age at time of execution:* 41.

Sentenced to death for: Convicted in the January 1988 shooting death of Vernon Hanan during the course of a bank robbery in San Antonio. Hanan, vice president of W. F. Castello & Associates, was shot to death in the foyer of Continental Bank when he attempted to stop Adanandus from escaping with $10,000 stolen from a bank teller. Adanandus was apprehended four hours later after police and FBI SWAT teams were called to the neighborhood residence where he had fled.

Received at Death Row: May 23, 1989. Time on death row: 3,050 days, (8.36 years).

Last meal: Cheeseburger, french fries, and iced tea.

Last statement: Ms. Croft and Mr. Betthi, I don't know what to say to you but I apologize for the pain I have caused you and your family over the years. I hope that you will accept my apology and that you will know that it is sincere. I hope this will allow you and your family to move on and I hope you will forgive me and I hope Mr. Hanan will forgive me for taking his life. Please accept my apology. I love you all. I am finished.

Pronounced dead: 6:16 P.M.

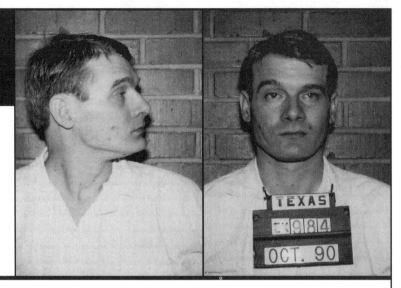

138

Ricky Lee Green

Executed: October 8, 1997

Personal Data: *Born:* December 27, 1960. *Race:* White. *Height:* 5'8". *Weight:* 170 lbs. *Education level:* 8 years. *Prior occupation:* Radiator repair. *County of conviction:* Travis. *Age at time of execution:* 36.

Sentenced to death for: Convicted in the September 1986 sexual mutilation and murder of 28-year-old Steven Fefferman, an advertising executive with KXAS-TV of Fort Worth. Fefferman was castrated and stabbed repeatedly with a butcher knife at his home after meeting Green and engaging in sex with him on a beach in Fort Worth. After killing Fefferman, Green stole the victim's car. Green was charged with the killing in April 1989 after his wife went to police with information. Green later confessed to three sexual mutilation slayings in 1985. His wife, Sharon Green, was convicted and sentenced to 19 years probation in one of the 1985 killings.

Received at Death Row: October 5, 1990. Time on death row: 2,558 days, (7.01 years).

Last meal: Five scrambled eggs, four sausage patties, eight slices of toast, six slices of bacon, and four pints of milk.

Last statement: I want to thank the Lord for giving me this opportunity to get to know him. He has shown me a lot and He has changed me in the past 2 months. I have been in prison 8 ½ years and on death row for 7 and I have not gotten into any trouble. I feel like I am not a threat to society any more. I feel like my punishment is over, but my friends are now being punished. I thank the Lord for all He has done for me. I do want to tell the families that I am sorry but killing me is not going to solve nothing. I really do not believe that if Jesus were here tonight that He would execute me. Jesus is all about love. I want to thank all of my friends for supporting me and for being here for me. Thank all of my friends on the row. Thank you, Lord. I am finished.

Pronounced dead: 6:31 P.M.

139

Kenneth Ray Ransom

Executed:
October 28, 1997

PHOTOGRAPHS NOT AVAILABLE

Personal Data: *Born:* May 15, 1963. *Race:* Black. *Height:* 5'9". *Weight:* 169 lbs. *Education level:* 12 years. *Prior occupation:* Plumber. *County of conviction:* Harris. *Age at time of execution:* 34.

Sentenced to death for: Convicted in the July 1983 stabbing death of 19-year-old Arnold Pequeno, an employee of the Malibu Grand Prix Race Track amusement center in Houston. Also slain were Anil Varughese, 18, a night manager, 22-year-old Roddy Harris, and Arnold Pequeno's 18-year-old brother Joerene Pequeno. All four victims died of multiple stab wounds to the upper body, neck, and head.
Co-defendant: Richard J. Wilkerson was convicted of capital murder in the stabbing death of Anil Varughese. Wilkerson had been fired from his job as a pit attendant at the raceway and amusement center located in the 6100 block of the Southwest Freeway about two weeks before the murders. Richard Wilkerson was sentenced to death, and executed by lethal injection on August 31, 1993 (See entry 67, Richard Wilkerson). James Edward Randle was convicted of capital murder and sentenced to life in prison.

Received at Death Row: September 13, 1984. Time on death row: 4,790 days, (13.12 years).

Last meal: Declined last meal.

Last statement: First and foremost I would like to tell the victims' families that I am sorry because I feel like I am guilty. I am sorry for the pain all of them have gone through during holidays and birthdays they are without their loved ones. I have said from the beginning and will say it again: I am innocent. I did not kill no one. I feel like this is the Lord's will that will be done. I love you all. You know it. Don't cry. Tell my brothers I love them. You all be strong.

Pronounced dead: 6:20 P.M.

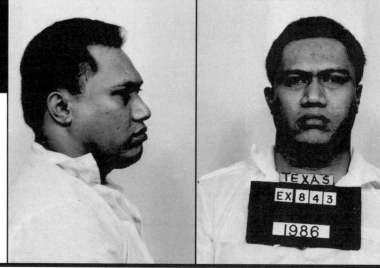

140

Aua Lauti

Executed: November 4, 1997

Personal Data: *Born:* June 18, 1954. *Race:* Other. *Height:* 5'10". *Weight:* 225 lbs. *Education level:* 11 years. *Prior occupation:* Landscaping. *County of conviction:* Harris. *Age at time of execution:* 43.

Sentenced to death for: Lauti was convicted of capital murder in the beating/strangulation death of his 9-year-old cousin Tara Lauti on December 19, 1985. Evidence showed that Lauti, despondent over a breakup with his girlfriend, kidnapped his cousin from her father's home and drove her to a field where she was beaten, sexually assaulted, and strangled. Police said Lauti knocked the girl unconscious with his fist while abducting her from the home at 11015 Maple Rock in Northeast Harris County and then twice more knocked her unconscious by hitting her on the head with a beer bottle and hitting her in the chest with his fist. She died of a skull fracture, strangulation, and a crushed right chest.

Received at Death Row: September 18, 1986. Time on death row: 4,062 days, (11.13 years).

Last meal: Double-meat cheeseburger, french fries, and soft drink.

Last statement: I would like to say that I have spent 11 years living on death row and during that time I have made a lot of friends. I do not feel anger and hatred. I feel love and forgiveness. I would like to say that I have come to realize that I have been blessed by God with good friends. I have friends on the inside and I have friends on the outside who support me. They write to me. I do not know them, and they do not know me. I have a wonderful family who loves me and supports me and who forgives me, and that is the most important thing. I am glad I found God and am so happy for it. I love my family and I want them to know that. That is about all I have to say.

Pronounced dead: 6:32 P.M.

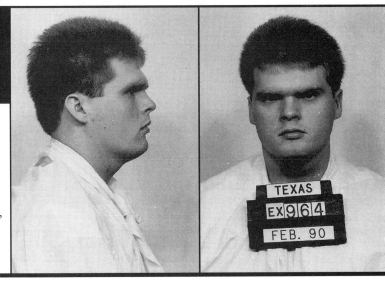

141

Aaron Lee Fuller

Executed:
November 6, 1997

Personal Data: *Born:* August 26, 1967. *Race:* White. *Height:* 5'11". *Weight:* 175 lbs. *Education level:* 11 years. *Prior occupation:* Diesel mechanic. *County of conviction:* Dawson. *Age at time of execution:* 30.

Sentenced to death for: Convicted in the March 1989 robbery and murder of 68-year-old Loretta Stephens. In a statement to police, Fuller said he decided to burglarize Stephen's residence in Lubbock after seeing her sleeping in a recliner in the living room. After finding more than $500 cash in the house, Fuller said he stood over Stephens for about 10 minutes and then started beating and choking her. He finally suffocated the woman with a pillow when he realized she had survived the beating. After tying her hands and feet with telephone cord and sexually assaulting the woman, Fuller placed the victim's body in the trunk of her car, and later, accompanied by a friend, drove to a spot eight miles north of Lamesa off Highway 87 and dumped it into a stand of weeds. Fuller and his friend then drove back to Lubbock where they abandoned the stolen vehicle in a parking lot across from the bus station.
Co-defendant: Juan Victor Gomez was reportedly charged with unauthorized use of a motor vehicle in connection with the case. Disposition of case unknown.

Received at Death Row: February 14, 1990. Time on death row: 2,281 days, (7.73 years).

Last meal: None.

Last statement: Jesus the Lord is everything to me. I am nothing without him. Praise Jesus. Praise God.

Pronounced dead: 6:20 P.M.

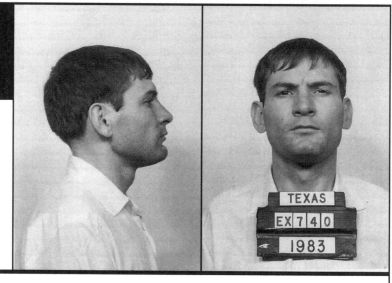

142

Michael Eugene Sharp

Executed:
November 19, 1997

Personal Data: *Born:* April 4, 1954. *Race:* White. *Height:* 5'1". *Weight:* 150 lbs. *Education level:* 13 years. *Prior occupation:* Oilfield worker. *County of conviction:* Crockett. *Age at time of execution:* 43.

Sentenced to death for: Convicted in the June 1982 abduction and stabbing death of 31-year-old Brenda Kay Broadway of Kermit. Broadway and her two daughters, ages 8 and 15, were reportedly abducted from a car wash and driven to a remote location in Ector County where they were sexually abused. Broadway and her 8-year-old daughter, Christie Michelle Elms, were then stabbed to death. Broadway's other daughter managed to escape during the stabbings. Naked and with her arms bound, she ran five miles through the desert before finding help at an oil rig. The bodies of the two victims were found buried in a shallow grave. Sharp was arrested five days after the bodies were found. In November 1982, Sharp was convicted of murder in Christie Elms' death and sentenced to life in prison. He was also a suspect in several other West Texas killings. In late November 1982, he led police to the grave of 18-year-old Blanca Guerrero of Odessa, who had been missing since May 17, 1982. Her body was found buried under a water tank in Andrews County.

Received at Death Row: June 6, 1983. Time on death row: 5,276 days, (14.45 years).

Last meal: Small pizza, dish of Italian spaghetti, marble cake, and punch.

Last statement: n/a.

Pronounced dead: 6:21 P.M.

143

Charlie Livingston

Executed:
November 21, 1997

Personal Data: *Born:* February 14, 1962. *Race:* Black. *Height:* 5'8". *Weight:* N/A lbs. *Education level:* 10 years. *Prior occupation:* Warehouseman. *County of conviction:* Harris. *Age at time of execution:* 35.

Sentenced to death for: Convicted in the robbery-murder of 38-year-old Janet Caldwell outside a grocery store in Houston. Livingston reportedly drove to the Weingarten's store at West 43rd Street and waited until he saw a woman, alone, drive up to the store and park. When Caldwell went inside, Livingston crawled underneath her van and waited until she returned with an armload of groceries. He then crawled from underneath her van, pointed a 9mm pistol at her, and attempted to steal her purse. As the two struggled, Livingston shot Caldwell twice in the throat and fled with her purse. He was apprehended a short time later and identified by witnesses.

Received at Death Row: July 25, 1985. Time on death row: 4,491 days, (12.33 years).

Last meal: Ribs smothered in onions and gravy, rice with butter, ice water, and Dr Pepper.

Last statement: You all brought me here to be executed, not to make a speech. That's it.

Pronounced dead: 6:17 P.M.

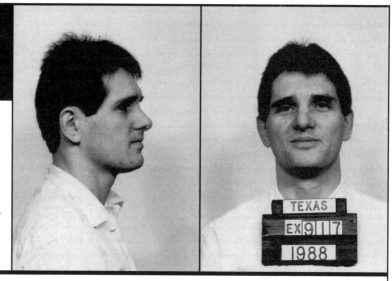

144

Michael Lee Lockhart

Executed:
December 9, 1997

Personal Data: *Born:* September 30, 1960. *Race:* White. *Height:* 5'10". *Weight:* 165 lbs. *Education level:* 11 years. *Prior occupation:* Laborer/truck driver. *County of conviction:* Bexar. *Age at time of execution:* 37.

Sentenced to death for: Convicted in the March 1988 shooting death of Beaumont police officer Douglas Hulsey, Jr. The officer was shot to death while attempting to arrest Lockhart for driving a stolen vehicle.
Note: Lockhart had been tied to a string of robberies and thefts across the country and also faced capital murder charges in Florida and Indiana.

Received at Death Row: October 26, 1988. Time on death row: 3,329 days, (9.12 years).

Last meal: Double-meat cheeseburger, french fries, and Coke.

Last statement: A lot of people view what is happening here as evil, but I want you to know that I found love and compassion here. The people who work here, I thank them for the kindness they have shown me. And I deeply appreciate all that has been done for me by the people who work here. That's all, Warden. I'm ready.

Pronounced dead: 6:24 P.M.

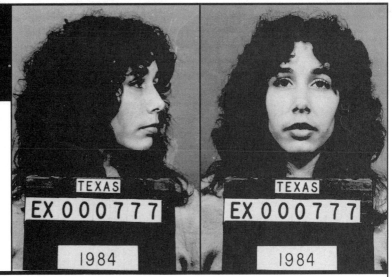

145

Karla Faye Tucker

Executed: February 3, 1998

Personal Data: *Born:* November 18, 1959. *Race:* White. *Height:* 5'3". *Weight:* 121 lbs. *Education level:* 7 years. *Prior occupation:* Office worker. *County of conviction:* Harris. *Age at time of execution:* 38.

Sentenced to death for: Convicted in the June 1983 pickax slaying of 27-year-old Jerry Lynn Dean at the victim's apartment on Watonga Drive in northeast Houston. Dean and his companion, 32-year-old Deborah Thornton, were hacked to death after Tucker and accomplice Daniel Ryan Garrett sneaked into the apartment, supposedly to steal some motorcycle parts. Tucker testified that she and Garrett confronted Dean in the bedroom and that Garret started beating Dean on the head with a hammer. Tucker said that she heard a "gurgling sound" coming from Dean and struck him in the back with a pickax she spotted in the room to stop him from making a sound. Tucker turned the pickax on Thornton when she was discovered beneath a blanket. The bodies of both victims had more than 20 stab or puncture wounds and the pickax was found embedded in Thornton's chest. Witnesses testified that Tucker later bragged about receiving gratification every time she hit her victims with the ax, a claim she later denied. She did admit to hating Dean because he had defaced photographs of her mother.
Co-defendant: Daniel Ryan Garret, was convicted of capital murder and sentenced to death. He died of liver disease in June 1993.

Received at Death Row: December 18, 1984. Time on death row: 4,979 days, (13.64 years).

Last meal: Banana, peach, and garden salad with ranch dressing.

Last statement: See Appendix 1.

Pronounced dead: 6:45 P.M.
Note: Tucker was the first woman executed in Texas since 1863. See Appendix 1 for a statement from Allan B. Polunsky, Chairman of the Texas Board of Criminal Justice, regarding Tucker's execution.

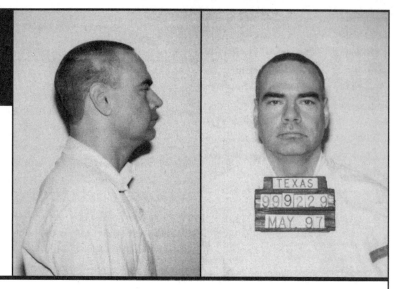

146

Steven Ceon Renfro

Executed:
February 9, 1998

Personal Data: *Born:* September 14, 1957. *Race:* White. *Height:* 6'1". *Weight:* 215 lbs. *Education level:* n/a. *Prior occupation:* Laborer. *County of conviction:* Harrison. *Age at time of execution:* 40.

Sentenced to death for: Convicted in the August 1996 slaying of three people in Marshall during a shooting spree that also left a city police officer wounded. Killed were Renfro's common-law wife, Rhena Fultner, 36; his aunt, Rose Rutledge, 66; and an acquaintance, George Counts, 40. Renfro reportedly dressed in camouflage clothing and armed himself with assault weapons after claiming to have seen his common-law wife having sex with two unidentified men. He drove to the house he shared with his aunt at 614 N. Washington and shot Fultner once in the forehead. He then walked to his aunt's bedroom and shot her once in the head while she watched television in bed. Renfro shot Fultner a second time in the forehead when he found her still alive in the living room of the home. Renfro then went to Counts' trailer home at 1000 Calloway and fired a barrage of bullets into the structure when Counts refused his admittance. Counts' body was found just inside the door of the bullet-riddled trailer. Renfro said he killed Counts because he had once struck Fultner. Renfro then opened fire on the squad car of Marshall police officer Dominick Pondant and reserve officer George Gill as they responded to reports of shots being fired near the intersection of Main and Calloway streets. Pondant was hit by gunfire, but managed to exit his vehicle and return fire, wounding Renfro in the arm and abdomen. At the hospital, Renfro reportedly told police, "I killed them all. I killed my whole family."

Received at Death Row: May 22, 1997. Time on death row: 263 days, (0.72 years).

Last meal: Bacon, lettuce, and tomato sandwich with extra bacon, cherry pie, vanilla ice cream, and two cans of Dr Pepper.

Last statement: I would like to tell the victim's families that I am sorry, very sorry. I am so sorry. Forgive me if you can. I know it's impossible, but try. Take my hand, Lord Jesus, I'm coming home.

Pronounced dead: 6:18 P.M.

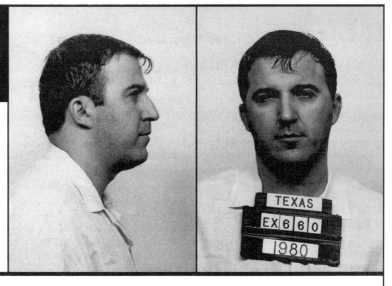

147

Jerry Lee Hogue

Executed: March 11, 1998

Personal Data: *Born:* September 26, 1950. *Race:* White. *Height:* 5'6". *Weight:* 170 lbs. *Education level:* 10 years. *Prior occupation:* Auto repossesser. *County of conviction:* Tarrant. *Age at time of execution:* 47.

Sentenced to death for: Hogue was convicted of capital murder in the January 1979 death of 27-year-old Jayne Markham in Arlington. Markham died in a house fire set by Hogue at 2412 Southcrest in Arlington. She had shared the rental house with her eight-year-old son and friends Mary Beth Crawford and Steve Renick. Hogue, who had lived in the same house a month before it was leased to the foursome in December 1978, apparently established some sort of amiable relationship with Markham and visited her on the last two days of her life. While Markham, Crawford, and Hogue were eating breakfast on January 12, he suddenly blurted out that he was a police officer and that he was arresting them for marijuana possession. Retrieving Renick's loaded pistol from a footlocker, Hogue later forced Crawford into an act of oral sodomy and then stabbed her in the stomach with a butcher knife. Markham was tied up and raped by Hogue prior to her death. Once Markham's son returned home from school and Renick returned from work, Hogue tied up or handcuffed the four inside the house and set it afire. All but Markham, whose hands and feet were tied behind her back with insulated wire, managed to escape. Hogue was arrested at a friend's home in Arlington on January 14.

Received at Death Row: June 6, 1980. Time on death row: 6,481 days, (17.76 years).

Last meal: Old-fashioned cheeseburger, french fries with catsup, chocolate cake and two cans of Coke.

Last statement: Mindy, I'm with you honey. I do not know why Mindy you are doing this but I will forgive you. You know he is a murderer. Why don't you support me? He will do it again. Mindy, you are lucky you are still alive. Give my love to my family. I love them. Mindy, you can stop this. OK. I'm ready.
Note: Mindy was a nickname for Mary Beth Crawford, who witnessed the execution.

Pronounced dead: 6:50 P.M.

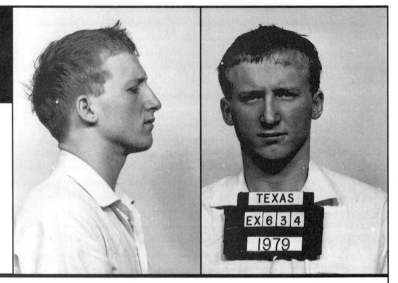

148

Joseph John Cannon

Executed: April 22, 1998.

Personal Data: *Born:* January 13, 1960. *Race:* White. *Height:* 6'1". *Weight:* 140 lbs. *Education level:* None. *Prior occupation:* Laborer. *County of conviction:* Bexar. *Age at time of execution:* 38.

Sentenced to death for: Convicted of capital murder in the slaying of San Antonio attorney Anne C. Walsh. Walsh was shot seven times with a .22-caliber pistol after she had returned home for lunch. Walsh was the sister of Dan Carabin, Cannon's court-appointed attorney on a burglary of a habitation charge. Carabin and Walsh took an interest in Cannon's welfare following a burglary conviction and he was permitted to live at the Walsh home while on probation. Cannon told police that he found several guns in a bedroom on the day of the murder and "just went crazy." He said he attempted to sexually assault Walsh after killing her. Cannon was arrested after seen driving a 1977 Maverick belonging to Walsh's daughter. He had taken several firearms from the house and stole two $250 travelers checks and a few dollars from Walsh's purse.
Note: Cannon committed the murder when he was 17 years old.

Received at Death Row: May 9, 1979. Time on death row: 6,918 days, (18.95 years).

Last meal: Fried chicken, barbecue ribs, baked potato, green salad with Italian dressing, chocolate cake or chocolate ice cream or both, a thick chocolate shake or malt, and iced tea.

Last statement: [Inmate was crying could not understand first words.] I am really sorry. I love you all. I love you, God.
Note: The first attempt at lethal injection failed when a vein in Cannon's arm collapsed, requiring the lethal needle to be removed. It took about 15 minutes for officials to establish another injection.
Second last statement: I am sorry for what I did to your mom. It isn't because I'm going to die. All my life I have been locked up. I could never forgive what I done. I am sorry for all of you. I love you all. Thank you for supporting me. I thank you for being kind to me when I was small. Thank you, God. All right.

Pronounced dead: 7:28 P.M.

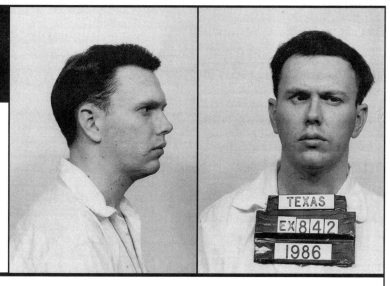

149

Lesley Lee Gosch

Executed: April 24, 1998

Personal Data: *Born:* July 8, 1955. *Race:* White. *Height:* 5'5". *Weight:* 140 lbs. *Education level:* n/a. *Prior occupation:* n/a. *County of conviction:* Victoria. *Age at time of execution:* 42.

Sentenced to death for: Gosch was convicted of capital murder in the shooting death of 43-year-old Rebecca Smith Patton of San Antonio in September 1985. Patton, married to the president of Castle Hill National Bank in San Antonio, was shot seven times in the head with a .22-caliber pistol fitted with a silencer during an extortion attempt in her Alamo Heights neighborhood home by Gosch and accomplice John Lawrence Rogers. The men attempted to kidnap Patton in order to demand ransom for her family. Gosch was arrested on September 25, 1985, at his home. His trial was moved from Bexar County to Victoria County in a change of venue. Co-defendant Rogers was convicted of extortion and sentenced to federal penitentiary.

Received at Death Row: September 15, 1986. Time on death row: 4,236 days, (11.61 years).

Last meal: Declined last meal.

Last statement: None.

Pronounced dead: 6:38 P.M.

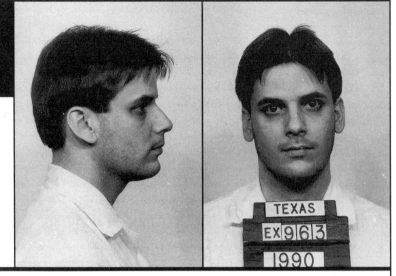

150

Frank Basil McFarland

Executed:
April 29, 1998

TEXAS EX963 1990

Personal Data: *Born:* October 7, 1963. *Race:* White. *Height:* 5'10". *Weight:* 160 lbs. *Education level:* 10 years. *Prior occupation:* Electrician. *County of conviction:* Tarrant. *Age at time of execution:* 34.

Sentenced to death for: Convicted in the February 1988 sexual assault and murder of 26-year-old Terri Lynn Hokanson of Arlington. Hokanson, who worked as a shoeshine girl at a Fort Worth bar, was found lying in the driveway of the First United Methodist Church in Hurst. Suffering from more than 50 stab wounds, Hokanson was alive when found and managed to tell police that two men had raped and stabbed her. She died the next morning at a local hospital. Witnesses told police that Hokanson was last seen with two men at a second Fort Worth bar that night of her disappearance. A knife and gold earring belonging to Hokanson were later found in McFarland's vehicle.
Co-defendant: Alleged co-defendant Ryan Michael Wilson was shot to death near Weatherford in Parker County on March 11, 1988.

Received at Death Row: February 12, 1990. Time on death row: 2,996 days, (8.20 years).

Last meal: Heaping portion of lettuce, a sliced tomato, a sliced cucumber, four celery stalks, four sticks of American or Cheddar cheese, two bananas, and two cold half-pints of milk. Asked that all vegetables be washed prior to serving. Also asked that the cheese sticks be "clean."

Last statement: I owe no apologies for a crime I did not commit. Those who lied and fabricated evidence against me will have to answer for what they have done. I know in my heart what I did and I call upon the spirit of my ancestors and all of my people and I swear to them and now I am coming home.

Pronounced dead: 6:27 P.M.

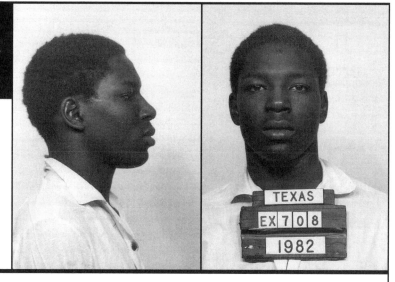

151

Robert Anthony Carter

Executed: May 18, 1998

Personal Data: *Born:* February 10, 1964. *Race:* Black. *Height:* 6'0". *Weight:* 156 lbs. *Education level:* 10 years. *Prior occupation:* Laborer. *County of conviction:* Harris. *Age at time of execution:* 34.

Sentenced to death for: Shooting death of Sylvia Reyes, 18, during a robbery. Reyes, manager of a Conoco service station in the 300 block of South Wayside in Houston was shot once in the chest with a .38-caliber revolver as she attempted to stop Carter from taking money ($150) from the cash register. Reyes died at a Houston hospital about an hour after the shooting. During his capital murder trial, Carter was also implicated in the June 18, 1981, slaying of R.B. Scott, 63, during a robbery of a beauty supply store in Houston.

Received at Death Row: : March 12, 1982. Time on death row: 5,907 days, (15.61 years).

Last meal: Fried fish fillet, french fries, orange juice, and German chocolate cake.

Last statement: I love all of you all. Thank you for caring so much about me. Keep the faith. I am going to a better place. I hope the victims' families will forgive me because I didn't mean to hurt no one or kill no one. I love you all.

Pronounced dead: 6:25 P.M.

152

Pedro Cruz Muniz

Executed:
May 18, 1998

TEXAS
EX 5 7 5
1977

Personal Data: *Born:* September 25, 1956. *Race:* Hispanic. *Height:* 5'4". *Weight:* 152 lbs. *Education level:* 10 years. *Prior occupation:* Laborer. *County of conviction:* Williamson. *Age at time of execution:* 41.

Sentenced to death for: Muniz was sentenced to die for the December 1976 rape/murder of 19-year-old Janis Carol Bickham, a student at Southwestern University in Georgetown.

Received at Death Row: October 7, 1977. Time on death row: 7,524 days, (20.61 years).

Last meal: Requested shrimp and salad. [Shrimp not available.] Served cheeseburger, french fries, and cola.

Last statement: I know you can't hear me now but I know that it won't matter what I have to say. I want you to know that I did not kill your sister. If you want to know the truth and you deserve to know the truth, hire your own investigators. That is all I have to say.

Pronounced dead: 6:20 P.M.

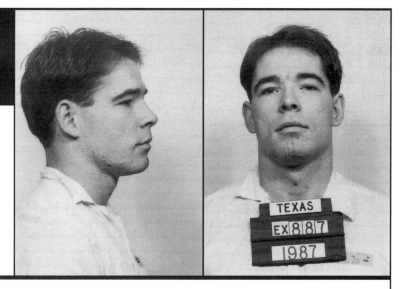

153

Clifford Boggess

Executed:
June 11,
1998

Personal Data: *Born:* June 11, 1965. *Race:* White. *Height:* 6'2". *Weight:* 232 lbs. *Education level:* 12 years. *Prior occupation:* Carpenter's helper. *County of conviction:* Clay. *Age at time of execution:* 32.

Sentenced to death for: Murder/robbery of Moses Frank Collier, 86, owner of Collier Grocery and Produce Store in Saint Jo. Mr. Collier was beaten and stabbed to death. Boggess left the scene with approximately $700.

Received at Death Row: October 23, 1987. Time on death row: 3,877 days, (10.62 years).

Last meal: Two double-meat cheeseburgers, salad, french fries with salt and catsup, chocolate fudge brownies, cherry cake, a Pepsi, and iced tea.

Last statement: I'd like to say that for the murders of Roy Hazelwood and Frank Collier, I'm sorry. For the pain it has caused you. To my friends, I'd like to say that I love you and I'm glad you've been a part of my life. Thank you. I'll miss you. Remember that today I'll be with Jesus in paradise. I'll see you again. Lord Jesus Christ, Son of Almighty God, mercy on me as a sinner, forgive me of my sins. I would like to offer up my death for the conversion of sinners on death row. Lord Jesus into your hands I command my spirit.
Note: At end of last statement, Boggess began praying "for the conversion of sinners on death row."

Pronounced dead: 6:21 P.M.

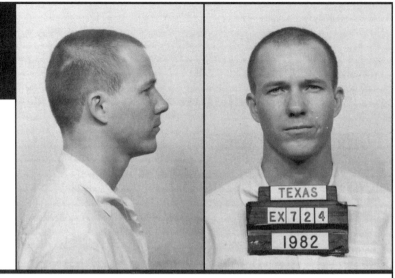

154

Johnny Dean Pyles

Executed: June 15, 1998

Personal Data: *Born:* December 30, 1957. *Race:* White. *Height:* 5'6". *Weight:* 155 lbs. *Education level:* 16 years. *Prior occupation:* Brick mason helper. *County of conviction:* Dallas. *Age at time of execution:* 32.

Sentenced to death for: Pyles was convicted and sentenced to death for the June 20, 1982, shooting death of a Dallas County sheriff's deputy, Ray Edward Kovar, 34. Kovar was shot in the chest at close range with a .38-caliber revolver.

Received at Death Row: October 21, 1982. Time on death row: 5,712 days, (15.65 years).

Last meal: Chicken-fried steak with gravy, potatoes, pineapple pie, and Coke.

Last statement: I want to tell you folks there, I have a love in my heart for you. I hope you don't look for satisfaction or comfort or peace in my execution. Jesus Christ is my Lord and Saviour and I want him to be yours. I'm sorry for the pain and heartache I've caused your family. Too many years I've caused all my family problems and heartache. I'm sorry. I wanted to let you know that the Lord Jesus is my life and I just want to say I'm gonna fall asleep and I'll be in His presence shortly. I got reason to rejoice and I pray to see all of you there someday.

Pronounced dead: 6:24 P.M.

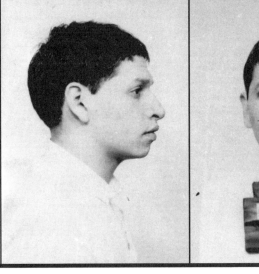

155

Leopoldo Narvaiz, Jr.

Executed:
June 26, 1998

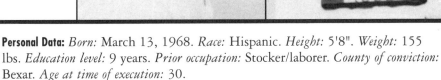

Personal Data: *Born:* March 13, 1968. *Race:* Hispanic. *Height:* 5'8". *Weight:* 155 lbs. *Education level:* 9 years. *Prior occupation:* Stocker/laborer. *County of conviction:* Bexar. *Age at time of execution:* 30.

Sentenced to death for: Convicted in the April 1988 stabbing deaths of his ex-girlfriend and her two sisters and brother inside their San Antonio home. Stabbed repeatedly with butcher knives were Narvaiz's ex-girlfriend Shannon Mann, 17; her two sisters, Jennifer Mann, 19, and Martha Mann, 15; and her brother, 11-year-old Ernest Mann, Jr. The victims suffered more than 100 wounds and some of the knife blades were broken and embedded in their bodies. Police responded to the victims' mobile home after Shannon placed a 911 emergency call and said her boyfriend was beating and killing them. Prosecutors charged that Narvaiz was angry over a spurned romance with Shannon and killed the siblings in a jealous rage.

Received at Death Row: November 22, 1988. Time on death row: 3,501 days, (9.69 years).

Last meal: None.

Last statement: None.

Pronounced dead: 6:29 P.M.

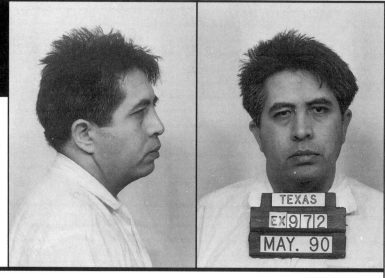

156

Genaro Camacho, Jr.

Executed:
August 26,
1998

Personal Data: *Born:* September 14, 1954. *Race:* Hispanic. *Height:* 5'7". *Weight:* 185 lbs. *Education level:* 13 years. *Prior occupation:* Produce baker. *County of conviction:* Dallas. *Age at time of execution:* 43.

Sentenced to death for: Convicted in the May 1988 slaying of 24-year-old David L. Wilburn. Wilburn was shot in the back of the head after interrupting the kidnapping of two persons from a home at 7917 Nassau Circle in Dallas. Sam Wright, the 57-year-old owner of the home, told police that Camacho and two unnamed accomplices forced their way into the home and attempted to kidnap him along with 31-year-old Evellyn Banks and her 3-year-old son Andre. Wright was able to escape the three intruders after they had shot Wilburn and called for police. Evellyn Banks, who was handcuffed, was taken from the home with her son and driven away in a car. Banks and her child reportedly were later killed by Comacho.
Co-defendants: Two unnamed accomplices.

Received at Death Row: May 9, 1990. Time on death row: 2,998 days, (8.21 years).

Last meal: Steak, baked potato, salad, and strawberry ice cream.

Last statement: I love you all. We had a good service and I'll be with you. I'll be waiting for you in heaven. OK. Adios. That's all I have to say.

Pronounced dead: 7:49 P.M.

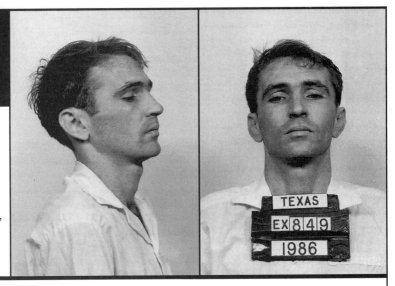

157

Delbert Boyd Teague, Jr.

Executed: September 9, 1998

Personal Data: *Born:* November 11, 1962. *Race:* White. *Height:* 5'8". *Weight:* 131 lbs. *Education level:* 10 years. *Prior occupation:* Construction worker. *County of conviction:* Tarrant. *Age at time of execution:* 35.

Sentenced to death for: Convicted in the April 1985 robbery-slaying of 21-year-old Kevin Leroy Allen at a park near Fort Worth. Allen, a Fort Worth resident, was one of three men shot at Marion Sansom Park after Teague and accomplice Robin Scott Partine robbed Thomas Emmitt Cox (DOB: 4-12-63) and his date, an 18-year-old white female at gunpoint. Cox had run over to the men's vehicle to ask for help when Teague and Partine robbed the couple of about $80 and then started to leave the park overlooking Lake Worth with the woman. At that point, Teague pulled up behind the men in the stolen pickup he was driving and shot each in the head with a .22-caliber pistol. Allen died at a local hospital of two gunshot wounds to the head. David Suson (DOB: 1-7-53) and James Bell (DOB: 12-20-54) recovered from head and facial wounds. Following the shootings, Cox's date (DOB: 12-20-66) was kidnapped and sexually assaulted by Teague and Partine. The two were arrested the following day after the woman was able to leave a note asking for help in a service station restroom near Ramah, Louisiana.
Co-defendant: Robin Scott Partine convicted of aggravated sexual assault with threat of violence and sentenced to life in prison.

Received at Death Row: November 11, 1986. Time on death row: 4,317 days, (11.83 years).

Last meal: None. Last minute he decided to eat a hamburger at his mother's request.

Last statement: I have come here today to die, not make speeches. Today is a good day for dying. Est sularus oth mithas [my honor is my life].

Pronounced dead: 6:24 P.M.

158

David Allen Castillo

Executed: September 23, 1998

Personal Data: *Born:* August 11, 1964. *Race:* Hispanic. *Height:* 5'6". *Weight:* 171 lbs. *Education level:* 9 years. *Prior occupation:* Electrician. *County of conviction:* Hidalgo. *Age at time of execution:* 34.

Sentenced to death for: Castillo was convicted and sentenced to death for the July 1983 stabbing of Clarencio Champion, 59, a cashier at the Party House Liquor Store in Mercedes. Castillo confronted Champion and demanded all of the cash. When Champion resisted, Castillo attacked him with a long solid knife stabbing him in the chest, abdomen and slashing him across the face. Castillo took an undetermined amount of cash. Champion died a week later.

Received at Death Row: September 12, 1984. Time on death row: 5,486 days, (15.03 years).

Last meal: Twenty-four soft shell tacos, six enchiladas, six tostados, two whole onions, five jalapenos, two cheeseburgers, one chocolate shake, one quart of milk, and one package of Marlboro cigarettes (prohibited by TDCJ policy).

Last statement: Keep it brief here. Just want to say, uh, family take care of yourselves. Uh, look at this as a learning experience. Everything happens for a reason. We all know what really happened. But there are some things you just can't fight. Little people always seem to get squashed. It happens. Even so, just got to take the good with the bad. There's no man that is free from all evil. Nor any man that is so evil to be worth nothing. But it's all part of life and my family take care of yourselves. Tell my wife I love her. I'll keep an eye on everybody, especially my nieces and nephews. I'm pretty good. I love y'all. Take care. I'm ready.

Pronounced dead: 6:23 P.M.

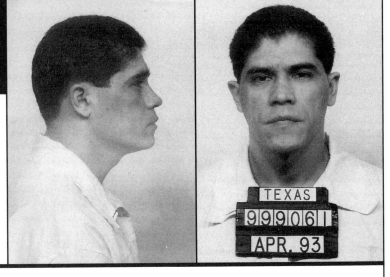

159

Javier Cruz

Executed: October 1, 1998

TEXAS
999061
APR. 93

Personal Data: *Born:* September 13, 1957. *Race:* Hispanic. *Height:* 5'7". *Weight:* 208 lbs. *Education level:* 9 years. *Prior occupation:* Feedstore clerk. *County of conviction:* Bexar. *Age at time of execution:* 41.

Sentenced to death for: Convicted in the strangulation murders of Louis Menard Neal, 71, and James Michael Ryan, 69, at the victims' homes in San Antonio. Neal was gagged and his hands bound behind his back with a sock before he was beaten with a hammer and strangled with a bathrobe belt. His decomposing body was found hanging by the neck from a towel rod inside his North Alamo Street apartment five days after the June 7, 1991, murder. Ryan's nude body was found inside his Mandalay Street residence the day after his July 14, 1991, murder. He was also strangled and his television and automobile stolen. Cruz's accomplice later told police they sold the tires off of Ryan's Cadillac to buy heroin. Cruz was arrested in the murders on October 22, 1991.
Co-defendant: Antonio Omero Ovalle agreed to testify against Cruz and plead guilty to murder, aggravated robbery, and attempted burglary in exchange for two life sentences.

Received at Death Row: June 7, 1991. Time on death row: 2,344 days, (6.42 years).

Last meal: Venison steak, baked potato, Lite beer, and Camel cigarettes (alcohol and tobacco prohibited by TDCJ policy).

Last statement: [written] Thank you for setting me free. God bless you all. I love you Miguel. Take care of my Angel Leslie. Love, Javier Cruz

Pronounced dead: 6:21 P.M.

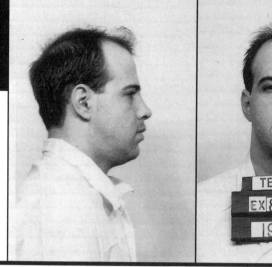

Jonathan Wayne Nobles

Executed: October 7, 1998

Personal Data: *Born:* August 27, 1961. *Race:* White. *Height:* 5'11". *Weight:* 202 lbs. *Education level:* 8 years (GED). *Prior occupation:* Electrician/marketing. *County of conviction:* Travis. *Age at time of execution:* 37.

Sentenced to death for: Convicted in the September 1986 stabbing deaths of Mitzi Johnson-Nalley, 21, and Kelly Farquhar, 24, at their rented home in Austin. Nobles, who was employed by the Central Texas Crime Prevention Association of Round Rock at the time of the killings, broke into the house at 5913 Sunshine Drive after consuming a combination of drugs and alcohol. Ronald Ross, Mitzi's 30-year-old date, was also stabbed in the assault, but survived his wounds. Nobles, who wounded himself in the arm during the assault, was arrested at his home on September 19, 1986, and confessed to police the same day.

Received at Death Row: October 15, 1987. Time on death row: 3,930 days, (10.77 years).

Last meal: Eucharist – Sacrament.

Last statement: See Appendix 1.

Pronounced dead: 6:25 P.M.

161

Kenneth Allen McDuff

Executed: November 17, 1998

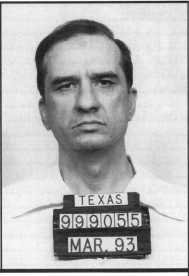

TEXAS
999055
MAR. 93

Personal Data: *Born:* March 21, 1946. *Race:* White. *Height:* 6'3". *Weight:* 255 lbs. *Education level:* 9 years (GED). *Prior occupation:* Machine operator. *County of conviction:* Harris. *Age at time of execution:* 52.

Sentenced to death for: Convicted in the March 1992 abduction and murder of 22-year-old Melissa Ann Northrup. Northrup was working in her job as a clerk at the Quic Pac convenience store, 4200 LaSalle in Waco, when she was abducted and driven from the location in her own vehicle, a 1977 Buick Regal. The car was found abandoned five days later near Seagoville, but it wasn't until April 26 that her body was found floating in a gravel pit about a mile from where the car was discovered. Her hands had been tied behind her back with shoestrings and a sock, and she had been strangled with a rope. Police were led to McDuff after his abandoned vehicle was found parked near the store. He had once worked with Northrup at the store and was arrested in Kansas City on May 4, 1992.
Note: McDuff was convicted of murder with malice and given the death sentence on October 9, 1968. His sentence was commuted to life on August 29, 1972. He was paroled December 6, 1990.

Received at Death Row: March 8, 1993. Time on death row: 1,460 days, (4.34 years).

Last meal: Two 16-ounce T-Bone steaks, five fried eggs, vegetables, french fries, coconut pie, and one Coke.

Last statement: I'm ready to be released. Release me.

Pronounced dead: 6:26 P.M.

162

Daniel Lee Corwin

Executed: December 7, 1998

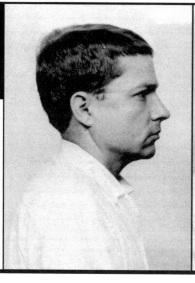 

Personal Data: *Born:* September 13, 1958. *Race:* White. *Height:* 5'9". *Weight:* 164 lbs. *Education level:* 15 years. *Prior occupation:* Cabinet maker. *County of conviction:* Montgomery. *Age at time of execution:* 40.

Sentenced to death for: Corwin was convicted in the deaths of Mary Risinger, 36, of Huntsville; Alice Martin, 72, of Normangee; and Debra Lynn Ewing, 26, of Conroe. Risinger was stabbed to death on October 31, 1987, while washing her vehicle at a car wash on FM 2821 in Huntsville. Risinger was stabbed in the neck while her 3-year-old daughter watched from inside the car. The young girl was not harmed. Martin was abducted while walking near her home on February 13, 1987. Her body was found the next day in a field in Robertson County. She had been raped, strangled, and stabbed. Ewing was abducted at gunpoint while working at the Vision Center in Huntsville on July 10, 1987. Her body was found two days later in an undeveloped subdivision in Montgomery County. Like Martin, Ewing had been raped, strangled, and stabbed.
Note: Corwin was the first person prosecuted under the state's serial killer statute.

Received at Death Row: February 13, 1987. Time on death row: 2,555 days, (7.34 years).

Last meal: Steak, potatoes, peas, cake, and root beer.

Last statement: See Appendix 1.

Pronounced dead: 6:33 P.M.

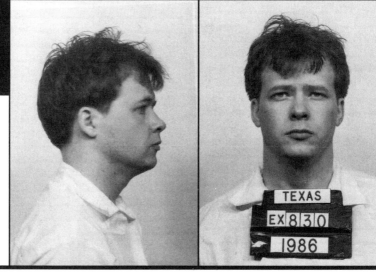

163

Jeff Emery

Executed:
December 8, 1998

Personal Data: *Born:* June 25, 1959. *Race:* White. *Height:* 5'8". *Weight:* 160 lbs. *Education level:* 8 years. *Prior occupation:* Air conditioner repairman. *County of conviction:* Brazos. *Age at time of execution:* 49.

Sentenced to death for: Convicted in the October 1979 stabbing death of 19-year-old LaShan Muhlinghaus, a Texas A&M student, at her College Station apartment. Prosecutors said Emery hid in a closet and attacked Muhlinghaus when she walked in while he was burglarizing her apartment. After death, Muhlinghaus was sexually assaulted and her lower body mutilated. The case went unsolved for four years until Emery's ex-wife, Debra, went to police in Milwaukee, Wisconsin. She later testified that her ex-husband came home the night of the murder covered with blood. Two of his friends testified that he admitted killing Muhlinghaus, a student from Rowlett. When charged with Muhlinghaus' murder, Emery was being held in St. Paul, Minnesota on three counts of murder.

Received at Death Row: October 12, 1979. Time on death row: 4,576 days, (12.54 years).

Last meal: Two T-bone steaks, french fries, salad, cake, chocolate ice cream, coffee, and Coke.

Last statement: I just want to tell Catharina I love you. Take care of yourself. That's all I have to say.

Pronounced dead: 6:24 P.M.

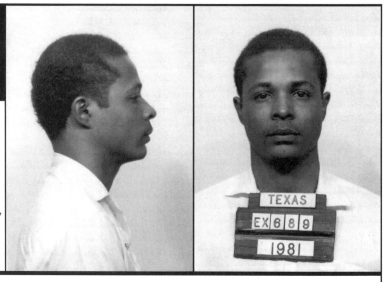

164

James Ronald Meanes

Executed: December 15, 1998

TEXAS
EX 6 8 9
1981

Personal Data: *Born:* June 8, 1956. *Race:* Black. *Height:* 5'8". *Weight:* 145 lbs. *Education level:* 12 years. *Prior occupation:* Welder. *County of conviction:* Harris. *Age at time of execution:* 42.

Sentenced to death for: Meanes was convicted of capital murder for the April 21, 1981, shooting death of Houston security guard Oliver Flores, 29, during a robbery of a Purolator Armored Inc. van containing more than one million dollars. Carlos Santana was also convicted in the Purolator incident, and given the death sentence. (See Entry 55, Carlos Santana.)

Received at Death Row: August 13, 1981. Time on death row: 6,330 days, (17.34 years).

Last meal: One bacon double cheeseburger, golden french fries, one tall strawberry milkshake, and six chocolate cookies.

Last statement: As the ocean always returns to itself, love always returns to itself, so does consciousness, always returns to itself. And I do so with love on my lips. May God bless all mankind.

Pronounced dead: 6:36 P.M.

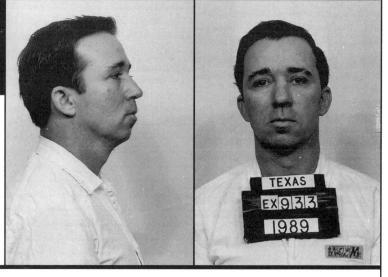

165

John Moody

Executed: January 5, 1999

Personal Data: *Born:* October 17, 1952. *Race:* White. *Height:* 5'10". *Weight:* 175 lbs. *Education level:* 12 years. *Prior occupation:* Landscaping. *County of conviction:* Taylor. *Age at time of execution:* 46.

Sentenced to death for: Convicted in the July 1988 robbery and murder of 77-year-old Maureen Louise Maulden in Abilene. Maulden was raped, beaten with a fireplace brush, and strangled with a telephone cord insider her home at 881 Elmwood Dr. A bloody fingerprint found on the telephone led police to Moody's residence where rings stolen from the house were recovered. Police said Moody had previously done yard work and odd jobs for Maulden.

Received at Death Row: March 6, 1989. Time on death row: 3,590 days, (9.84 years).

Last meal: Two T-bone steaks, salad with french onion dressing, rolls, french fries with catsup, five soft tacos, angel food cake, one pint white chocolate-almond ice cream, and a six-pack of Pepsi.

Last statement: I'd like to apologize and ask forgiveness for any pain and suffering I have inflicted upon all of you, including my family, all of you, I am very sorry. There is a point where a man wants to die in judgment, though my judgment is merciful. I hope and pray that all those involved as well as the judgment upon y'all will one day be more merciful than mine. God bless you all. God speed, I love you. Remain strong, ask God to give mercy. I love you all too. I'm very sorry. I've got to go now, I love you.

Pronounced dead: 8:33 P.M.

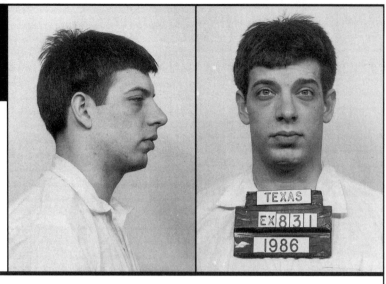

166

Troy Dale Farris

Executed: January 13, 1999

Personal Data: *Born:* February 26, 1962. *Race:* White. *Height:* 6'0". *Weight:* 185 lbs. *Education level:* 12 years. *Prior occupation:* Electrician/truck driver. *County of conviction:* Tarrant. *Age at time of execution:* 36.

Sentenced to death for: Convicted in the December 1983 shooting death of 28-year-old Clark Murell Rosenbaum, Jr., a Tarrant County deputy sheriff. Rosenbaum was shot twice in the chest after he had driven up on Farris and co-defendants Vance Nation and Charles Lowder during a drug buy on Old Decatur Road. Nation, who with Lowder had met Farris to buy 3/4 pounds of marijuana, told police that Farris shot Rosenbaum as the officer reached inside his car for the radio. As the officer fell and reached for his gun, Farris shot him a second time, Nation said. One of the .38-caliber bullets was stopped by Rosenbaum's bulletproof vest. The second bullet entered the deputy's shoulder and passed through his heart and lungs.
Co-defendants: Charges against Lowder were dismissed and he was granted immunity from prosecution. File records indicate that a capital murder case against Nation is still pending.

Received at Death Row: June 3, 1986. Time on death row: 4,616 days, (12.64 years).

Last meal: None.

Last statement: First off, to the Rosenbaum family, to Cindy, to Scott, to everyone, I just want to say I have nothing but love for you and I mean that from the deepest part. I can only tell you that Clark did not die in vain. I don't mean to offend you by saying that. But what I mean by that is, through his death, he led this man to God. I have nothing but love for you. To my family, my soul beloved, you're so beautiful. For all you love and support is just miraculous. Everything that y'all have done. Be sure and tell T.D. he's in my heart. I send my love to Jay, to everyone. To Roger Burdge. I have nothing but love for all of you. Like they say in the song I guess, I just want to go out like Elijah, on fire with the spirit of God. I love you. I'm done.

Pronounced dead: 7:16 P.M.

167

Martin Sauceda Vega

Executed: January 26, 1999

Personal Data: *Born:* October 17, 1946. *Race:* Hispanic. *Height:* 5'10". *Weight:* 165 lbs. *Education level:* 3 years. *Prior occupation:* Laborer. *County of conviction:* Caldwell. *Age at time of execution:* 52.

Sentenced to death for: Convicted in the murder-for-hire killing of 36-year-old James William Mims. Vega told authorities that he and Mims' wife, Linda, plotted to kill Mims in order to collect approximately $250,000 in life insurance. Mims was beaten and shot seven times with a .22-caliber pistol. Vega went to authorities in Luling on January 2, 1988, and confessed his role in the murder. He later led police to an area where the murder weapon was found.

Received at Death Row: February 16, 1989. Time on death row: 3,296 days, (9.03 years).

Last meal: T-Bone steak, shrimp, and a Coke.

Last statement: See Appendix 1.

Pronounced dead: 6:22 P.M.

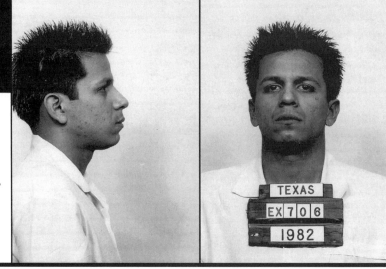

168

George Cordova

Executed:
February 10, 1999

TEXAS
EX 7 0 6
1982

Personal Data: *Born:* March 26, 1959. *Race:* Hispanic. *Height:* 5'8". *Weight:* 140 lbs. *Education level:* 6 years (GED). *Prior occupation:* Laborer. *County of conviction:* Bexar. *Age at time of execution:* 39.

Sentenced to death for: August 4, 1979, Manuel Villanueva and two unidentified males approached Jose "Joey" Hernandez, 19, and Hernandez's date, Cynthia West, as they sat in their car. Cordova asked Hernandez to take him to a station for gas. Hernandez refused because he noticed Villanueva had a knife. Cordova pulled Hernandez from his car and beat him in the head with a tire tool. Villanueva stabbed Hernandez in the neck. The other two men pulled West from the car and forced her into the woods and raped her, then Villanueva raped her. They ran to Hernandez's car and drove it away.
Co-defendants: Mauel Villanueva was convicted of murder and sentenced to life in prison. The two other people involved in the incident were never identified.

Received at Death Row: March 4, 1982. Time on death row: 6,184 days, (16.94 years).

Last meal: None.

Last statement: For the pain I have caused you. I am ashamed to even look at your faces. You are great people. To my brothers on death row. Mexico, Mexico. [Spoke in Spanish, not translated.]

Pronounced dead: 6:30 P.M.

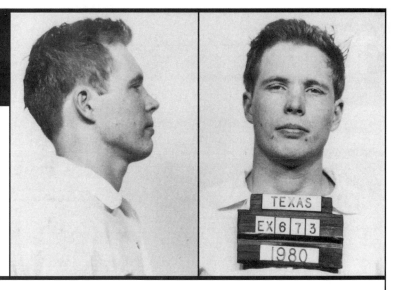

169

Danny Lee Barber

Executed: February 11, 1999

Personal Data: *Born:* May 8, 1955. *Race:* White. *Height:* 5'7". *Weight:* 140 lbs. *Education level:* 12 years. *Prior occupation:* Roofer. *County of conviction:* Dallas. *Age at time of execution:* 43.

Sentenced to death for: Barber was convicted in the October 8, 1979, slaying of Janice Louise Ingram at her home in Balch Springs. Barber reportedly broke into Ingram's home on Lake June Road and repeatedly struck her in the head and face with a piece of pipe when she surprised him. Ingram was also stabbed in the throat. Her leather purse, clock radio, and calculator were stolen from the home. Barber was also serving life sentences for three other murders, including the January 17, 1979, slaying of 48-year-old Mercedes Mendez, aka Mercy Mendez. The woman's body was dumped on a road in a wooded area near Mesquite after she had been beaten, sexually molested, and shot three times in the head. Barber was charged with the woman's murder on May 6, 1980, while being held in the Dallas County jail on other charges. He confessed to the murder the next day and later pleaded guilty to two other Dallas County murders committed on June 18, 1978, and April 21, 1980. Records indicate neither the victims nor the circumstances in those two cases.

Received at Death Row: October 31, 1980. Time on death row: 6,674 days, (18.28 years).

Last meal: Two steaks, baked potato, chef salad, tea, and chocolate ice cream.

Last statement: Hello, Ms. Ingram, it is good to see you. I said I could talk but I don't think I am gonna be able to. I heard one of your nieces had some angry words. I didn't have anything to do with the stay. I spent the last twenty years waiting to figure out what's going on. I pray that you get over it and that's the only thing I can think to say. I'm regretful for what I done. But I'm a different person from that time. If you could get to know me over the years, you could have seen it. I've got some people over here that believes that. I want to talk to my friends over here for a second. Well it's good to see you guys. Look after Mar Lynn for me. Like I said, I've called my mother already so she knows. Good bye.

Pronounced dead: 6:26 P.M.

Andrew Cantu

Executed: February 16, 1999

Personal Data: *Born:* December 5, 1967. *Race:* Hispanic. *Height:* 5'7". *Weight:* 155 lbs. *Education level:* 11 years. *Prior occupation:* Construction. *County of conviction:* Taylor. *Age at time of execution:* 30.

Sentenced to death for: Convicted in the stabbing deaths of three people inside an Abilene home in what authorities claim was a murder-for-hire scheme. Killed were Helen Summers, Mandell Eugene Summers, and Billy Mack Summers. All three were stabbed with a knife and then their home was set afire. Prosecutors charged that the three were killed for the promise of remuneration from co-defendant Gregory Lynn Summers. Two other co-defendants, Ramon Gonzales and Paul Flares, testified that Cantu stabbed the three victims. He later admitted the murders to family members and friends.
Co-defendants: Cases pending against Ramon Gonzales, Paul Flares, and Gregory Summers.

Received at Death Row: June 6, 1991. Time on death row: 2,811 days, (7.70 years).

Last meal: Pork baby-back ribs, hard shell tacos, corn tortillas, french fries, salad with ranch dressing, red and green chili sauce, jalapenos and tomatoes boiled with garlic and comino, root beer, and chocolate ice cream.

Last statement: None.

Pronounced dead: 9:37 P.M.

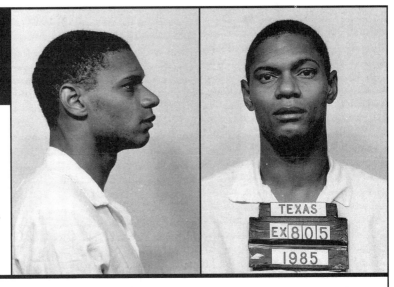

171

Norman Evans Green

Executed: February 24, 1999

Personal Data: *Born:* November 7, 1960. *Race:* Black. *Height:* 6'1". *Weight:* 160 lbs. *Education level:* 14 years. *Prior occupation:* Hotel housekeeper. *County of conviction:* Bexar. *Age at time of execution:* 38.

Sentenced to death for: Convicted in the February 1985 shooting death of 19-year-old Timothy Adams during an attempted robbery of an electronics store in San Antonio. Green and accomplice Harold Bowens waited for the manager of Dyer Electronics, 9402 Perrin Beitel, to leave for lunch before entering the store to confront Adams, a clerk, with a .38-caliber pistol. When Adams was slow to follow instructions, Green fired four times striking Adams in the arm, chest, and abdomen. He died 12 hours later. Witnesses identified Green and Bowens, who escaped from the scene empty-handed. Green reportedly surrendered to authorities on February 21, 1985.
Co-defendant: Harold Bowens testified against Green and pleaded guilty to a lesser charge of murder in exchange for a life sentence.

Received at Death Row: September 27, 1985. Time on death row: 4,906 days, (13.44 years).

Last meal: Barbeque ribs, pork chops, salad with french dressing, baked potato, Texas toast, and Coke.

Last statement: None.

Pronounced dead: 6:17 P.M.

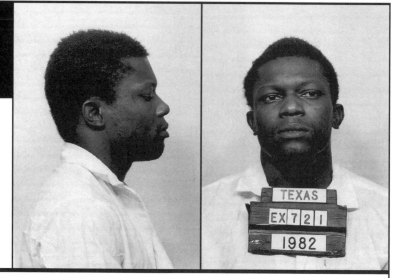

172

Charles Henry Rector

Executed: March 26, 1999

Personal Data: *Born:* April 16, 1954. *Race:* Black. *Height:* 5'8". *Weight:* 160 lbs. *Education level:* 8 years. *Prior occupation:* Paint and body repairman. *County of conviction:* Travis. *Age at time of execution:* 44.

Sentenced to death for: Rector was convicted and sentenced to death for the October 17, 1981, shooting, rape and drowning death of Carolyn Kay Davis, 22. Her bruised and naked body was found in Town Lake [Austin]. Rector was arrested the same night near the apartment complex where Davis lived. He was wearing the victim's blue jeans, and carrying her rings and necklace.
Note: On March 28, 1986, Rector used a razor blade to inflict a 4-inch laceration to his right wrist. On April 25, 1986, he attempted suicide by inflicting a large laceration to the right side of his neck and several lacerations to both arms. (Rector has a history of self-mutilations.) On October 25, 1983, Rector was stabbed by former death row inmate Jay Kelly Pinkerton (since executed) (See Enty 13, Jay Kelly Pinkerton) in the back and upper chest region with a homemade shank.

Received at Death Row: September 2, 1982. Time on death row: 6,044 days, (16.56 years).

Last meal: Three beef enchiladas, three tacos, french fries, and one strawberry shake.

Last statement: See Appendix 1.

Pronounced dead: 6:22 P.M.

173

Robert Excell White

Executed:
March 30, 1999

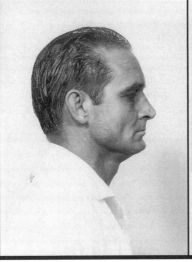

Personal Data: *Born:* March 14, 1938. *Race:* White. *Height:* 6'1". *Weight:* 172 lbs. *Education level:* 10 years. *Prior occupation:* Auto mechanic. *County of conviction:* Collin. *Age at time of execution:* 61.

Sentenced to death for: Convicted in the execution-style slaying of three men at the Hilltop Grocery, a rural country store near the communities of McKinney and Princeton. Killed were store owner Preston Broyles, 73, and store customers Gary Coker and Billy St. John, both 18 and residents of Princeton. All three were riddled with bullets from a .30-caliber machine gun stolen a day earlier from a Waco gun collector, who was found stabbed to death in his apartment. White and two accomplices left the store with $6 taken from the cash register and about $60 taken from the wallets of the victims. While White confessed to shooting all three men, he was tried and convicted only in Broyles' death. *Co-defendants*: James Owen Livingston was convicted of capital murder and originally sentenced to death. Death sentence commuted to life in April 1983. Gary Dale Livingston was convicted of murder (3) in May 1975 and sentenced to 20 years. Discharged July 28, 1984.

Received at Death Row: August 26, 1974. Time on death row: 8,977 dys, (24.59 years).

Last meal: Two hamburgers, double order of french fries, and fried onion rings.

Last statement: Send me back to my maker, Warden.

Pronounced dead: 6:17 P.M.

174

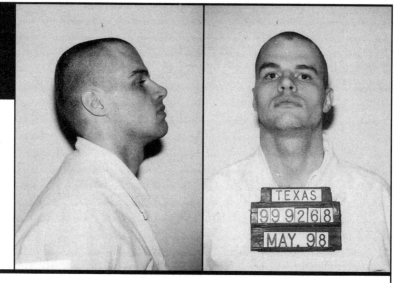

Aaron Christopher Foust

Executed:
April 28, 1999

Personal Data: *Born:* July 28, 1972. *Race:* White. *Height:* 6'0". *Weight:* 180 lbs. *Education level:* n/a. *Prior occupation:* Laborer. *County of conviction:* Tarrant. *Age at time of execution:* 26.

Sentenced to death for: Convicted in the May 1997 robbery and murder of 43-year-old David S. Ward in Fort Worth. Stereo speaker wire was used to bound Ward's hands and feet before he was strangled inside his apartment at 5624 Blue Ridge Ct. Ward's credit cards were stolen and later used by Foust. Ward's BMW was also stolen. It was found on fire in Arlington two days after the murder. Before leaving the apartment, Ward's killer and an accomplice sprayed words and letters to make the murder appear gang related.
Co-defendant: Jamal Brown was charged with capital murder. Disposition not immediately known.

Received at Death Row: May 19, 1998. Time on death row: 345 days, (.93 years).

Last meal: Cheeseburger, french fries, and Coke.

Last statement: Adios, amigos. I'll see you on the other side. I'm ready when y'all are.

Pronounced dead: 6:22 P.M.

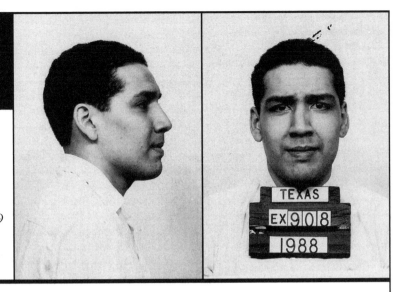

175

Jose De La Cruz

Executed:
May 4, 1999

Personal Data: *Born:* April 26, 1968. *Race:* Hispanic. *Height:* 5'9". *Weight:* 139 lbs. *Education level:* 10 years. *Prior occupation:* Forklift operator/mechanic. *County of conviction:* Nueces. *Age at time of execution:* 31.

Sentenced to death for: Convicted in the June 1987 robbery-slaying of 24-year-old Domingo Rosas in Corpus Christi. De La Cruz, boyfriend of Rosas' cousin, stabbed the victim six times with a kitchen knife and broke his neck before robbing him of his driver's license and credit cards. The murder weapon was found in the car De La Cruz was driving the day after the murder when arrested for public intoxication. De La Cruz was arrested and charged with capital murder on June 3, 1987, when he attempted to withdraw money from Rosas' savings account at the Nueces National Bank by presenting Rosas' identification and forging his signature. Rosas was an epileptic who lived primarily off of Social Security benefits due to a physical handicap. His body was found inside his apartment at 4702 Old Brownsville Rd. when family members complained he had not contacted them over a two-day period.

Received at Death Row: June 16, 1988. Time on death row: 3,972 days, (10.88 years).

Last meal: None.

Last statement: None.

Pronounced dead: 6:23 P.M.

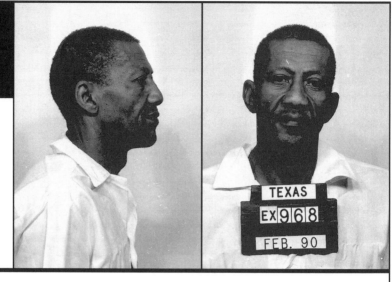

Clydell Coleman

Executed:
May 5, 1999

TEXAS
EX968
FEB. 90

Personal Data: *Born:* October 1, 1936. *Race:* Black. *Height:* 6'1". *Weight:* 160 lbs. *Education level:* 11 years. *Prior occupation:* Janitorial. *County of conviction:* McLennan. *Age at time of execution:* 62.

Sentenced to death for: Convicted in the February 1989 robbery and murder of 87-year-old Leethisha Joe. Coleman and accomplice Yolanda Phillips entered Joe's home at 706 Dawson through the back door and confronted the victim. Coleman covered the victim's head with a blanket, hit her with a hammer, and then strangled her with her own stocking. Property stolen from the home included a television, clock radio, sheets, cooler, floor fan, and ladder. Phillips was arrested after her fingerprints were found inside the home. She then implicated Coleman in a statement to police.
Co-defendant: Yolanda Phillips was convicted of burglary of a habitation and sentenced to 30 years in prison.

Received at Death Row: March 1, 1990. Time on death row: 3,350 days, (9.18 years).

Last meal: Salmon croquettes, scrambled eggs, french fries, and biscuits.

Last statement: None.

Pronounced dead: 6:30 P.M.

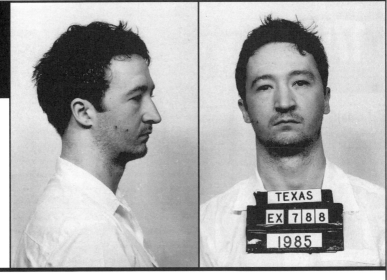

177

William Hamilton Little

Executed: June 1, 1999

TEXAS
EX 7 8 8
1985

Personal Data: *Born:* October 25, 1960. *Race:* White. *Height:* 6'1". *Weight:* 191 lbs. *Education level:* 9 years. *Prior occupation:* Roofer. *County of conviction:* Liberty. *Age at time of execution:* 38.

Sentenced to death for: Convicted in the stabbing death of 23-year-old Marilyn Peters at her rural Cleveland, Texas, home. Peters was raped, stabbed more than 19 times with a kitchen knife, and then raped a second time after her death. Her nude body was found on the living room floor of her home in the Old Snake River Lake subdivision. Robbery was not a motive in the murder since Peters was still wearing her jewelry and nearly $500 was found in her bedroom dresser. Authorities also found nearly two pounds of marijuana inside the residence. Little claimed he had become acquainted with the victim through her sale of marijuana to him. Bloodstained blue jeans and towels were found at Little's residence on Buckley Drive. He was arrested there on December 6, 1983.

Received at Death Row: April 15, 1985. Time on death row: 5,158 days, (14.13 years).

Last meal: Fifteen slices of cheese, three fried eggs, three buttered toasts, two hamburger patties with cheese, half tomato sliced, one slice onion, french fries with salad dressing, half a pound of crispy fried bacon, one quart chocolate milk, and one pint of fresh strawberries.

Last statement: None.

Pronounced dead: 6:20 P.M.

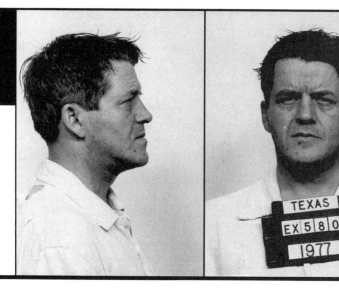

178

Joseph Stanley Faulder

Executed: June 17, 1999

Personal Data: *Born:* October 19, 1937. *Race:* White. *Height:* 5'7". *Weight:* 171 lbs. *Education level:* 10 years. *Prior occupation:* Auto mechanic. *County of conviction:* Gregg. *Age at time of execution:* 61.

Sentenced to death for: Convicted in the July 1975 beating-stabbing death of 75-year-old Inez Phillips at her Gladewater home. Faulder and accomplice Linda "Stormy" Summers (aka Linda "Stormy" McCann) broke into Phillips' home believing she had money hidden in a floor safe. When Faulder found no money in the safe, he stole other household valuables, including Phillips, wedding ring. She was bound and gagged with tape and beaten on the back of the head with a blackjack when she resisted. Faulder later stabbed the elderly widow in the chest with a knife. Phillips' maid found her body the morning of July 9 with the knife still imbedded in her chest. Faulder, an acquaintance of Phillips' former employee, was charged in the murder in April 1977 while being held on unrelated charges in Colorado. The Texas Court of Criminal Appeals ruled Faulder's written confession inadmissible and reversed his first conviction. He was again convicted in 1981 and sentenced to death a second time. Records do not indicate that his accomplice was incarcerated.

Received at Death Row: December 9, 1977. Time on death row: 8,221 days, (22.52 years).

Last meal: None.

Last statement: None.

Pronounced dead: 6:18 P.M.

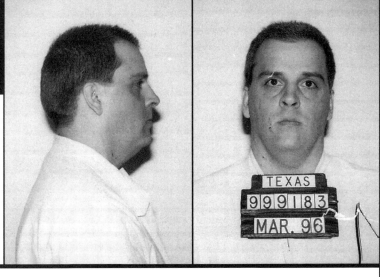

179

Charles Daniel Tuttle

Executed:
July 1, 1999

Personal Data: *Born:* June 26, 1964. *Race:* White. *Height:* 5'8". *Weight:* 212 lbs. *Education level:* 10 years (GED). *Prior occupation:* Construction worker. *County of conviction:* Smith. *Age at time of execution:* 35.

Sentenced to death for: Convicted in the beating death of 42-year-old Cathy Harris of Tyler. Harris was beaten to death with a hammer and her body placed in a closet in an effort to conceal the crime. Before fleeing, Tuttle took the victim's purse and a handgun from the residence off CR 1148. Tuttle had been staying with Harris a week prior to the killing but was told to leave for failing to pay his share of the bills. Tuttle was arrested four days later while visiting at a Beaumont hospital. He had Harris' .357-caliber revolver and two of her credit cards in his possession when arrested.

Received at Death Row: March 26, 1996. Time on death row: 1,192 days, (3.26 years).

Last meal: Four fried eggs sunny-side up, four sausage patties, one chicken-fried steak patty, one bowl of white country gravy, five pieces of white toast, five tacos with meat and cheese only, four Dr Peppers with ice on the side, and five mint sticks.

Last statement: To Cathy's family and friends that were unable to attend today, I am truly sorry. I hope my dropping my appeals has in some way begun your healing process. This is all that I am going to do to help you out in any way for the nightmare and pain that I have caused you. But I am truly sorry and I wish I could take back what I did, but I can't. I hope this heals you. To my family – I love you, when the tears flow let the smiles grow. Everything is alright. To my family, I love you. Warden, ATW.

Pronounced dead: 6:28 P.M.

180

Tyrone Leroy Fuller

Executed:
July 7,
1999

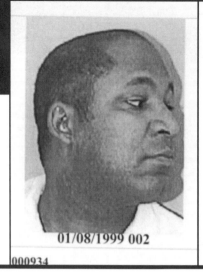

01/08/1999 002
000934

000934
01/08/1999 001
ID Numb

Personal Data: *Born:* August 1, 1963. *Race:* black. *Height:* 6'0". *Weight:* 212 lbs. *Education level:* 11 years (GED). *Prior occupation:* Coaching. *County of conviction:* Grayson. *Age at time of execution:* 38.

Sentenced to death for: Convicted in the January 1988 capital murder of 26-year-old Andrea Lea Duke of Paris. Duke, a medical technologist working at McCuiston Hospital, was raped, tortured, and stabbed to death after Fuller and two accomplices broke into her apartment at 1050 34th St. in Paris. Duke's car, jewelry and credit cards were stolen. Her body was found on the front lawn of the apartment complex.
Co-defendants: John Earl McGrew reportedly received a life sentence as part of a plea bargain. Charges against Kenneth Wayne Harmon are pending.

Received at Death Row: March 31, 1989. Time on death row: 3,749 days, (10.27 years).

Last meal: One bacon, ham and cheese omelet with diced onion and peppers, one cinnamon roll, three slices of toast, three milks, two orange juices, hot sauce, grape jelly, butter, salt and pepper, and fruit.

Last statement: To my family I love you. Please do not mourn my death or my life. Continue to live as I want you to live. I hold no bitterness toward no one. Just remember the light. I'm gonna let this light shine. Let it shine. Let the light shine.

Pronounced dead: 6:20 P.M.

181

Ricky Don Blackmon

Executed: August 4, 1999

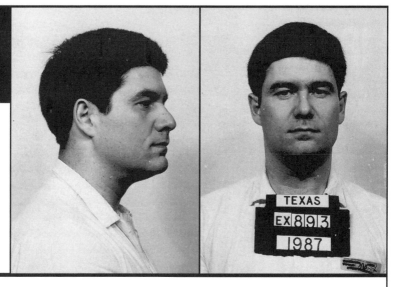

Personal Data: *Born:* November 21, 1957. *Race:* White. *Height:* 6'1". *Weight:* 214 lbs. *Education level:* n/a. *Prior occupation:* Cook. *County of conviction:* Shelby. *Age at time of execution:* 42.

Sentenced to death for: Convicted of capital murder in the robbery-stabbing death of Carl Joseph Rinkle, 26. Rinkle was slashed numerous times with a sword or machete and robbed.
Co-defendant: Donna Mae Rogers was convicted of murder and sentenced to life in prison.

Received at Death Row: December 7, 1987. Time on death row: 4,255 days, (11.66 years).

Last meal: No last meal requested, only requested something to drink.

Last statement: None.

Pronounced dead: 6:22 P.M.

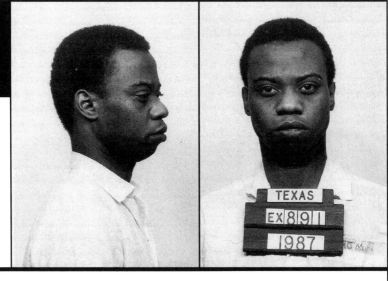

182

Charles Anthony Boyd

Executed: August 5, 1999

Personal Data: *Born:* August 17, 1959. *Race:* Black. *Height:* 5'9". *Weight:* 148 lbs. *Education level:* 12 years. *Prior occupation:* Janitor. *County of conviction:* Dallas. *Age at time of execution:* 39.

Sentenced to death for: Convicted of capital murder in the April 13, 1987, strangulation-drowning death of Mary Milligan. Milligan was found dead in her bathtub, and her 1984 Cadillac had been stolen.

Received at Death Row: December 3, 1987. Time on death row: 4,260 days, (11.67 years).

Last meal: None.

Last statement: I want you all to know I did not do this crime. I wanted to wait for a thirty-day stay for a DNA test so you know who did the crime.

Pronounced dead: 6:22 P.M.

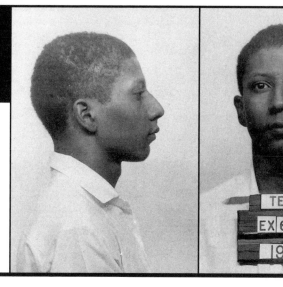

183

Kenneth Dunn

Executed:
August 10,
1999

Personal Data: *Born:* October 3, 1959. *Race:* Black. *Height:* 5'6". *Weight:* 130 lbs. *Education level:* 9 years. *Prior occupation:* Laborer. *County of conviction:* Harris. *Age at time of execution:* 39.

Sentenced to death for: Dunn was convicted of the March 17, 1980 shooting death of bank teller Madeline Peters, 21, during a robbery at the Bank of Almeda. Dunn received the death penalty in November 1980, but the sentence was overturned because a court reporter lost part of the trial transcript.

Received at Death Row: December 19, 1980. Time on death row: 6,812 days, (18.66 years).

Last meal: Beef fajitas, stir-fried beef, six cinnamon rolls, one pecan pie, one cherry pie, one diet cream soda, and three eggs.

Last statement: None.

Pronounced dead: 7:30 P.M.

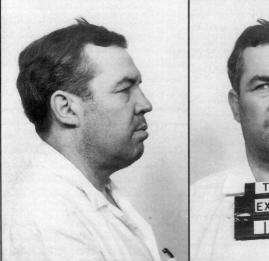

184

James Otto Earheart

Executed:
August 11, 1999

TEXAS
EX905
1988

Personal Data: *Born:* April 29, 1943. *Race:* White. *Height:* 5'9". *Weight:* 258 lbs. *Education level:* 7 years. *Prior occupation:* Sales/appliance repair. *County of conviction:* Lee. *Age at time of execution:* 56.

Sentenced to death for: Convicted in the May 1987 abduction and slaying of 9-year-old Kandy Janell Kirtland of Bryan. Kandy was abducted from her home at 3210 Deer Trail on May 12, 1987, after being dropped off by the school bus. Her parents found Kandy's backpack on the front porch, the front door open, and the keys to the home on the kitchen stove. Her decomposed body was found on May 26, 1987, along a creek in the 2500 block of East Villa Maria Road. She had been shot once in the head after her hands had been tied behind her back with electrical cord. Earhart was arrested in Walker County's Stubblefield Lake Park the same day Kandy's body was found. Police learned Earhart had gone to the Kirtland home on May 4, 1987, in response to a newspaper ad about a paint spray gun for sale. He returned on the day Kandy disappeared, asking a neighbor when the Kirtlands would be home.

Received at Death Row: May 27, 1988. Time on death row: 4,091 days, (11.22 years).

Last meal: Steak, french fries, and one vanilla shake.

Last statement: None.

Pronounced dead: 6:24 P.M.

185

Joe Mario Trevino

Executed: August 18, 1999

Personal Data: *Born:* July 25, 1962. *Race:* Hispanic. *Height:* 5'10". *Weight:* 165 lbs. *Education level:* 12 years. *Prior occupation:* Paint and body work. *County of conviction:* Tarrant. *Age at time of execution:* 37.

Sentenced to death for: Convicted in the January 1983 rape-slaying of 80-year-old Blanche Miller at her home in Haltom City. Trevino broke into Miller's home at 4901 Broadway through a kitchen window while she was away and killed her when she returned home. She was raped and then strangled to death. Trevino stole Miller's car after loading it with jewelry, a color television, stereo equipment, and other items from the house. Miller's car was recovered on Diamond Oaks drive hours later and police discovered the stolen property at Trevino's residence at 5129 Jerri Lane.

Received at Death Row: July 10, 1984. Time on death row: 5,515 days, (15.11 years).

Last meal: Fried chicken, watermelon, salad with Italian dressing, raw carrots, raw cucumbers, and a strawberry shake.

Last statement: None.

Pronounced dead: 6:25 P.M.

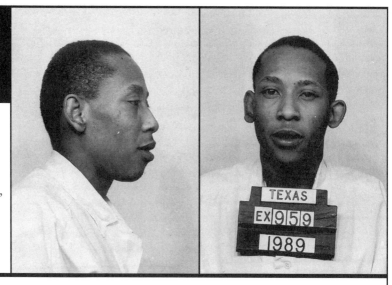

186

Raymond Jones

Executed: September 1, 1999

TEXAS
EX959
1989

Personal Data: *Born:* 1960. Race: Black. *Height:* 5'11". *Weight:* 150 lbs. *Education level:* 8 years. *Prior occupation:* Laborer. *County of conviction:* Jefferson. *Age at time of execution:* 39.

Sentenced to death for: Convicted in the June 1988 robbery and murder of 51-year-old Su Van Dang at the victim's residence in Port Arthur. Dang was stabbed to death during a robbery of his home at 2348 8th St. His body was found in a closet and had been partially burned in an attempt to destroy evidence.

Received at Death Row: December 20, 1989. Time on death row: 3,567 days, (9.67 years).

Last meal: Double-meat cheeseburger, french fries, ice cream, and a soda.

Last statement: None.

Pronounced dead: 6:17 P.M.

187

 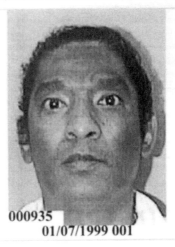

Willis Jay Barnes

Executed: September 10, 1999

01/07/1999 002

000935

000935 01/07/1999 001

ID Numb

Personal Data: *Born:* August 13, 1948. *Race:* Black. *Height:* 5'11". *Weight:* 153 lbs. *Education level:* 11 years (GED). *Prior occupation:* Antique refinisher. *County of conviction:* Harris. *Age at time of execution:* 51.

Sentenced to death for: Convicted in the February 1988 strangulation death of 84-year-old Helen Greb. Barnes cut the telephone line to Greb's home before breaking into the residence. Once inside, Barnes brutally beat and raped Greb before strangling her to death with his hands. An autopsy revealed that Greb suffered 20 broken ribs, a broken back, a crushed chest, and numerous lacerations. Police later traced two guns and a television set stolen from the residence to a fence who bought the items from Barnes.

Received at Death Row: April 3, 1989. Time on death row: 3,810 days, (10.44 years).

Last meal: Three fried chicken breasts, three jalapenos, five rolls, and one soda.

Last statement: Yes. I would like to give love to my mother, sisters, and brothers and let them know that I am thinking of them right now and I want to thank God for giving me such a loving family. To the victim's family I hope you find it in your heart to forgive me as I have forgiven you. I'm ready, Warden.

Pronounced dead: 6:19 P.M.

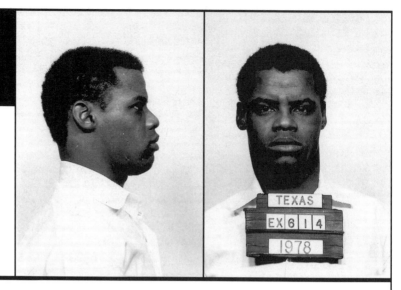

188

William Prince Davis

Executed: September 14, 1999

Personal Data: *Born:* April 24, 1957. *Race:* Black. *Height:* 5'7". *Weight:* 142 lbs. *Education level:* 7 years. *Prior occupation:* Roofer. *County of conviction:* Harris. *Age at time of execution:* 42.

Sentenced to death for: Convicted in the June 1978 robbery-slaying of a man identified as the 60-year-old manager of the Red Wing Ice Cream Company in Houston. Records indicate the victim, identified only by the last name of Lang, was receiving cash receipts from three drivers when Davis entered the company office with a pistol and shot Lang once. David fled with $712 and a shotgun taken from the office. He was later identified by the three company drivers and gave a written confession to police.

Received at Death Row: October 10, 1978. Time on death row: 7,639 days, (20.9 years).

Last meal: Chicken-fried drumsticks, one bowl of chili, one bowl of cheese, five rolls, two bags of barbecue chips, six-pack of Coke, one pack of Palmer cigarettes (prohibited by TDCJ regulations), one lighter (prohibited by TDCJ regulations).

Last statement: See Appendix 1.

Pronounced dead: 6:19 P.M.

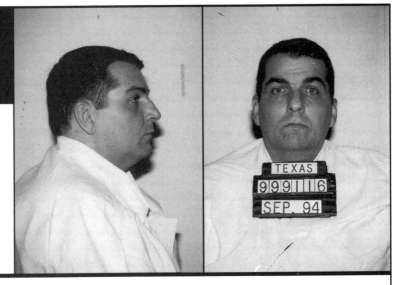

189

Richard Wayne Smith

Executed:
September 21, 1999

Personal Data: *Born:* January 12, 1956. *Race:* White. *Height:* 5'8". *Weight:* 246 lbs. *Education level:* 14 years. *Prior occupation:* Electrician. *County of conviction:* Harris. *Age at time of execution:* 43.

Sentenced to death for: Convicted in the murder of Karen Birky, a Baytown convenience store clerk. Birky was working at the Stop-N-Go convenience store at 3312 Decker when Smith robbed her at gunpoint and attempted to abduct her in the stolen vehicle he was driving. When Birky refused to get in the vehicle, Smith shot her once in the neck, killing her. He was arrested a short time later with the pistol and stolen cash in his pockets.

Received at Death Row: September 2, 1994. Time on death row: 1,845 days, (5.06 years).

Last meal: Three bacon, lettuce and tomato sandwiches, french fries, one small bowl of pickles, one half onion, and one cup of iced tea.

Last statement: None.

Pronounced dead: 6:25 P.M.
Note: Smith dropped all appeals when he learned he was dying of liver failure.

190

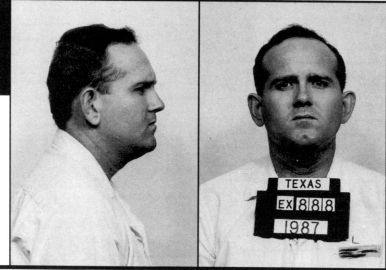

Alvin Crane

Executed: October 12, 1999

Personal Data: *Born:* May 6, 1958. *Race:* White. *Height:* 6'. *Weight:* 204 lbs. *Education level:* 8 years. *Prior occupation:* Oil field operator. *County of conviction:* Denton. *Age at time of execution:* 41.

Sentenced to death for: Convicted in the March 1987 shooting death of Melvin Kenneth Drum, an Ochiltree County deputy sheriff. Deputy Drum, responding to a disturbance call, was shot once in the face after stopping Crane's vehicle on the roadway. Crane exited his vehicle and shot Drum while he was still seated inside his patrol car. The officer died before he could be transported to a hospital. Crane was arrested for the killing on April 15, 1987.

Received at Death Row: November 12, 1987. Time on death row: 4,349 days, (11.91 years).

Last meal: Fried chicken, mashed potatoes with gravy, corn on the cob, cauliflower, and chocolate cake.

Last statement: I would like to say a little something. I just want to say I'm sorry to the family. I know I caused you a lot of pain and suffering and I hope that you will find some peace and comfort in this. That if there is any anger you can let it go. Not let it come between you and God. Sorry for causing everybody such trouble tonight, Bruce, Joe, y'all all treat me with respect I appreciate it. I really do. I just want to tell my family, everybody I love and I want you to know that I love you, and that God loves you too. Everything is going to be just fine, just fine. I love y'all. That's it.

Pronounced dead: 6:23 P.M.

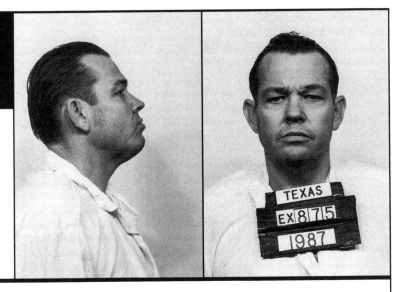

191

Jerry McFadden

Executed: October 14, 1999

Personal Data: *Born:* March 21, 1948. *Race:* White. *Height:* 5'9". *Weight:* 208 lbs. *Education level:* 7 years. *Prior occupation:* Telephone cable installer. *County of conviction:* Bell. *Age at time of execution:* 51.

Sentenced to death for: Convicted in the abduction, raped and strangulation death of 18-year-old Suzanne Denise Harrison of Hawkins. Harrison and companions Gena Turner, 20, and Bryan Boone, 19, were abducted during an outing to Lake Hawkins. McFadden raped and sodomized Harrison and then strangled her with her panties. Her body was found atop Barnwell Mountain in Upshur County. The bodies of Turner and Boone were found five days later. Both had been shot to death execution-style with a .38-caliber pistol.
Note: On July 8, 1986, while being held in the Upshur County Jail, McFadden overpowered a male jailer and escaped in the car of a female jailer he took hostage. The hostage, eventually kept in an abandoned railroad box car in Big Sandy, escaped McFadden after 28 hours. He was captured after three days of an extensive manhunt.

Received at Death Row: July 15, 1987. Time on death row: 4,471 days, (12.22 years).

Last meal: BLT with pickles and onions, french fries, one pint of butter pecan ice cream, and Coke.

Last statement: None.

Pronounced dead: 6:16 P.M.

192

Domingo Cantu, Jr.

Executed: October 28, 1999

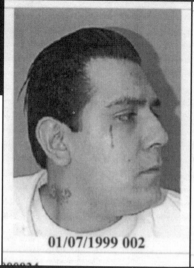

01/07/1999 002

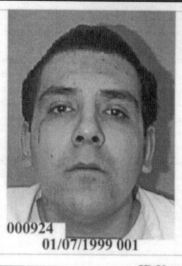

000924
01/07/1999 001

Personal Data: *Born:* June 7, 1968. *Race:* Hispanic. *Height:* 5'8". *Weight:* 178 lbs. *Education level:* n/a. *Prior occupation:* n/a. *County of conviction:* Dallas. *Age at time of execution:* 31.

Sentenced to death for: Convicted in the June 1988 sexual assault and slaying of 94-year-old Suda Eller Jones in Dallas. Cantu sexually assaulted the victim and then beat her head against a concrete sidewall outside a residence at 1139 North Madison. Jones died from multiple head injuries. Cantu was arrested after being spotted running from the scene. He later confessed to police.

Received at Death Row: December 1, 1988. Time on death row: 4,282 days, (11.73 years).

Last meal: Fried chicken (12 pieces white/dark meat), mashed potatoes with gravy, 14 jalapenos, orange juice, chocolate milk, buttermilk biscuits, and strawberry ice cream.

Last statement: [In English] I love you. I will be waiting for you on the other side. Son be strong no matter what happens, know that God is looking over you. Jesus mercy, Jesus mercy, Jesus mercy! [In Spanish] Brother-in-law, take care of the family and let it be united. Yoli. [In German] Menic schone prizessin. Du list all mine herz and seele, rind ich liele dich so sehm! [Translation: My beautiful princess. You are all my heart and soul and I love you so much.]

Pronounced dead: 6:23 P.M.

193

Desmond Jennings

Executed:
November 16, 1999

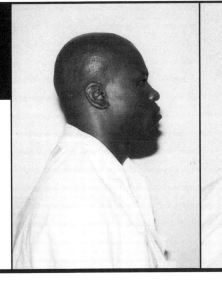

Personal Data: *Born:* October 4, 1971. *Race:* Black. *Height:* 5'6".*Weight:* 183 lbs. *Education level:* 9 years. *Prior occupation:* Nurse's aid. *County of conviction:* Tarrant. *Age at time of execution:* 28.

Sentenced to death for: Convicted in the shooting deaths of Sylvester Walton, 44 and Wonda Matthews, 27, at a Fort Worth residence. Both Walton and Matthews were shot in the head with a .32-caliber pistol inside the residence at 2614 Langston. Walton's pockets were emptied by Jennings following the double murders. Police indicated that the killings were drug related.

Received at Death Row: August 22, 1995. Time on death row: 6,059 days, (16.6 years).

Last meal: None.

Last statement: None.

Pronounced dead: 6:22 P.M.
Note: Jennings refused to exit his cell at the Ellis Unit for transportation to the death house. A chemical agent was applied and a use of force team entered the cell and applied restraints.

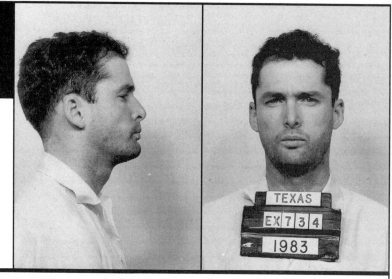

194

John Lamb

Executed: November 17, 1999

Personal Data: *Born:* July 24, 1957. *Race:* White. *Height:* 5'10". *Weight:* 145 lbs. *Education level:* 11 years. *Prior occupation:* Laborer. *County of conviction:* White. *Age at time of execution:* 42.

Sentenced to death for: Lamb admitted he shot Virginia businessman Jerry Harrison Chafin, 30, to steal his wallet, shaving kit, and car. Chafin was found dead by a cleaning woman the morning of November 6, 1982, two days after he had left Virginia for a new job in San Antonio. Lamb was arrested five days later near Perry, Florida, in Chafin's car. Lamb was released November 5, 1982, from a state prison in Searcy, Arkansas, hitchhiked to Greenville, and met Chafin later that day in the parking lot of a Greenville Motel. Lamb said the two men talked in Chafin's room for 30-minutes, and then he found Chafin's automatic pistol.

Received at Death Row: April 12, 1983. Time on death row: 6,059 days, (16.6 years).

Last meal: Ten pieces of large deep-fried jumbo shrimp, two pieces of garlic bread, two pieces of fried chicken (dark meat), one tossed salad with thousand island dressing, and one chocolate milkshake.

Last statement: I'm sorry, I wish I could bring them back. I'm done, let's do it.

Pronounced dead: 6:19 P.M.

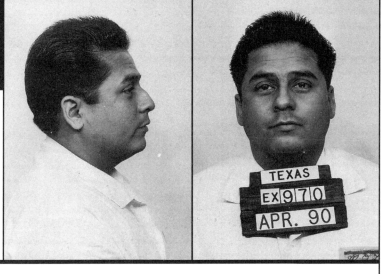

195

Jose Gutierrez

Executed:
November 18, 1999

Personal Data: *Born:* October 14, 1960. *Race:* Hispanic. *Height:* 5'4". *Weight:* 189 lbs. *Education level:* 8 years. *Prior occupation:* Construction. *County of conviction:* Brazos. *Age at time of execution:* 39.

Sentenced to death for: Convicted in the September 1989 robbery and murder of 42-year-old Dorothy McNew, a College Station store clerk. McNew was working the counter at the Texas Coin Exchange, 404 University, when Gutierrez and his brother Jessie entered shortly after 10 A.M. When McNew saw one of the men pull a handgun from his coat, she attempted to flee inside an office but was shot in the head. The Gutierrez brothers fled the store with gems and jewelry worth approximately $500,000. Both were traced to Houston, where they were arrested on September 1, 1989. Approximately $375,000 worth of the stolen merchandise was recovered. *Co-defendant*: Jessie Gutierrez was convicted of capital murder, sentenced to death, and executed by lethal injection on September 16, 1994. (See Entry 80, Jessie Gutierrez)

Received at Death Row: April 27, 1990. Time on death row: 3,491 days, (9.56 years).

Last meal: Two double-meat cheeseburgers with all vegetables and bacon, french fries, two cans of Coke, five jalapeno peppers, five pieces of fried chicken (white/dark meat), three buttermilk biscuits, and a steak.

Last statement: Mama Isabel told me to tell you hello. Holy, holy, holy! Lord God Almighty! Early in the morning our song shall rise to Thee; Holy, holy, holy, merciful and mighty! God in three Persons, blessed Trinity. Holy, holy, holy! Merciful and mighty. All Thy works shall praise Thy name, in earth, and sky, and sea; Holy, holy, holy, merciful and mighty! God in three Persons, blessed Trinity. Oh, our Father who art in heaven, holy, holy, holy be Thy name. Thy kingdom come, Thy will be done, on earth as it is in heaven. Give us this day our daily bread and forgive us our sins as we forgive our debtors. Lead us not into temptation, but deliver us from evil, for Thine is the kingdom and the power and the glory forever and ever. Now, Father, into Thy hands I commit my spirit. Amen.

Pronounced dead: 6:22 P.M.

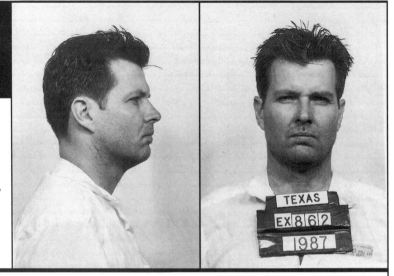

196

David Long

Executed:
December 8,
1999

Personal Data: *Born:* July 15, 1953. *Race:* White. *Height:* 5'9". *Weight:* 181 lbs. *Education level:* 13 years. *Prior occupation:* Cable TV technician. *County of conviction:* Dallas. *Age at time of execution:* 46.

Sentenced to death for: Convicted in the hatchet slaying of three women in Lancaster, a Dallas suburb. Killed were Donna Sue Jester, 38; her blind cousin Dalpha Lorene Jester, 64; and Laura Lee owens, a 20-year-old drifter from Florida who lived with the Jesters and Long in a house at 1010 Bayport. All were hacked to death with a hatchet by Long after he grew tired of hearing them argue. Long had lived at the house since September 19, 1986. He stole a purse, money and a car from the residence after the killings. He was arrested about a month later in Austin.
Note: During his trial, Long, who called the triple homicide "a satanic" experience, said he would kill again if not given the death penalty. In a statement to police, Long also claims to have killed his former boss in Bayview in 1983 and a gas station attendant in San Bernardino, California in 1978.

Received at Death Row: February 17, 1978. Time on death row: 4,657 days, (12.81 years).

Last meal: Four bacon, lettuce, and tomato sandwiches, iced tea, and potato chips.

Last statement: Ah, just ah sorry y'all. I think I've tried everything I could to get in touch with y'all to express how sorry I am. I, I never was right after that incident happened. I sent a letter to somebody, you know a letter outlining what I feel about everything. But anyway I just wanted, right after that apologize to you. I'm real sorry for it. I was raised by the California Youth Authority, I can't really pinpoint where it started, what happened but really believe that's just the bottom line, what happened to me was in California. I was in their reformatory schools and penitentiary, but ah they create monsters in there. That's it, I have nothing else to say. Thanks for coming, Jack.

Pronounced dead: 6:19 P.M.

197

James Beathard

Executed:
December 9, 1999

Personal Data: *Born:* February 23, 1957. *Race:* White. *Height:* 5'10". *Weight:* 197 lbs. *Education level:* 15 years. *Prior occupation:* Motorcycle mechanic. *County of conviction:* Trinity. *Age at time of execution:* 42.

Sentenced to death for: Beathard, along with Gene Hathorn, Jr., murdered Gene Hathorn, Sr., 45, Linda Sue Hathorn, 35, and their son, Marcus, 14, in their Trinity County home. The pair ransacked the home and took VCRs, several guns, and a van to make it look like a robbery. Beathard's motive was the promise of remuneration ($12,500) from the estate valued at $150,000. Only after the killings did Gene Hathorn discover that weeks before his father had cut him out of his will.
Co-defendant: Gene Hathorn was convicted of capital murder and sentenced to death.

Received at Death Row: March 5, 1985. Time on death row: 5,389 days, (14.76 years).

Last meal: Fried catfish, fried chicken, french fries, onion rings, green salad, fresh carrots, and Coke.

Last statement: See Appendix 1.

Pronounced dead: 6:21 P.M.

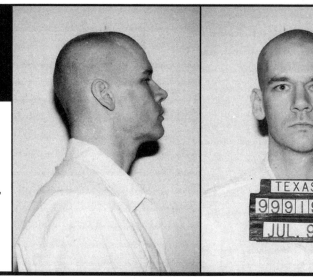

198

Robert Atworth

Executed: December 9, 1999

Personal Data: *Born:* August 18, 1968. *Race:* White. *Height:* 6'1". *Weight:* 170 lbs. *Education level:* 11 years (GED). *Prior occupation:* Laborer. *County of conviction:* Dallas. *Age at time of execution:* 30.

Sentenced to death for: Convicted in the April 1995 robbery and murder of 56-year-old Thomas Carlson in Richardson. Carlson's body was found between two trash dumpsters behind the President's Health Club at 110 W. Campbell Road. He had suffered multiple gunshot wounds to the head, torso, and groin area as well as knife wounds to the abdomen and chin. His wallet was missing and his right little finger where he had worn a ring had been severed. Atworth was arrested the next day when caught burglarizing a residence in Garland. He was driving Carlson's car and had in his possession the 9mm murder weapon as well as the Manurhin .380-caliber pistol Carlson had carried for protection. Knives were also found in Atworth's pants pocket and boot.

Received at Death Row: July 18, 1996. Time on death row: 1,245 days, (3.41 years).

Last meal: Grilled chicken, salad with ranch dressing, nachos and cheese with picante sauce, cookies and ice cream, two root beers.

Last statement: Well, first, my people, you guys have heard everything I needed to say today. I hope I said the right things. I hope you heard me. And I hope you go beyond here and do what you need to do, do the right thing. Strength in numbers. Look out for each other. You still got a chance with Shawn. Edwin you know what you gotta do. You have my love. It's the right thing. And for everybody else, those people who have malice in their heart, allow ambitions to over ride what they know. Be right. Even though they just gotta do their job. For all of you with hatred in their veins, and think this is a sham. You've done nothing. I did this, I chose this, you've done nothing. Remember this, if all you know is hatred, if all you know is blood love, you'll never be satisfied. For everybody out there that is like that and knows nothing but negative, kiss my proud white Irish ass. I'm ready, Warden, send me home.

Pronounced dead: 6:21 P.M.

199

Sammie Felder, Jr.

Executed:
December 15, 1999

TEXAS
EX 550
1976

Personal Data: *Born:* August 23, 1945. *Race:* Black. *Height:* 6'0". *Weight:* 190 lbs. *Education level:* 7 years. *Prior occupation:* Attendant. *County of conviction:* Harris. *Age at time of execution:* 54.

Sentenced to death for: Convicted in the February 1975 stabbing death of 42-year-old James Hanks, a paraplegic living at the Independent Life Style Apartment Complex in Houston. Hanks was reportedly stabbed with a pair of scissors and money taken from his apartment in the 5100 block of South Willow. Felder was working as an attendant at the complex at the time. He was arrested by Idaho police for a traffic violation a month after the killing. Felder's 1976 conviction was overturned by the Fifth Circuit Court of Appeals because of an improperly admitted confession. He was again convicted in September 1986 and sentenced to death a second time.

Received at Death Row: June 19, 1976. Time on death row: 8,565 days, (23.47 years).

Last meal: One pound of chitterlings, ten pieces fried chicken (dark meat), ten pieces of bacon, one raw onion, 15 pieces fried shrimp, peach cobbler, and one pitcher of whole milk.

Last statement: Like to tell my friends that I love them. Appreciate them being here to support me. Alison, I love you.

Pronounced dead: 6:15 P.M.

200

Earl Carl Heiselbetz, Jr.

Executed: January 12, 2000

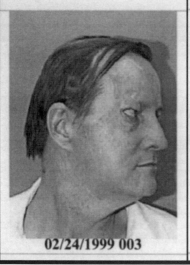

02/24/1999 003

999014
02/24/1999 002

Personal Data: *Born:* April 1, 1951. *Race:* White. *Height:* 6'2". *Weight:* 210 lbs. *Education level:* 11 years. *Prior occupation:* Truck driver. *County of conviction:* Sabine. *Age at time of execution:* 48.

Sentenced to death for: Convicted in the abduction and murder of 27-year-old Rena Whitten Rogers and her 2-year-old daughter, Jacy. The two were taken from their home in Pineland and driven to Tyler County where their skeletal remains were found in a barn on June 27, 1991. Both victims had been strangled. Heiselbetz lived next door to the victims and was unemployed at the time of the killing. Rena Rogers' husband reported a jar containing $8 in change, a .38-caliber pistol, and his wife's purse missing from the home. Police later found the victim's purse and the missing jar in a pond next to the home. Heiselbetz confessed after failing three polygraph tests.

Received at Death Row: November 22, 1991. Time on death row: 2,972 days, (8.14 years).

Last meal: Two breaded pork chops, three scrambled eggs, french fries, and milk.

Last statement: Love y'all, see you on the other side.

Pronounced dead: 6:19 P.M.

201

Spencer Corey Goodman

Executed:
January 18, 2000

02/26/1999 003

999031
02/26/1999 002

Personal Data: *Born:* October 28, 1968. *Race:* White. *Height:* 5'10". *Weight:* 200 lbs. *Education level:* 12.5 years. *Prior occupation:* Restaurant manager. *County of conviction:* Fort Bend. *Age at time of execution:* 31.

Sentenced to death for: Convicted in the abduction and murder of 18-year-old Cecile Ham, wife of entertainment manager Bill Ham. Goodman approached Ham as she was getting into her car in the parking lot of a Walgreen's store at Dairy Ashford and Memorial in Houston. He knocked her unconscious, pushed her into her red Cadillac, and drove into Fort Bend County before stopping and breaking the woman's neck. Police tracked Ham's killer through his use of her credit cards in Central Texas. Goodman, still driving Ham's car, was finally captured following a high-speed chase with police in Eagle County, Colorado, on August 7, 1991. He later confessed and directed authorities to where he had dumped Ham's body at a remote site near Pearsall in West Texas.

Received at Death Row: July 7, 1992. Time on death row: 2,751 days, (7.54 years).

Last meal: Double cheeseburger, french fries topped with onions and cheese, baked potato topped with sour cream, cheese, and butter, two fried pork chops, three beef enchiladas, and chocolate cake.

Last statement: To my family, I love them. To Kami, I love you and will always be with you. That's it, Warden.

Pronounced dead: 6:22 P.M.

202

David Hicks

Executed: January 20, 2000

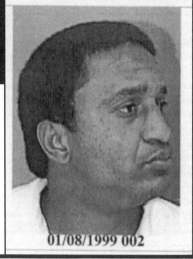

01/08/1999 002

000930
01/08/1999 001

Personal Data: *Born:* January 15, 1962. *Race:* Black. *Height:* 5'8". *Weight:* 148 lbs. *Education level:* 11 years. *Prior occupation:* Laborer. *County of conviction:* Freestone. *Age at time of execution:* 38.

Sentenced to death for: Convicted in the April 1988 sexual assault and beating death of his 87-year-old grandmother, Ocolor Hegger, at her residence in Teague. Hegger suffered eight to ten blows to the head with a blunt instrument after being sexually assaulted. Hicks was seen at or near the scene of the crime, and prosecutors later discovered that his DNA matched semen found in the body of the victim. Hicks was was charged with capital murder following his arrest in August 1988 on an outstanding misdemeanor warrant for theft.

Received at Death Row: February 2, 1989. Time on death row: 4,003 days, (10.97 years).

Last meal: Fish, fries, and soda.

Last statement: Hey, how y'all doin' out there? I done lost my voice. Y'all be strong now. All right. I love all of y'all. Don, thanks, man. I love you, Gloria, [to his wife, Gloria Hicks, a witness] always baby. That's all I gotta say. Hey, don't y'all worry about me. OK?

Pronounced dead: 7:29 P.M.

203

Larry Keith Robison

Executed:
January 21, 2000

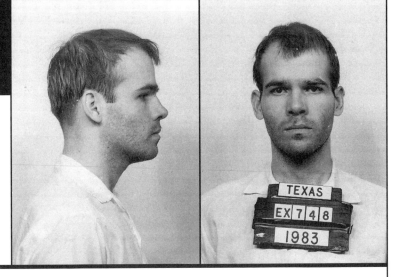

TEXAS
EX 7 4 8
1983

Personal Data: *Born:* August 12, 1957. *Race:* White. *Height:* 6'0". *Weight:* 150 lbs. *Education level:* 13 years. *Prior occupation:* Carpenter. *County of conviction:* Tarrant. *Age at time of execution:* 42.

Sentenced to death for: Convicted in the August 1982 stabbing-shooting death of 33-year-old Bruce M. Gardner, one of five persons killed by Robison in two adjacent Lake Worth cottages. Robison, a former mental patient, also killed Georgia Ann Reed, 34; her son, Scott Reed, 11; her mother, Earline H. Barker, 55; and Rickey Lee Bryant, 31. Bryant, who shared his home with Robison and who was portrayed by witnesses as Robison's lover, was decapitated and sexually mutilated. Robison fled in Gardner's car to Wichita, Kansas, following the mass murder.

Received at Death Row: September 9, 1993. Time on death row: 5,991 days, (16.41 years).

Last meal: None.

Last statement: None.

Pronounced dead: 6:16 P.M.

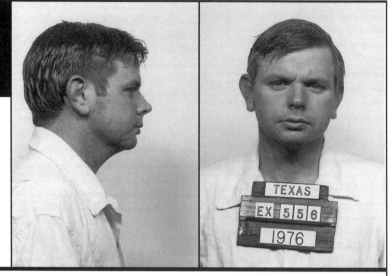

204

Billy George Hughes, Jr.

Executed:
January 24, 2000

Personal Data: *Born:* January 28, 1952. *Race:* White. *Height:* 5'10". *Weight:* 165 lbs. *Education level:* 12 years. *Prior occupation:* Horseshoer. *County of conviction:* Matagorda. *Age at time of execution:* 47.

Sentenced to death for: Convicted of capital murder in the April 4, 1976, shooting death of state trooper Mark Frederick of Bellville. Frederick was killed on I-10 in Sealy as he walked toward Hughes' car to question him about a stolen credit card at a Brookshire motel.

Received at Death Row: September 17, 1976. Time on death row: 8,525 days, (23.36 years).

Last meal: Chicken-fried steak with white gravy (2), french fries, four pieces of white bread, peaches, and two Cokes.

Last statement: I want to tell you all how much I love you all, how much I appreciate everything. I love you all and my family. I treasure every moment that I have had. I want the guys to know out there not to give up, not to give in, that I hope someday the madness in the system, something will come about, something will be resolved. I would gladly trade the last 24 years if it would bring back Mark Frederick. Give him back his life, give back my father his life, and my mother her health. All I ask is that I have one day and all the memories of you and my family and all the things that have happened. They are executing an innocent man because things did not happen as they say they happen and there's. The truth will come out someday. I am not the same person as I was 24 years ago. Who would have thought it would have taken 24 years to get to this moment? Don't give up, don't give in. If I am paying my debt to society, I am due a rebate and a refund, but I love you all and you all watch out for Mom and you all keep up, keep going. Thank you, Warden.

Pronounced dead: 6:18 P.M.

205

Glen Charles McGinnis

Executed: January 25, 2000

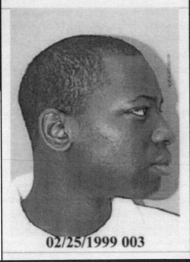 

02/25/1999 003

999039   02/25/1999 002

Personal Data: *Born:* January 11, 1973. *Race:* Black. *Height:* 6'0". *Weight:* 172 lbs. *Education level:* 10 years. *Prior occupation:* Laborer. *County of conviction:* Montgomery. *Age at time of execution:* 27.

Sentenced to death for: Convicted in the robbery and murder of 30-year-old Leta Ann Wilkerson of Conroe. Wilkerson was working as a clerk at Wilkins Cleaners & Laundry, 1200 South Frazier, when McGinnis walked in and shot her once in the head and three times in the back with a .25-caliber pistol he had taken from his aunt's apartment. McGinnis took $140 from the cash register and fled in Wilkerson's GMC Safari van. The van was recovered along I-45 and McGinnis was arrested the following morning at his aunt's apartment. His thumb print was found on the victim's wallet and $105 was recovered from his pants pocket. He was also serving a 10-year sentence for theft.

Received at Death Row: August 3, 1992. Time on death row: 2,731 days, (7.48 years).

Last meal: Cheeseburger with lettuce, tomato, bacon, onion rings, and catsup.

Last statement: None.

Pronounced dead: 6:17 P.M.

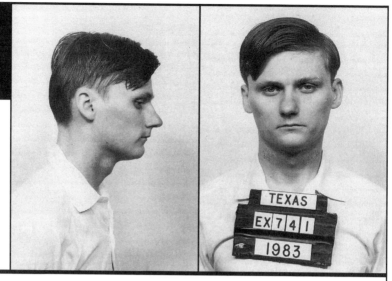

206

James Moreland

Executed:
January 27, 2000

TEXAS EX 7 4 1 1983

Personal Data: *Born:* May 15, 1960. *Race:* White. *Height:* 5'7". *Weight:* 126 lbs. *Education level:* 8 years. *Prior occupation:* Laborer. *County of conviction:* Henderson. *Age at time of execution:* 39.

Sentenced to death for: Moreland was convicted and sentenced to death for the October 9, 1982 stabbing death of Clinton Corbet, 53. He was also indicted in the death of John Royce Cravey, 41. A Dallas pathologist testified that the pair had been stabbed multiple times in the back. A court prosecutor said that since the jury returned a death penalty punishment, Moreland would not be tried in Cravey's death.

Received at Death Row: June 17, 1983. Time on death row: 6,081 days, (16.66 years).

Last meal: Three fried eggs over-easy, hash browns, several strips of bacon, toast (white bread), and orange juice.

Last statement: Dad, I love you both. You've been the best. All of you, all of you have truly been the best. And ah, I believe I'm going home. I'm sorry, and I really mean that, it's not just words. My life is all I can give. I stole two lives and I know it was precious to y'all. That's the story of my whole life, that's what alcohol will do for you. Oh Jesus, Lord God, take me home. Precious Lord. Take me home, Lord. Take me home. Yes, sir. Take me home, oh Lord.

Pronounced dead: 6:21 P.M.

207

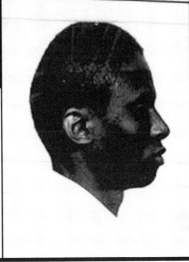

Cornelius Goss

Executed:
February 23, 2000

Personal Data: *Born:* May 24, 1961. *Race:* Black. *Height:* 5'9". *Weight:* 135 lbs. *Education level:* 11 years. *Prior occupation:* Laborer. *County of conviction:* Dallas. *Age at time of execution:* 38.

Sentenced to death for: Convicted in the May 1987 beating death of Carl Leevy in Dallas. Goss broke into Leevy's home at 10443 Heather Lane through a bedroom window and beat Leevy to death with a board. Goss then stole a $10 gold piece, a lady's bracelet, a camera, a necklace, a Rolex watch, and two men's rings. His fingerprints were found inside the home, and he later gave a voluntary statement to police.

Received at Death Row: May 24, 1961. Time on death row: 4,197 days, (11.50 years).

Last meal: One apple, one orange, one banana, coconut, and peaches.

Last statement: I'd like to apologize to the victim's family. Ah, no ah, I really can't say, I don't think I can say anything that will help, but I hope through your God, you can forgive me. I'm definitely not the person now that I was then. I was sick, afraid, and looking for love in all the wrong ways. I've caused you pain and grief beyond ever dreaming to cause someone of. I hope you will be able to forgive me. To my mother, I love you very much. Thanks, Jones.

Pronounced dead: 6:17 P.M.

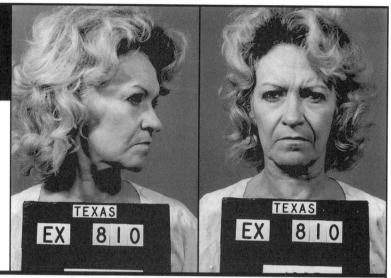

208

Betty Lou Beets

Executed:
February 24, 2000

Personal Data: *Born:* March 12, 1937. *Race:* White. *Height:* 5'2". *Weight:* 118 lbs. *Education level:* 10 years. *Prior occupation:* Cashier/waitress. *County of conviction:* Henderson. *Age at time of execution:* 62.

Sentenced to death for: Convicted in the 1983 shooting death of her fifth husband, Jimmy Don Beets, at the couple's home near Gun Barrel City. Prosecutors said Beets killed her husband, a firefighter, to collect $100,000 in insurance and pension benefits. His body was found buried in a wishing well used as a flower garden at the home. Police also found the skeletal remains of Beets' fourth husband, Doyle Wayne Baker, buried under a storage shed at the home. Baker, who disappeared in 1981, had also been shot to death.
Note: The press dubbed Beets "the Black Widow."

Received at Death Row: October 14, 1985. Time on death row: 5,258 days, (14.41 years).

Last meal: No final meal requested.

Last statement: None.

Pronounced dead: 6:18 P.M.

209

Odell Barnes, Jr.

Executed:
March 1, 2000

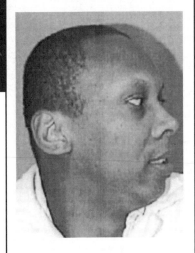

Personal Data: *Born:* March 22, 1968. *Race:* Black. *Height:* 6'2". *Weight:* 171 lbs. *Education level:* 11 years. *Prior occupation:* Construction worker. *County of conviction:* Lubbock. *Age at time of execution:* 31.

Sentenced to death for: Convicted in the November 1989 robbery and murder of Helen Bass. Bass was killed inside her home at 1221 Harding. She was beaten with a lamp and rifle, stabbed in the neck, and then shot in the head. Her nude body was found on her bed, where she had been sexually assaulted prior to her death. Barnes stole a .32-caliber pistol and an undetermined amount of money from the home. He was later observed trying to sell the gun to different people.

Received at Death Row: May 20, 1991. Time on death row: 3,211 days, (8.8 years).

Last meal: Justice, Equality, World Peace.

Last statement: I'd like to send great love to all my family members, my supporters, my attorneys. They have all supported me throughout this. I thank you for proving my innocence, although it has not been acknowledged by the courts. May you continue in the struggle and may you change all that's being done here today and in the past. Life has not been that good to me, but I believe that now, after meeting so many people who support me in this, that all things will come to an end, and may this be fruit of better judgments for the future. That's all I have to say.

Pronounced dead: 6:34 P.M.

210

Ponchai Wilkerson

Executed:
March 14, 2000

TEXAS
999011
NOV. 91

Personal Data: *Born:* July 15, 1971. *Race:* Black. *Height:* 5'8". *Weight:* 140 lbs. *Education level:* 11 years. *Prior occupation:* Laborer. *County of conviction:* Harris. *Age at time of execution:* 28.

Sentenced to death for: Convicted in the November 1990 robbery and shooting death of Chung Myong Yi, a Houston jewelry store clerk. Wilkerson reportedly watched co-defendant Wilton Bethany buy pieces of jewelry at Royal Gold Wholesale, 9889 Harwin, and then returned with a pistol and shot Yi once in the head. Following his arrest, police found that Wilkerson had committed three additional burglaries, three auto thefts, and had shot four other people in two separate drive-by shootings. Prosecutors also claimed that Wilkerson was a party to attempted capital murder when another store clerk was shot with a shotgun.
Note: On Thanksgiving Day 1998, Wilkerson along with six other death row inmates cut through a recreation yard fence at the Ellis Unit and made it onto the roof. Wilkerson and five of the inmates were caught after guards started firing, but inmate Martin Gurule escaped, becoming the first inmate in 64 years to get out of death row. Gurule's body was found a week later in a creek not far from the prison. He had drowned. In 1999, Wilkeson and death row inmate Howard Guidry, 23, took a female prison guard, Jeanette Bledsoe, 57, hostage for nearly 13 hours to demand better living conditions.

Received at Death Row: July 15, 1971. Time on death row: 3,043 days, (8.34 years).

Last meal: No final meal requested.

Last statement: None.
Note: Wilkerson refused to leave his cell at the Ellis unit for transport to the death room. He was gassed before transport, refused to leave his holding cell near the death chamber, and was bound to the gurney with additional velcro bands. As the lethal drugs began to take effect, Wilkerson spit out a universal handcuff and leg restraint key he had been holding in his mouth. It was unknown how Wilkerson obtained the key.

Pronounced dead: 6:24 P.M.

211

Timothy Gribble

Executed: March 15, 2000

Personal Data: *Born:* August 27, 1963. *Race:* White. *Height:* 5'10". *Weight:* 204 lbs. *Education level*: 11 years. *Prior occupation:* Mechanic/roofer. *County of conviction:* Galveston. *Age at time of execution:* 36.

Sentenced to death for: Convicted in the September 1987 rape and strangulation of 36-year-old Elizabeth "Libby" Jones of Clear Lake Shores. Gribble was working as a roofer at Jones' home, which was being remodeled at the time of the murder. He told police he returned to the home at 304 Queen St. several hours after work and raped Jones after she let him in to search for a billfold he claimed to have left behind. He said he later drove her to an isolated area near League City and strangled her with the sash from the robe she was wearing. Gribble was arrested on September 30, 1987, and led police to Jones' remains after confessing. Police found a cloth sash knotted around neck vertebrae at the site and later recovered Jones' purse from a nearby creek.

Received at Death Row: January 11, 1989. Time on death row: 4,080 days, (11.18 years).

Last meal: No final meal requested.

Last statement: Okay, thank you. To the Weiss family, and ah I just want you to know from the bottom of may heart that I am truly sorry. I mean it, I'm not just saying it. Through the years of being in prison I have come to hear and respect our life. It was wrong what I did. I know you had to go through a lot of pain and I'm sorry. To the Jones family, the same is true, I am truly, truly sorry. I wanted to prepare a longer statement but time ran out. I had the chaplain write down a few words for my friends and for you, my family. I would like him to read them for me, and ah, just please find peace. [Chaplain Brazzil recites written statement, See Appendix 1.] (last verbal statement) No sir, I just want to pray a chant, do what you have to do.

Pronounced dead: 6:19 P.M.

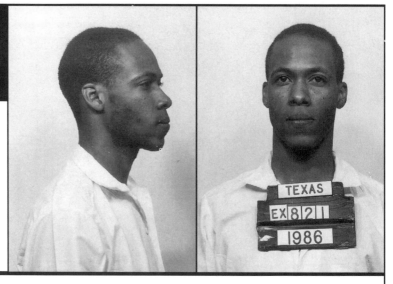

212

Tommy Ray Jackson

Executed:
May 4, 2000

Personal Data: *Born*: November 15, 1956. *Race*: Black. *Height*: 5'7". *Weight*: 120 lbs. *Education level*: 14 years. *Prior occupation:* Computer technician. *County of conviction:* Williamson. *Age at time of execution*: 43.

Sentenced to death for: Convicted in the November 1983 abduction and shooting death of Rosalind Robison, a 24-year-old University of Texas student from Terre Haute, Indiana. Robison, an engineering student, was reportedly kidnapped from the UT campus in Austin and forced to withdraw money from a bank teller machine. She was then driven to a rural location between Pflugerville and Round Rock and shot once in the head with a .25-caliber pistol. Her body was found a month later beneath a gravel pile. Jackson was arrested four days later outside an Austin grocery in the victim's car.

Received at Death Row: February 28, 1986. Time on death row: 5,189 days, (14.22 years).

Last meal: None.

Last statement: See Appendix 1.

Pronounced dead: 6:24 P.M.

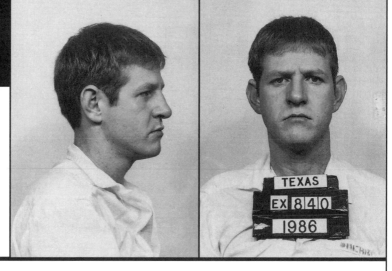

213

William Joseph Kitchens

Executed: May 9, 2000

TEXAS
EX 8 4 0
1986

Personal Data: *Born*: April 26, 1963. *Race*: White. *Height*: 6'3". *Weight*: 185 lbs. *Education level*: 8 years. *Prior occupation*: Painter. *County of conviction*: Taylor. *Age at time of execution*: 37.

Sentenced to death for: Convicted of capital murder in the death of Patricia Leann Webb neat Abilene on May 17, 1986. Webb, who had met Kitchens at an Abilene bar on the day of her death, was raped and then driven to a secluded area 11 miles from Abilene where she was severely beaten, strangled, and shot in the head with a .22-caliber pistol. Kitchens stole Webb's car along with her money, credit cards and checkbook. Kitchens was arrested in his hometown of Blanchard, Oklahoma on May 18 in possession of Webb's property.

Received at Death Row: September 2, 1986. Time on death row: 4,995 days, (13.68 years).

Last meal: ½ dozen sunny side up fried eggs, eight pieces of pan sausage, six slices of toast with butter and grape jelly, crispy hash browns, milk and orange juice.

Last statement: See Appendix 1.

Pronounced dead: 6:22 P.M.

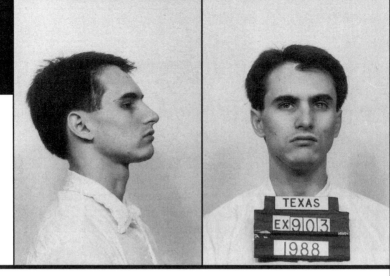

214

Michael Lee McBride

Executed: May 11, 2000

TEXAS
EX903
1988

Personal Data: *Born*: January 3, 1967. *Race*: White. *Height*: 5'4". *Weight*: 141 lbs. *Education level:* 12 years. *Prior occupation:* Bar manager/bartender. *County of conviction:* Lubbock. *Age at time of execution*: 33.

Sentenced to death for: Convicted in the October 1985 shooting deaths of Christian Fisher and James Alan Holzler, both 18, in Lubbock. Fisher, McBride's ex-girlfriend, and her companion were shot to death with a .30-caliber rifle outside McBride's residence at 1903 26th Street. Witnesses said Fisher had gone to the residence to pick up some things and was killed by a volley of shots after challenging McBride to shoot. McBride then walked to the victim's car and shot Holzler, who was seated in the driver's seat, in the head and chest. Both died at the scene. McBride then turned the rifle on himself, shooting himself once in the head. Police found him lying on the ground and reaching for the rifle.

Received at Death Row: May 26, 1988. Time on death row: 4,377 days, (11.99 years).

Last meal: Two chicken patties with Swiss cheese, stuffed baked potato with jalapeno peppers and sour cream, milk.

Last statement: Thank you, um, I anticipated that I would try to memorize and recite beatitudes New Testament, more or less, Luke's beatitudes, I should say, and ah, a chapter on love in 1st Corinthians chapter 13, ah, I pretty much knew that I would not be able to memorize so much. There was also a poem that went along with it and in anticipation of not being able to, um, fulfill that desire, I provided a written statement that will be made available to anybody that wants it, I believe. Isn't that correct? So, uh, I wanted you to hear me say that and I apologize and for any other grief I have caused you know, including the, ah, what you're about to witness now. It won't be very long. As soon as you realize that appear I am falling asleep. I would leave because I won't be here after that point. I will be dead at that point. It's irreversible. God bless all of you. Thank you. [See Appendix 1 for written last words.]

Pronounced dead: 6:21 P.M.

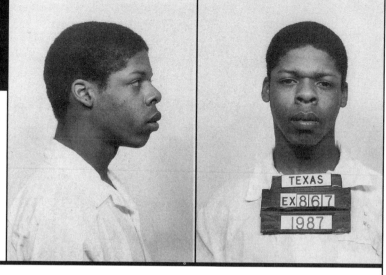

215

James David Richardson

Executed: May 23, 2000

Personal Data: *Born*: September 7, 1967. *Race*: Black. *Height*: 5'9". *Weight*: 170 lbs. *Education level:* 11 years. *Prior occupation:* Construction. *County of conviction:* Navarro. *Age at time of execution:* 32.

Sentenced to death for: Convicted of capital murder in the shooting death of 35-year-old Gerald Abay during an armed robbery at Gusher Liquor Store in Angus on December 17, 1986. Richardson was with two other men who had picket out some beer and were about to pay for it when Richardson pulled out a pistol and shot Abay in the throat and chest. Abay, of Corsicana, managed to fire several shots at the suspects and did hit Richardson in the left hand. Approximately $1,000 was taken from the liquor store cash register. Abay died about an hour after the shooting. Richardson was arested the next afternoon after evading authorities on foot.
Co-defendants: Michael James Ellison received a life sentence for murder. James McHenry received a life sentence for capital murder.

Received at Death Row: May 1, 1987. Time on death row: 4,759 days, (13.04 years) .

Last meal: Fresh fried chicken (no skin, 5 breasts and 20 wings), carrot cake, white coconut cake, cheesecake with cherry topping.

Last statement: See Appendix 1.

Pronounced dead: 6:32 P.M.

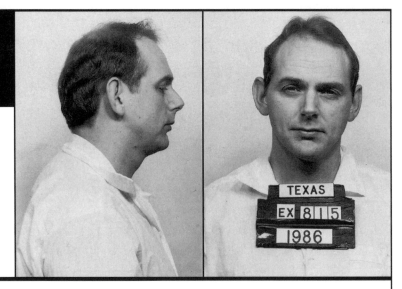

216

Richard Donald Foster

Executed: May 24, 2000

Personal Data: *Born*: August 16, 1952. *Race*: White. *Height*: 5'9". *Weight*: 195 lbs. *Education level:* 11 years (GED). *Prior occupation:* Roofer/auto paint & body. *County of conviction:* Parker. *Age at time of execution:* 47.

Sentenced to death for: Convicted in the April 1984 shotgun slaying of Gary Michael Cox, owner of Cox's Feed and Farm Supply located two miles outside of Springtown on SH 199. Cox was shot once in the back of the head with a shotgun during a robbery of his store that netted $250. Foster was apprehended May 5, 1984 after holding seven employees of Citizen's National Bank in Breckenridge hostage for 12 hours. Foster was sentenced to four life terms on aggravated kidnapping charges in connection with the hostage incident. In August 1986, Foster, accompanied by a female inmate, escaped form the Stephens Co. Jail, where he was awaiting trial on the kidnapping charges. Police shot out the tires of the stolen vehicle he was driving and recaptured him near Possum Kingdom Lake on August 7. He was given a 20-year sentence in Palo Pinto County in connection with the escape.

Received at Death Row: January 7, 1986. Time on death row:5,260 days, (14.41 years).

Last meal: Beef fajita, blooming onion, fried chicken (white meat), jalapeno peppers, large Caesar salad with blue cheese dressing, bread rolls with butter, vanilla ice cream, three bananas, one Coke, a pot of coffee, a pack of cigarettes (prohibited by TDCJ regulations).

Last statement: I have been crucified with Christ. It is no longer I who lives, but Christ who lives in me. So for the life for which I live now in the flesh, I live by faith in the Son of God who loved me and gave himself for me. I love you, Annie. You have been the best friend I have ever had in the world. I'll see you when you get there, okay? I am ready, Warden.

Pronounced dead: 6:23 P.M.

217

James Edward Clayton

Executed: May 25, 2000

Personal Data: *Born*: December 30, 1966. *Race*: Black. *Height*: 5'11". *Weight*: 188 lbs. *Education level:* 14 years. *Prior occupation:* Clerical. *County of conviction:* Taylor. *Age at time of execution:* 33.

Sentenced to death for: Convicted in the September 1987 abduction and slaying of 27-year-old Lori M. Barrett of Abilene. Barrett was reportedly abducted from her apartment at 1734 Ave. D after Clayton managed to break in through a bedroom window. Her body, tied at the hands with telephone cord and wrapped in a blanket, was found on September 29, 1987, off the side of a rural road three miles north of the Jones-Taylor county line. She had been shot in the head, neck, and left shoulder with a .243-caliber rifle. Clayton was arrested in connection with Barrett's disappearance on September 23, 1987.

Received at Death Row: November 14, 1988. Time on death row: 4,222 days, (11.57 years).

Last meal: Three chicken breasts (fried), fresh lettuce and cucumber salad with light vinegar salad dressing on the side, a large pitcher of ice water.

Last statement: I would like to take this time to, ah, to use this moment an example for Christ. I would like to follow his example and leave with peace in my heart and forgiveness. There is no anger in my heart about this entire situation. I just want to testify to all of y'all that I have loved you. I appreciate your concern and genuine love for me. God bless you. I love all of all. Jesus is Lord.

Pronounced dead: 6:17 P.M.

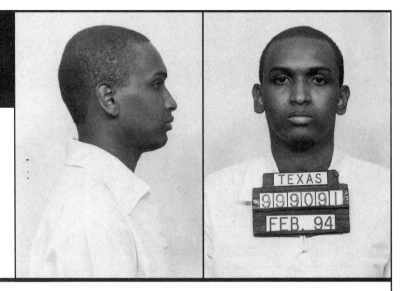

218

Robert Earl Carter

Executed: May 31, 2000

Personal Data: *Born*: March 7, 1966. *Race*: Black. *Height*: 5'9". *Weight*: 171 lbs. *Education level*: 12 years. *Prior occupation*: Correctional officer. *County of conviction*: Burleson. *Age at time of execution*: 34.

Sentenced to death for: Convicted in the deaths of six people in Somerville. Killed were Bobbie Davis, 45, her daughter Nicole Davis, 16, and her grandchildren De 'Nitra Davis, 9, Lea'Erin Davis, 5, and Brittany Davis, 6. Also killed was 4-year-old Jason Davis who was stabbed to death as he cowered beneath a pillow at his grandmother's home. With the exception of Nicole, each victim died of multiple stab wounds. Nicole was killed by five gunshots to the head. Following the killings, the elder Davis' home was set afire in an effort to conceal the murders. Carter, who had recently been named in a paternity suit by Davis' daughter, attended funeral services for the victims wrapped in bandages for severe burns apparently suffered in the house fire.
Co-defendant: Anthony Graves was convicted of capital murder and given the death penalty. He is awaiting an execution date.

Received at Death Row: February 23, 1994. Time on death row: 2,293 days, (6.28 years).

Last meal: Double-meat cheeseburger (all the way), fries.

Last statement: To the Davis family, I am sorry for all of the pain that I caused your family. It was me and me alone. Anthony Graves had nothing to do with it. I lied on him in court. My wife had nothing to do with it. Anthony Graves don't even know anything about it. My wife don't know anything about it. But, I hope that you can find your peace and comfort in strength in Christ Jesus alone. Like I said, I am sorry for hurting your family. And it is a shame that it had to come to this. So I hope that you don't find peace, not in my death, but in Christ. Cause He is the only one that can give you the strength that you need. And to my family, I love you. Ah, you have been a blessing to me and I love you all and one day I will see y'all, so I hope y'all find y'all peace, comfort, and strength in Christ Jesus alone, because that's where it's at. Abul, behold your son, and Anitra, behold your mother. I love you. I am ready to go home and be with my Lord. I'm sorry for all the pain I've caused your family. It was me and me alone. Anthony Graves [his codefendant] had nothing to do with it. I lied on him in court. I hope you will find peace and comfort with Christ Jesus. It's a shame it has come to this. I'm ready to go home with my lord.

Pronounced dead: 6:20 P.M.

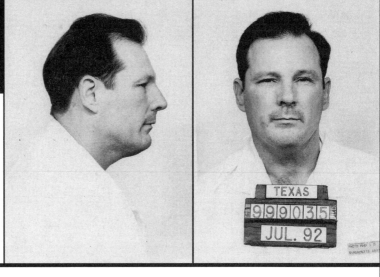

219

Thomas Wayne Mason

Executed: June 12, 2000

Personal Data: *Born*: December 31, 1951. *Race*: White. *Height*: 6'1". *Weight*: 217 lbs. *Education:* 9 years. *Occupation*: Drywaller. *County of conviction:* Smith. *Age at time of execution:* 48.

Sentenced to death for: Convicted in the October 1991 shotgun slayings f his mother-in-law, 55-year-old Marsha Yvonne Brock, and her 80-year-old mother, Sybil Mares Dennis, at Brock's home in Whitehorse. Brock, a nurse, called 911 from her home at 113 Robinwood and screamed for help when Mason showed up brandishing a 12-gauge shotgun. Both victims were shot in the head at close range. The killings apparently stemmed from Mason's separation from Brock's daughter. Two months earlier, police had placed Brock's home under surveillance after she reported that Mason threatened to burn it down.

Received at Death Row: July 14, 1992. Time on death row: 2,896 days, (7.93 years).

Last meal: None.

Last statement: See Appendix 1.

Pronounced dead: 6:24 P.M.

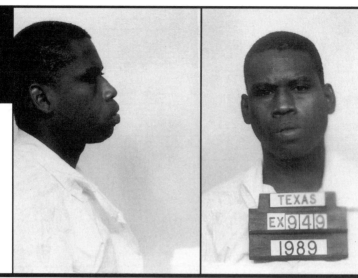

220

John Albert Burks

Executed: June 14, 2000

TEXAS
EX 949
1989

Personal Data: *Born*: January 18, 1956. *Race*: Black. *Height*: 5'6". *Weight*: 155 lbs. *Education level:* 9 years. *Prior occupation:* Cement finisher. *County of conviction:* McLennan. *Age at time of execution:* 44.

Sentenced to death for: Convicted in the January 1989 murder of Jesse Contreras during the armed robbery of Jesse's Tortilla Factory at 1226 Webster in Waco. Contreras was shot in the mouth and chest with a .25-caliber pistol during the robbery. He died of his wounds at a Waco Hospital on February 16, 1989. *Co-defendant*: Mark McConnell was convicted of robbery and burglary and given a 40-year sentence.

Received at Death Row: October 5, 1989. Time on death row: 3,905 days, (10.70 years).

Last meal: Fried chicken (two thighs and wings), one pound of bacon, 16-ounce T-bone steak, Big Red, coffee.

Last statement: Hey, how are y'all doing? Alright, it's gonna be alright. There's some guys I didn't get a chance to visit with, ah I met when I first drove up here...Lester Byers, Chris Black, Alba, John Alba, and Rosales Rock. You know who you are. The Raiders are going all the way, y'all [mumbles...] Mo-B. Y'all pray for me. And it's going to be alright. That's it and it's time to roll up out of her. It's going down, let's get it over with. That's it.

Pronounced dead: 6:18 P.M.

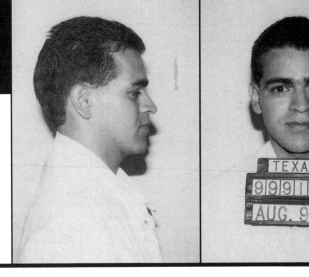

221

Paul Selso Nuncio

Executed: June 15, 2000

Personal Data: *Born*: October 20, 1968. *Race*: Hispanic. *Height*: 5'4". *Weight*: 130 lbs. *Education level:* n/a. *Prior occupation:* Clerk. *County of conviction:* Hale. *Age at time of execution:* 32.

Sentenced to death for: Convicted in the strangulation death of 61-year-old Pauline Crownover Farris in Plainview. Nuncio broke into Farris' home at 708 Beech through the back door and beat the resident before sexually assaulting her and strangling her to death with his hands. He then stole several items from the home, including two television sets, a stereo, VCR, several rings and a watch. Nuncio was arrested five days later after selling one of the stolen televisions. He told police he broke into Farris' home in order to steal items he could sell for money to buy drugs.

Received at Death Row: August 2, 1995. Time on death row: 1,782 days, (4.88 years).

Last meal: Enchiladas, burritos, chocolate ice cream, cantalope (whole, split in half).

Last statement: See Appendix 1.

Pronounced dead: 7:17 P.M.

222

Gary Lee Graham

Executed:
June 22, 2000

Personal Data: *Born*: September 5, 1960. *Race*: Black. *Height*: 5'10". *Weight*: 155 lbs. *Education level*: 9 years. *Prior occupation*: Laborer. *County of conviction*: Harris. *Age at time of execution*: 39.

Sentenced to death for: Convicted in the May 1981 robbery and fatal shooting of 53-year-old Bobby Grant Lambert of Tucson, Arizona outside a Houston supermarket. A witness testified Lambert was coming out of a Safeway store in the 8900 of the North Freeway when Graham reached into Lambert's pockets and then shot Lambert with a pistol as they scuffled. Lambert, who staggered back into the store where he died, was robbed only of change from a $100 bill, even though police found $6,000 in $100 bills on his body. Testimony showed Graham had been charged in ten separate robberies and suspected in two shootings, ten car thefts and eight more robberies in Houston.

Received at Death Row: November 9, 1981. Time on death row: 6,814 days, (18.67 years).

Last meal: None.

Last statement: See Appendix 1.

Pronounced dead: 8:49 P.M.
Note: Graham's execution was postponed due to last minute legal delays. The U.S. Supreme Court declined in a 5-4 vote to hear Graham's appeal, the Texas Court of Criminal Appeals denied an appeal, and Texas Federal District Judge James Nowlin rejected a civil lawsuit against the Texas Board of Pardons and Paroles by Graham's attorneys.

3. Ronald Clark O'Bryan (written): What is about to transpire in a few moments is wrong! However, we as human beings do make mistakes and errors. This execution is one of these wrongs. Yet doesn't mean our whole system of justice is wrong. Therefore, I would forgive all who have taken part in any way in my death. Also, to anyone I have offended in anyway during my 39 years, I pray and ask your forgiveness, just as I forgive anyone whose offended me in anyway. And, I pray and ask God's forgiveness for all of us respectively as human beings. To my loved ones, I extended my undieing [*sic*] love. To those close to me, know in your hearts I love you one and all. God bless you all and may Gods best blessings be always yours. Ronald C. O'Bryan P.S. During my time here, I have been treated well by all T.D.C. personnel.

10. Charles Francis Rumbaugh (written): I am currently scheduled to be executed before sunrise on the morning of September 11th, 1985. This is my third scheduled execution date and I therefore believe it is highly probable it will be carried out this time. This knowledge does not in any way disturb me; I feel comfortable with myself and my situation. I acknowledge my responsibility for causing a man's death almost 10½ years ago and I am prepared to die for that even though it resulted from a situation I was not in control of and in which I had to either kill or be killed. Regardless of the circumstances, however, I do acknowledge my responsibility because I realize and admit it would not have occurred if I had not been in that place at that time with the intention of committing a robbery; I have no excuse and do not try to claim any.

Because of the offense I committed, my background, my rebellious character, and my alleged remorselessness, society – through it's judicial system – has condemned me to die. Just as I realize and acknowledge that I can proffer no excuse for my actions in causing the death of a human being, so must I state my clear and emphatic belief that neither can society proffer any righteously acceptable or defensible excuse for the imposition of the death penalty. My crime was an individual one committed by me alone and the responsibility is therefore mine alone, whereas society's crimes are concerted ones committed in the name of and by the authority of each and every citizen and therefore the responsibility is that of each and every citizen. Murder is Murder! Just as society condemns me, so must it condemn itself. Just as society labels me a "murderer" for causing the death of a human being, so must it label itself for knowingly, intentionally, premeditatedly and hypo critically causing the deaths of each an every human being throughout this country whom it has put to death. And the only possible "right" that society can claim in the RIGHT of MIGHT!

Just as the State of Texas has indicted me for the offense of Capital Murder, so do I indict each and every adult citizen of the State of Texas for the premeditated murders of nine men thus far and, further, for conspiring to murder over 200 others hwo are now incarcerated under sentence of death. (The only exception to this indictment are those persons of conscience who recognize the hypocrisy inherent in capital punishment, recognize "legalized" murder for what it really is and actively work in opposition to it.) Just as the State of Texas has convicted me of my crime, so does each and every adult citizen of the State of Texas stand convicted of their crimes. And, finally, just as the State of Texas has condemned me to die, so do I condemn each and every adult citizen of the State of Texas to serve the remainder of their lives contemplating their misdeeds – the rest of their lives contemplating the blood on their hands.

I leave you with one last thought: My life has taught me that violence does indeed beget violence, and capital punishment only perpetuates the vicious cycle and contributes to the list of victims of violence. I have no answers and I have no solutions, but I do know that only through the powers of love, caring, understanding, compassion, and reconciliation can you ever hope to find a solution.

35. Johnny R. Anderson (written): My final statement to the people…
I just want the public to know that I am not guilty of this crime and am being used as an excape goat, and all the people that were suppose to be involved in this case are out in the free world. I also want the public to know that in Capitol cases, the person getting killed by the state for revenge of the victim and there family, may satisfy the victim's family, but no one looks at what it puts my family through. The state puts my family in the same place as the victim's family. There are a lot of people on death row (that if people could meet would know that either they are not guilty or don't belong on death row). This is not a fair system they use to put people here, and instead of trying to shorten their appeals, you should try and get a specal court to look over all cases that involve the death sentence. Look at all the mistakes the state has made so far in some of these cases, and you will understand how bad the system is. People's lives ar on the life here, (Wake up out there People) some are guilty, but some are not, your killing the not guilty just as much as the state is by not helping find the not guilty one's. How would you

like to get locked up for something you know you didn't do, and be killed for it, just because people think they that when you get locked up your guilty and that's the end of it regardless. The higher courts are so full that they are killing people left and right without really looking at the cases or the law, either they will change the law to fit the cases, or they will say when they find out later afterh they kill them and find out they shouldn't of, the one out of Ten is't bad, or try to hide it from the public. People what about that one person and his family?? And the victim's family that helped kill someone that wasn't guilty, through the state, What?? Keep killing people unitl you get the right one and play the odds. You people out there don't understand, any of this, either because you don't care enough to check, or you will have to wait until you're the one on the table getting killed, then as always it will be to late, then you understand how unfair the system really is for all parties involved. And stop killing people that kill people. What kind of masage is this sending to people, (That killing is okay for some people and not others??) That's why death row is full and shows no sign of slowing down, WRONG MASAGE, [sic] PEOPLE!!!!!!
The excape goat Johnny R. Anderson Ex #000732

36. Jones Smith (portion of spoken last statement, most of which was not recorded): I have already spoken the truth but because the truth was spoken by one of the accused, the truth was not respected so for that to set me free it must come from the one who spoke a lie. I am not the killer. I myself did not kill anyone. But I go to my death not begging for my life. I will not humiliate myself. I'll let no man break me…When people wake up to the reality of execution, the price the will be paid will be a dear one. Hare Krishna.

67. Richard J. Wilkerson (written by his sister): This execution is not justice; This execution is an act of revenge! If this is justice, then justice is blind. Take a borderline retarded young male Who for the 1st time ever committed a felony Then contaminate his true tell all confession Add a judge who discriminates Plus an ALL-WHITE jury Pile on an ineffective assistance of counsel And execute the option of rehabilitation Persecute the witnesses And you have created a death sentence or a family lasting over 10 years I will say this again…..This execution isn't justice — but an act of revenge. Killing RJ will not bring Anil back, it only justifies "an eye for an eye and a tooth for a tooth." Its too late to help RJ, but maybe this poem will help someone else out there. *Note:* The following statement was also written prior to the execution. Seeing Through The Eyes of a Death Row Inmate Sometime I wonder why, why he? Why did he go out inot the world to see? To be out there and see what really id exist, now his name is written down on the Death Row List. I can only imagine how lonesome he was all by himself. We both knew he had no future left! His hopes and dreams became a fantasy. He often said, "There's nothing left of me." I have asked myself, why did he get involved with drugs? He could never explain why he hung around with thugs? Did it really make him feel like a king – Did he actually think he as capable of getting away with anything? He knew the thought of life wasn't ticking in his head. There's nothing left but the memory of those who lay dead. What was done, cannot be undone. He confessed he was one of the guilty ones. What would he say to the victims family? - I'm sorry and my head wasn't on straight. I hope you will accept my apology, even though its too late. I never knew I would take a life and commit a crime. I regret it because now I have to face the lethal injection while doing death row time. I knew I would pay with struggle and strife, but I never thought the cost would be losing my life.

Richard J. Wilkerson
Written through his sister, Michelle Winn

79. Robert Nelson Drew (written): It is now the second of August 1994 and tonight the state of Texas committed murder. The state took the life of Robert Nelson Drew Sr. age 35 for a crime he did not commit and had the evidence to prove it. The state fought for his life/execution with tax payers money that could have been better spent on schools or many other worth while endeavors that the entire state could have benefited from. Instead, one Harris county district attorney is gloating in his victory of not having to admit he made a mistake and sent an innocent man to death row for 11 years of his life. The district attorney would rather murder and innocent person than admit he made this mistake.

I hope that my death will serve as a catalyst to all people world wide to speak up and fight together as one to do away with the crime of judicial murder at the hands of any state. The facts of my case showed that I was and always will be innocent of the crime the state of Texas murdered me for. Yet due to the unjust 30 day low on newly discovered evidence I was unable to get a court to hear the evidence of my innocence. Now, as of April 20th, 1994, this law has been done away with by the court of criminal appeals of Texas and still the district attorney would rather waste the tax payers money to execute an innocent man then agree to a hearing. This tells the truth about the states case, if the state was so sure they were correct in their conviction they would allow a hearing cause they would know they had had nothing to hide. Since the truth of my innocence has come to light the state has fought twice as hard to execute me since they know their case would crumble under their own feet when the judge saw the evidence all presented by competent attorney's and not the incompetent ones they appoint at trial to those of us who were unable to retain our own for one reason or the other.

I think the words of Robert Alton Harris, executed in California, tell it best. "It you're a king or a street sweeper, one day we all dance with the grim reeper." This will include the district attorneys who fought for my judicial murder to be carried out on August second 1994. From this day on they will have the blood of an innocent man on their hands and my name in their lives til the day they stand before a higher power to be judged for the things they've done in their lives on this earth.

But, always remember the words spoken by Jesus Christ, "Forgive them father for they know not what they do." He has the power to forgive what they are doing by taking all the human lives they are taking by judicial murder, 80 in Texas alone since the death penalty was brought back into the law. This includes the murder of me tonight.

I'd like to let all my supporters know I'm very grateful for everything they've done for me over the years. Your kindness and compassion for truth in justice will never go unnoticed by others. I would like you to all remember that if you see another case that makes you feel this way to please stand up and yell long and loud til your heard world wide and justice is served. Not just sitting by is what it takes to change this world and you have to power to do it. Please be heard and fight for the death penalty to be abolished for good. This will be for the good of all humans in the world and not just a couple thousand men and women on death rows world wide. Everyone should remember it could very well be them or one of their loved ones in my place and for this reason everyone should stand now and be heard screaming to the world, "STOP THIS MADNESS, LET NO MORE BLOOD FLOW IN THE NAME OF JUSTICE, JUDICIAL MURDER MUST STOP NOW AND NEVER START AGAIN."

How many innocent people must die at the hands of states before the people all come together to fight for a just cause and do away with this madness? Don't let the politicians ruin your country and what it stands for. Tell them you know the truth and would rather see the two to three million or more that is spent to kill someone, when it would cost less than half a million to keep that person locked up for 40 calendar years or longer, spent on the things needed to ensure the future of the country. This money they have spent to murder an innocent man tonight could have been spent on schools for eh children who are the future of this country. This way it was wasted to murder someone who did nothing, but let the fear of his own death and the drunken haze of a day of drinking cloud his better judgement to not get killed himself to save someone else.

I am truly sorry I was to drunk to stop the killing of that young man that night in 1983, but, should I have been killed for being drunk and not getting myself killed to stop the murder that took place that night? Ask yourself if you'd back the state in this jucidial murder process if you could have seen all the evidence in court and not just what the district attorney wanted you to see. Should people die at the hands of the district attorneys just so they can add to their political endevors to become attorney general or a judge. Do you peole really want to be part of this judicial murder process? You are unless you join the world wide fight now tot do away with this unjust, barbaric, senseless law called the death penalty.

To all my friends I've left behind. I'd like you to always remember the fight must go on and never give up for any reason. Let no man tell you other wise. Always remember that quitters never are winners in anything and if you quit fighting for life and what is right you'll never win the battle. The battle will be won if you continue to fight. The cause is a just one, your own life, so fight with everything you have and win the fight. Carry on and hold your heads high knowing you are going the right thing.

To all my loved ones I left behind. I was taken from this life to satisfy a states governments blood lust but don't ever think of those who di ti cause they are not worthy of your thoughts. Remember I love every one of you from the bottom of my heart and always will. I'll be looking down on you from a better place and I now rest at peace and hope you'll find some comfort knowing these people have not killed me, they killed themselves cause I will never die to those who care and love me for me and not something else. I ask you to remember the good times from years gone by and know we'll be together again.

To all my friends on the "Row", don't give up. Fight his war an dwin it like I know in my heart that you can. Every one or you are worhty of this battle it will take to win, so fight on my brothers and know I'm fighting with you from a better place. Con'd let these bastards get you down.

To my road dog Robert "Shorty" Ramos, keep your head high and remember to do time and don't ever let time do you. Play your own game and don't ever give up the fight. It takes time but it can be won so don't let these bastards ever get you down. Keep yourself well, my brother. Your dog know you can do it so stick with it and you'll win the war.

Remember the good times Shorty and eat some candy for me once in a while. Don't let this shit get you down cause your dog is at peace and in a better place. I did my time in hell and now its time for something better. I'm gone in body but I'll never leave you in spirit, we'll fight together side by side.

To my dearest Judith. You've brought my love and happiness in the time we've been together and that will always be ours if we're together now or later. Remember our times and smile cause you know I'm looking over you from above. I'll hold you in my arms tenderly one day soon. We'll walk in the summer sun and frolic in the fields of morning glories yet to grow in the fields of tomorrow and those fields will be ours. Give the children and grandchildren my love. Let your mum know I'm at peace but never give up the fight. My love is unconditional and never ending.

To George, your love, understanding, help, care, hard never ending work, and compassion have touched me deeply to depths I had forgotten even I had. Your loved dearly and there is no real way I could tell you in words how deeply grateful I am for everything you and your family have done over the years for me and the cause. Never give up the fight for the death penalty to be abolished once and for all and to never be brought back on the law books in this world again.

To my lawyers, Ron, Bill, Rob and the many others who worked for justice to be done in my case and worked so hard to save my life from this judicial murder. You have my undieing gratitude for everything you've done. Stay involved in capitol cases til the end of this judicial murder has come. Maybe we could've done more, maybe we could've done something differently, we'll never know and I don't want you to think about it. We fought it hard and long and with everything we had. Don't kid yourselves cause the bastards didn't win, they never beat us.

Now that this twelve year nightmare has come to an end let it be rememberd that the state of Texas has taken the life of an innocent man on August second nineteen ninety four and their true colors have been shown for what they are, blood thirsty politicians who will murder the innocent rather then say they made a mistake. May they rest in peace cause every time they close their eye lids I'll appear! I will not go away!!

Peace, Love and Much Respect to All My Comrades, Loved Ones, Fellow Abolishest, And Of Course My Road Dog!!!

Robert "Frenchy" Nelson Drew Sr. – Execution #79, August 2, 1994

85. Raymond Kinnamon (spoken last statement: the recording official noted "portions of last statement of Raymond Kinnamon, #808 that I could hear and understand"): Yes, warden, I would like to say a few words. I would like to say goodbye to my two boys in Indiana. I would like to tell them that I love them. I love all of my family members. I want my friends and family to keep working on the Death Penalty here in the State of Texas. I also want to thank my lawyers. I don't understand Judge Poe and Judge Higginbotham (Fifth Circuit) and I don't understand why Governor Richards did nothing. I also want to thank Kent Ramsey, the warden, Mr. Nunneles, etc. Sharon Longmier also treated me good. If any of this makes anyone feel good, then something is wrong with society. Also, thanks to Liz Cohen, Rob Owens and Marsa Rutenbaum, my lawyers. I appreciate their hard work on my case. I love them all. Goodbye to Joey and all of my friends overseas, and I know there are a few more people I am missing. I'm not trying to delay this; there are just so many people I want to remember; there are so many friends on death row that I can't mention them all. I have never seen so many people who do not want me to be executed. I apologize for anything I have done that is wrong. I am not sure where I am going of if there is an afterlife. I just want one question answered, "What is capital punishment for?" Is it for someone like me to be executed? I also want to thank Kathy Fair, although she is no longer there. I want to thank the radio stations. I want to thank my Aunt Pat and my brother, and I don't want him to let this bother his illness; and Carol and Ron — take care of the boys. This coughin is due to cigarettes and the flu I just got over. There are lots of friends out there on the row that I would like to say goodbye to: Vanderbilt, B.J., Carl Buntion (although he isn't a very popular person on death row because he killed a cop); but he's been a real good friend. The warden wanted me to be short, but shoot, this is my last chance. I want to thank Pete Gaylord for his support and help and old Robert Valentine; he needs to take it easy; I appreciate all of the letters and everything. If I left anyone out, it's due to extenuating circumstances beyond my control. I want to thank everyone back here with me; I don't see how nice guys like them got tied up in something like this. Thank Chaplain Taylor and Jane. I just got your letter. Thanks to Carolyn and Gloria who have been my friends for over four years. I want to remember Patsy Buntion, Gladys and a lot more friends. I want to thank the prosecutor in my case; it took courage for him to do what he did but he did what he did because he believed in the judicial system. I'm not ready to go, but I have no choice; I sent several letters to my family; they'll be very moving when you get them. I want to say goodbye again to my boys. I know I'm missing somebody, but if there's anything I have left to say, it would be that I wish I had a Shakesperean vocabulary but since I was raised in TDC, I missed out on some of my vocabulary.

If my words can persuade you to discontinue this practice of executing people; please do so. If the citizens don't do away with the death penalty, Texas won't be a safe place to be. I have no revenge because hate won't solve anything. [last comment from official recording the last statement: I gave Warden Hodges the phone at this time and he listened for 5-10 minutes. When he returned the phone to me, I could hear Kinnamon talking, but evidently the phone was not close to the mike, because I could not understand him.]

86. Jesse Dewayne Jacobs (spoken): I would like to say that I see there are a number of you gathered here tonight to witness an execution by the State of Texas. However, I have news for you. There is not going to be an execution. This is premeditated murder by the appointed district attorney and the State of Texas. I am not guilty of this crime. I hope that my death will snowball an avalanche that will stop all executions in the State of Texas and elsewhere. If my death serves this purpose, then maybe it will be worthwhile. I hope my [official record is illegible]. I have committed lots of sin in my life but I am not guilty of this crime. I would like to tell my son, daughter, and wife that I love them. Eden, if they want proof of them give it to them. Thanks for being my friend.

118. Clifton Eugene Belyeu (written): First of all I want to thank the LORD, my family and my wife Nora for all the support and encouragement they've shown through all this. I love you!! Now I want to thank all of you that came here today to be with me. Iknow most of you are here to see me suffer and die but your in for a big disappointment because today is a day of joy. Today is the day I'll be set free from this pain and suffering. Today I'm going to HEAVEN to live for all eternity with my HEAVENLY FATHER JESUS CHRIST and as I lay here taking my last breath, I'll be praying for all of you because your here today with anger and hatred in your hears letting satan deceive you into believing that what your doing is right and just. GOD help you, because what your doing here today and what's in your hearts here today makes you no better than any man or woman on death-rows across this country. Today your commiting murder too!!! I pray on my own behalf for forgiveness for any and all of the pain I've caused you, I pray that some day you'll realize your own mistakes and ask GOD to forgive you as I have because there is no peace without GOD's forgiveness........AMEN

145. Karla Faye Tucker (spoken): Yessir, I would like to say to all of you - the Thornton family and Jerry Dean's family — that I am so sorry I hope God will give you peace with this. Balu [spelling?], I love you. Ron, give Peggy a hug for me. Everybody has been so good to me. I love all of you very much. I am going to be face to face with Jesus now. Warden Taggett, thank all of you so much. You have been so good to me. I love all of you very much. I will see you all when you get there. I will wait for you.

Note: There was a tremendous amount of controversy about the Tucker execution, largely because many believed Tucker had become a Christian and changed her life. Allan B. Polunksy, Chairman of the Texas Board of Criminal Justice issued the following statement after her execution: "The issues here were not religious conversion or gender but rather culpability and accountability. Karla Faye Tucker brutally murdered two innocent people and was found guilty by the court and afforded all legal processes. Although I believe she finally found God, her religious awakening could in no way excuse or mitigate her actions in the world she just left, but hopefully will provide her redemption in the world she just entered."

160. Jonathan Wayne Nobles (spoken): Paula, I love you and I'm sorry. These two weeks have been a huge blessing. Kim, hi, I'm so sorry. Kyra, you made me hope you received my love, it's yours. I'm so sorry I'm a source of pain. David, thank you for everything. I took so much from you. There's nothing I can to do give it back to you. I love you, I love all of you. Steve, it took me this to get you in a suit coat (laughs). Don't worry about the phone number. Everything is going to be fine. I love you, man. I love you with all my heart. Father Walsh my spirit has grown because of you. Father Fitzgerald, thank you for being my friend. I'll see all of y'all at the church later on. Richard, thank you for everything you brought to Alice to help all of us. To my darling, what would life have been without you. I would still be in the dark night of the soul, I think. Thank you, Donna. Y'all wrap your arms around yourselves and give yourselves a great big hug for me. You know the routine. I want to share my favorite scriptures with y'all. Chaplain, help me through this. [See below for scriptures read by chaplain.] I ask God to take my death as sacrifice for all the abuses directed toward the Holy Virgin. I ask this sacrifice in Christ. (Nobles then sang the hymn "Silent Night.") [Scriptures read by chaplain: the text of 1 Corinthians 12:31B-13:13 (NIV) And now I will show you the most excellent way. If I speak in the tongues of men and angels, but have not love, I am only a resounding gong or a clanging cymbal. If I have the gift of prophecy and can fathom all mysteries and knowledge, and I have a faith that can move mountains, but have not love, I am nothing. If I give all I possess to the poor and surrender my body to the flames, but have not love, I gain nothing.

Love is patient, love is kind. It does not envy, it does not boast, it is not proud. It is not rude, it is not self-seeking, it is not easily angered, it keeps no record of wrongs. Love does not delight in evil but rejoices with the truth. It always protects, always trusts, always hopes, always perseveres.

Love never fails. But where there are prophecies, they will cease; where there are tongues, they will be stilled; where there is knowledge, it will pass away. For we know in part and we prophesy in part, but when perfection comes, the imperfect disappears.

When I was a child, I talked like a child, I thought like a child, I reasoned like a child. When I became a man, I put childish ways behind me. Now we see but a poor reflection as in a mirror; then we shall see face to face. Now I know in part; then I shall know fully, even as I am fully known.

And now these three remain: faith, hope and love. But the greatest of these is love.]

162. **Daniel Lee Corwin** (spoken): I guess the first thing I want to do is thank some very special people, Sara and Sabrina. And for affording me the opportunity that y'all did. It made a real big difference in my life. I thank you. Thank you again from the deepest part of my heart. I'm sorry. The biggest thing I wanted to say was to you and family and I know I haven't had a chance to talk with y'all in any form or fashion or way or manner. And I regret what happened and I want you to know I'm sorry. I just ask and hope that sometime down the line you can forgive me. I think in a lot of ways that without that it becomes very empty and hollow and the only thing we have is hatred and anger. I guess the only thing I have to say about the death penalty is that a lot of times people think of it as one-sided, but it's not. It's two-sided. There is pain on both sides and it's not an issue that people just sit there and voice off and say well this is a good thing or this is a bad thing. But it's something that's you know needs to be looked at and desired in each heart. I just hope that all of you can understand and someday forgive me. I want to thank y'all for affording me the opportunity to talk and meet with y'all. It meant so much. Thank you so much for being with me and my family. Thank you. I love you.

167. **Martin Sauceda Vega** (spoken): I really don't have much to say. All I want to say is that when the state introduced my sister and my niece as state

witness, it's not that they testified against me. The thing is, my lawyers would not subpoena anyone, so they allowed the state to subpoena them to paint a picture to the jury that my own sister and niece was testifying against me. Linda is innocent of this. I am innocent of this. Now all you all are seeing in this process is a perfect example of the ole freaky deaky Bill Clinton, when he signed that anti-terrorism law to shorten the appeals. This is a conspiracy. They used false testimony of a woman that said I had raped her. When the test showed that the foreign pubic hair that was found on her body belonged to no one in that room. They found a drop of sposmosa in the crotch of her pants that was tied to blood type B. My blood type is A. Now the same woman there they brought to testify during this murder case. That woman was under indictment for possession of methamphetamine, delivery of methamphetamine. She could have gotten out of both those cases. Yet, she swore under oath that she had never been in trouble with the law and none of that mattered. So what does that make this great state? A very high priced prostitute that sells itself called justice to the highest bidder. I am being charged under article 19.83 of the Texas Penal Code, of murder with the promise of renumeration. That means they got to have three people, the one that paid, the one that killed, and the deceased. And the alleged renumerator is out on the streets. So how come I'm being executed today, without a renu-merator? This is a great American justice. So if you don't think they won't, believe me they will. Ain't no telling who gonna be next. That's all I have to say. Especially for the people of the deceased. Sims is innocent and so am I. So the murderer is still out there. Today you are a witness. The state...(cough). Bye.

172. **Charles Henry Rector** (spoken): (the words of the song "God Living With Us 24 Hours")

GOD LIVING WITH US 24 HOURS
Intro......   "Listen People" no man can stand all on his own and
     No man has to stand alone.
       The Father gave his Son so that all mankind never
     Have to stand alone.
       He's with you the day you are born up until the day
     You die, "LISTEN."
GOD LIVING WITH US 24 HOURS
Chorus......   Yes Sister... what dwells inside of you
       Brother ... he dwells inside of me

Yes-Yes-Yes ... that mighty mighty power
The spirit of God ... living with us 24 hours

Verse......   Come on ... reach out and touch his hand
#1:   Come on ... and make a definite friend
Repeated   Yes he will all way's ... be there around
Yes he never, never ... gonna let you down

Verse......   When you paining ... when you in trouble
#2:   Look to him ... to deal with the problem
Repeated   All he won't from you ... is your love to be true
Call on him ... he's there inside of you
Chorus......   Yes Sister ... what dwells inside of you
Brother ... he dwells inside of me
Yes-Yes-Yes ... that mighty mighty power
The spirit of God ... living with us 24 hours
Verse......   Let him take control ... give him your body
#3;   Offer your soul ... Yes you got the power
The spirit of God ... living with us 24 hours
Yes-Yes-Yes ... that mighty, mighty power
Chorus......   Yes Sister ... what dwells inside of you
Brother ... he dwells inside of me
Yes-Yes-Yes ... that mighty mighty power
The spirit of God ... living with us 24 hours
Verse #1 Repeated
Verse #2 Repeated
Chorus repeated
Bridge......   Once you had a taste ... of heaven
Nothing on earth can ... replace it
Check him out for yourself ... Yes-Yes
His love is really ... something else
Verse #1 Repeated
Verse #2 Repeated
(FADE –OUT)
Chorus Repeated
Chorus Repeated

188. William Prince Davis (spoken): I would like to give thanks to God Almighty by whose grace I am saved through his son Jesus Christ without whom I would be nothing today. Because of this mercy and grace I have come a long way. And I would like to thank God and others who have been instrumental. I would like to say to the Lang family how truly sorry I am in my soul and in my heart of hearts for the pain and misery that I have caused from my actions. I am truly sorry. And to my family I would also like to extend to them the same apology for the pain and misery that I have put them through and I love them dearly from the bottom of my heart and one day I would like to see them on the other side. Some I will. Some I won't. I would like to thank all of the men on death row who have showed me love through the years but especially the last two or three weeks and I hold nothing against no man. I am so thankful that I have lived as long as I have. I hope that I have helped someone. I hope that donating my body to science that some parts of it can be used to help someone. And I just thank the Lord for all that He has done for me. That is all I have to say, Warden. Oh, I would like to say in closing, "What about those Cowboys?"

197. Jones Beathard (spoken): I want to start out by acknowledging the love that I've had in my family. No man in this world has had a better family than me. I had the best parents in the world. I had the best brothers and sisters in the world. I've had the most wonderful life any man could have ever had. I've never been more proud of anybody than I have of my daughter and my son. I've got no complaints and no regrets about that. I love everyone of them and have always been loved all of my life. I've never had any doubts about that. Couple of matters that I want to talk about since this is one of the few times people will listen to what I have to say. The United States has gotten to a now where they zero respect for human life. My death is just a symptom of a bigger illness. At some point the government has got to wake up and stop doing things to destroy other countries and killing innocent children. The ongoing embargo and sanctions against places like Iran and Iraq, Cuba and other places. They are not doing anything to change the world, but they are harming innocent children. That's got to stop at some point. Perhaps more important in a lot of ways is what we are doing to the environment is even more devastating because as long as we keep going the direction we're going the end result is it won't matter how we treat other people because everybody on the planet will be on their way out. We have got to wake up and stop doing that. Ah, one of the few ways in the world the truth is ever going to get out, or people are ever going to know what's happening as long as we support a free press out there. I see the press struggling to stay existent as a free institution. One of the few truly free institutions is the press in Texas. People like the *Texas Observer* and I want to thank them for the job they've done in keeping me and everybody else informed. I hope people out there will support them, listen to them, and be there for them. Without it, things like this are going to happen and nobody will even know. I love all of you. I always have I always will. I would like to address the State of Texas and specially Joe Price, the District Attorney who put me here. I want to remind Mr. Price of the mistake he made at Gene Hathorn's trial when he said that Gene Hathorn was telling the truth at my trial. Mr. Price is a one-eyed hunting dog. He in fact is not a one-eyed hunting dog, and in fact Gene Hathorn lied at my trial. Everybody knew it. I'm dying tonight based on testimony, that all parties, me, the man who gave the testimony, the prosecutor he used knew it was a lie. I am hoping somebody will call him to the floor for recent comments he's made in the newspaper. It's bad enough that a prosecutor can take truth and spin on it and try to re-doctor it. But when they actually make facts up and present to the public as trial's evidence. That goes beyond fail, that's completely unforgivable and I hope somebody makes Mr. Price account for or explain the tennis shoes he is talking about that put me here. I'm still completely lost on that and I'm hoping that somebody will go back and verify the trial record and make him accountable for lying to the public and the press that way. That's really all I have to say except that I love my family and nobody, nobody has got a better family than me. I love you, booger bear. I love doodle bug, too. Don't let them ever forget me. I'll never forget them. I'll see you on the other side, okay. Bye bye, Debbie. Bye, bro; bye, booger bear. Father Mike, Father Walsh, love you all. That's all, sir.

211. **Timothy Gribble** (written by chaplain): To the Jones Family: Please accept my sincerest apology and requests for what happened to your loved one. It was truly a horrible thing that I did and I regret it deeply. I do not know if this will ease your pain but I truly pray that this will help you find peace. I am sincerely truly sorry. For the Weis Family: The same is true. I regret what happened. I have lived with the guilt and the pain in my heart for taking Donna away from you. There is no way that I can know your pain and sorrow for losing someone so close to you. I truly hope that you will find peace. Please know that I am sorry. I feel that I have to speak out against the practice of the death penalty, although I have no regrets in my case. The death penalty is an unnecessary punishment for society who has other means to protect itself. You cannot rectify death with another death. Whenever the state chooses to take a life and take the power of God into their own hands, whenever our leader's kill in the name of justice, we are all diminished. To my family and friends, father, sister

and brother, those that have traveled so far to be here today, please just know that I am at peace. You have all been so good to me through this whole ordeal. I can never find the words to express my love for all of you. Just know that I go with God. Oum – Nama Shiveya I go with God.

212. **Tommy Ray Jackson** (spoken): Yes sir, I would like to address the Robinson family. There is nothing I can say here or anything I could probably do. Now you are all probably mad at me and I would probably be in the same situation you all in if anybody I thought killed anybody in my family ahh. If I knew who killed Rosalyn I would let you know, but, I am going to say this: I am going to heaven with God as my witness. Ros was a personal friend of mine. She was a beautiful person, very educated, her. I'm very tight with the Robinson family. She was proud that she had a father that was a doctor. My family is not here present and that is by my wish and my wish only. Now the tables is turned. You are all here, the Robinson family is her to see me executed. That is something that I would not want for my family. In no form or fashion would I have ever want to see Rosalyn dead. I left the scene of where the incident happened. I guarantee you if I would have been there you would not be standing where you are if I would have been there. You all have some very serious look on your face and something very serious fixin' to happen now. I will say this on my own behalf but then again I know it is not going to make any difference but what you fixing to witness is not a nice thing. It's not nice. It's not nice. The media. I would just like to address to the media with everybody's permission. I would like to say before I go that it has been said that I have shown no remorse, but if you look at my record and my background, ask anybody that know me that in order for me to show any kind of remorse for killing that ever been done, this one time I can't show no remorse for something that I did not do and if I did I would be faking. I would totally be faking and believe me there is nothing fake about me. Nothing fake. I've done wrong, sure, I've paid the time. This is one time that I know I cannot show no remorse for something that I did not do. I am at peace, please believe me. Wherefore, I figure that what I am dying for now is what I have done in my past. This is what I am dying for. Not for killing Rosalyn. I don't know what y'all call her but I call her Ros, I call her Ros. That's it.

213. **William Kitchens** (spoken): Yes, sir. James Webb, I don't know which one you are out there. I can't remember from the trial. I personally just want to let you know if there has ever been any doubt in your mind at all of what happened, I want you to know that Patty was always faithful to you, that I forced her for everything that she did and I am sorry. I just don't know how

to tell y'all I am sorry for what I did. There is no way for expressing I am sorry. I just hope that in some kind of way that y'all can move on and find peace in your life. The Lord has given me peace and that is all that I pray for is that y'all can find that peace. I just want you to know that I am sorry for what I done. I can't change that, all I can do is say I am sorry, that's nothing for what I have done. I can't replace your loss. I am sorry. I just want you to know that I love all of y'all. It's been a pleasure, y'all just keep on with life, it's gonna be good. The Lord's gonna be with us. If it's alright, I just want to say a prayer first. Father, God, I just thank you for the time that you have given me on this earth, for having mercy on somebody like me for all the despicable thing's I've done in my life, Father, but you still with your love and your mercy reach down into my heart and changed it before it's too late. I ask that you bestow peace upon the family of Patricia Webb, that you let them know, Father, that you are in a place where they can obtain that peace, and you will help them move on in their life, Father. Help them, Father, to find it in their hearts, not for my sake, but for yours, and their sake to, Father, find it in their heart to forgive me for what I have done. Father, I just ask that you be with my family and comfort them to move on Father. Father, we are all here today for the mistake that I have made and I thank you for your mercy for sending your Son into this life, that we might come to know you, Father. Father, I pray for these Wardens and the officers and the people that deal with all of this, Father, I ask that you touch their hearts, Father, and if there is any wrong to it, that you will forgive them, Father. Just let them know that you love them, Father, and that You are the way. I just thank you and in Jesus' name, I pray, Amen. I love y'all, y'all take care. I am so sorry.

214. **Michael McBride** (written): The following is the personal final statement of and by Michael L. McBride. The Beatitudes: Jesus lifted up his eyes on His disciples, and said, "Blessed be the poor: for yours is the kingdom of God. Blessed are ye that hunger now: for ye shall be filled. Blessed are ye that weep now: for ye shall laugh. Blessed are ye, when men shall hate you, and they shall separate you from their company, and shall reproach you, and cast out your name as evil for the Son of Man's sake. Rejoice ye in that day, and leap for joy: for behold, your reward is great in Heaven: for in the like manner did their fathers unto the prophets. But woe unto you that are rich! for ye have received your consolation. Woe unto you that are full! for ye shall hunger. Woe unto you that laugh now! for ye shall moan and weep. Woe unto you, when all men shall speak well of you! for so did their fathers to the false prophets.

The supremacy of love over gifts: I Corinthians, Chapter 13: 4-8: Love is patient, love is kind, and is not jealous, love does not brag and is no arrogant, does not act unbecoming; it does not seek its own, is not provoked, does not take into account a wrong suffered, does not rejoice in unrighteousness, but rejoices with the truth; bears all things, believes all things, hopes all things, endures all things. Love never fails; but if there are gifts of prophecy, they will be done away; if there tongues, they will cease. Now abide faith, hope, love, these three: but the greatest of these is love.

   Poem:

Do not stand at my grave and weep,
I am not there I do not sleep.
I am the diamond glints in the snow,
I am the sunlight on the ripened grain.
I am the gentle autumn rain.
When you awaken in the morning's hush,
I am the swift uplifting rush
of quiet birds in circled flight,
I am the soft stars that shine at night.
Do not stand at my grave and cry,
I am not there. I did not die.
Signed
Michael L. McBride #903
May 11, 2000, Huntsville, Texas

215. James David Richardson (spoken): Can they talk back? Say I pray for it, I accept it. Pray with me. This is still a statement. Ready? Dear Heavenly Father, forgive us, Lord. I ask that you watch over my Mama and over my sister. I ask this in the name of Christ. I also repent for all my sins, Lord. I pray that you will bring me home tonight. Please, I ask that I rest in your arms in the name of Christ Jesus I pray this. I truly believe that Jesus died for my sins that I may be resurrected, Lord, that you would do that much. Please, I ask that you not let me down and that I will be with you today in Heaven. Christ Jesus name I pray this. Donna and everybody else, Mr. Johnson, I ask that y'all will pray for me and that God will bring me home tonight, that he will keep me in Heaven, that I will still be in heaven. Please Lord, I don't want to be in Heaven, I mean I don't want to be in Hell. And, please Lord, I confess my sins. This is your son, Lord Jesus, this is your servant, please, this is your slave. I love you, too. Donna and Mama and Mr. Johnson, I wrote a message. Don't give up, love you all, even the ones that are my enemies. I truly forgive all of y'all in Christ Jesus, we pray. I ask God that he take all the hate out of my heart and away from my soul. Please, please, Lord, don't fail me. I don't know is Margie here now? But if she is, I ask her forgiveness. I ask that you not hold nothing against me or my family from this day forward, and hold no hate toward them. I don't know. I can't hear you, you may forgive me, and you may not. Forgive Mike Allison, forgive McHenry, forgive us all. Whatever the cost may be I love you. Take care of my Mama. Donna, I ask you to take care of my Mama, too. Whenever you get mad at her, you remember me. Remember I may be back. Mama, I am going to try to make that promise to you. I gonna ask God to allow his child to come back to see you. Cause I am in Heaven. At time I can come (unintelligible). Okay, Mr. Johnson, you take care, let my Mama's will be done. One more prayer, then we may proceed. Heavenly Father, I confess my sins, really I do. Let me know that I will be in Heaven tonight. Please let me know. I don't want to be in Hell with Satan or anyone else. Please, that is something I need to know. I ask that Jesus give me help. In Jesus precious name, I pray this. I ask that you give me those promises, that you assure me that those promises are real. That I am praying right. In Jesus precious name, I pray this. Goodbye, Mama. Goodbye, Donna.

219. **Thomas Wayne Mason** (spoken): I understand that Michael Skains is supposed to be here somewhere. They did everything but make sure I got a fair trial to prove I was innocent. I wasn't the one who had the gun to give to police and all these altered records from the District Attorney's office and the Attorney General's office, that's why Michael Sputnick got fired and ran off when I filed these appeals. Not one of my sell out lawyers would use this evidence, because they all work as a conspiracy with the court. No doubt about it. Jack King did everything he could to keep me from making arms and showing this evidence. They wait till the hearing was over and then make the arguments in the court or on paper where nobody can rebut it or contradict the testimony or arguments. There's more than 30 altered and falsified records saying I told so and so this or that, but you go look in their record, it does not say Thomas Mason called them at all and told them anything. But that's okay. All this evidence is being saved, so Jack King can laugh all he wants like he's the big hero, after this is over with, that's fine. But the person that had the gun, they know was not Thomas Mason, so who's getting the last laugh after all? The guy that got away. But Jack King knows he illegally convicted me of all these falsified altered records. My sister's got the document that my lawyer filed, but he didn't file with the court. It's got the signature on it. He put this all in one record. So it's going to be saved. It ain't going to be destroyed just because I'm dead. Everybody's got to go sooner or later and sooner or later everyone of y'all will be along behind me. That's all I got to say.

221. **Paul Selso Nuncio** (spoken): I have a written statement for the press. It will be released as soon as they can. And I also responded to a comment to me from Sandy, daughter of Ms. Farris. I have felt deeply sorry for the deceased. But I'm sorry that I wasn't the one that did it or anything. She will tell you that when she gets a chance to. When the time comes. I just wish just to be patient when the time for each and everyone of y'all individually have y'all time. But I'm not putting pressure on either one of y'all being having any guilt. I just want to say two thing, executing someone that is innocent, cause even though I am. The burden will be wiped away and you will be at ease to know that I know how it is and they will pay for it when their time comes. And all I have to say is that right now I'm sorry that it happened and I was part, not part in it but, part responsible for not properly getting the word out in time to get the right victim or the right convict or the right person that did it. I just wish to say a little prayer for the family for their appearance and forgiveness in this matter. Our Father, who art in heaven, hallowed by thy name. Thy kingdom come, thy will be done, on earth as it is in Heaven. Give this day your daily bread and forgive us our trespasses as we forgive those who trespass against us. Lead us not into temptation, but deliver us from evil. Our Lord, Amen. And ah, don't be surprised if your Mom be the helper of God that would grab my hand and say "You are now into eternal life with God." This is her being one of the chosen ones to give as proof of innocence. That's what I meant by telling you I don't mean to injure you anymore. When your time comes that she would let you know, if I was innocent or guilty. That about all I have to say. Love you all.

(written): I wish the public to see my point of inside view that the officers of Death Row of the State of Texas. All the years of 5 or 6 years of my first time being locked up for not doing a crime of this sort. Now, officers of Texas TDCJ are of Terrell Unit, Walls Unit and some of Ellis I are just doing their job for their family. Now there are also respectful inmates death row and population that I've meet, now I say to all of you just realizing what crime is about, don't do it. One way I've thought of was having your friends "inmate" to witness your execution talking about those of population and first timers. I just want to give those officers that respected me while in prison of TDCJ Death Row. May God bless you all of TDCJ and inmates especially the free-world population. With Gods and my words of faith, Paul Selso Nuncio

222. **Gary Graham** (spoken): I would like to say that I did not kill Bobby Lambert. That I'm an innocent black man that is being murdered. This is a

lynching that is happening in America tonight. There's overwhelming and compelling evidence of my defense that has never been heard in any court of America. What is happening here is an outrage for any civilized country to anybody anywhere to look at what's happening here is wrong. I thank all of the people that have rallied to my cause. They've been standing in support of me. Who have finished with me. I say to Mr. Lambert's family, I did not kill Bobby Lambert. You are pursuing the execution of an innocent man. I want to express my sincere thanks to all of y'all. We must continue to move forward and do everything we can to outlaw legal lynching in America. We must continue to stay strong all around the world, and people must come together to stop the systematic killing of poor and innocent black people. We must continue to stand together in unity and to demand a moratorium on all executions. We must not let this murder/lynching be forgotten tonight, my brothers. We must take it to the nation. We must keep our faith. We must go forward. We recognize that many leaders have died. Malcom X, Martin Luther King, and others who stood up for what was right. They stood up for what was just. We must, you must brothers, that's why I have called you today. You must carry on that condition. What is here is just a lynching that is taking place. But they're going to keep on lynching us for the next 100 years, if you do not carry on that tradition, and that period of resistance. We will prevail. We may loose this battle, but we will win the war. This death, this lynching will be avenged. It will be avenged, it must be avenged. The people must avenge this murder. So my brothers, all of y'all stay strong, continue to move forward. now that I love all of you. I love the people, I love all of you for your blessing, strength, for your courage, for your dignity, the way you have come here tonight, and the way you have protested and kept this nation together. Keep moving forward, my brothers. Slavery couldn't stop us. The lynching couldn't stop us in the south. This lynching will not stop us tonight. We will go forward. Our destiny in this country is freedom and liberation. We will gain our freedom and liberation by any means necessary. By any means necessary, we keep marching forward. I love you, Mr. Jackson. Bianca, make sure that the state does not get my body. Make sure that we get my name as Shaka Sankofa. My name is not Gary Graham. Make sure that it is properly presented on my grave. Shaka Sankofa. I died fighting for what I believe in. I died fighting for what was just and what was right. I did not kill Bobby Lambert, and the truth is going to come out. It will be brought out. I want you to take this thing off into international court, Mr. Robert Mohammed and all y'all. I want you, I want to get my family and take this down to international court and file a law suit. Get all the video tapes of all the beatings. They have beat me up in the back. They have beat me up at the unit over there. Get all the video tapes supporting that law suit. And make the public exposed to the genocide and this brutality world, and let the world see what is really happening here behind closed doors. Let the world see the barbarity and injustice of what is really happening here. You must get those video tapes. You must make it exposed, this injustice, to the world. You must continue to demand a moratorium on all executions. We must move forward Minister Robert Mohammed. Ashanti Chimurenga, I love you for standing with me, my sister. You are a strong warrior queen. You will continue to be strong in everything that you do. Believe in yourself, you must hold your head up, in the spirit of Winnie Mandela, in the spirit of Nelson Mandela. Y'all must move forward. We will stop this lynching. Reverend Al Sharpton, I love you, my brother.

Appendix 2

Adanandus, Dwight Dwayne 137
Allridge, Ronald Keith 95
Amos, Bernard Eugene 101
Anderson, Johnny R. 35
Anderson, Larry Norman 75
Andrade, Richard 20
Atworth, Robert 198
Autry, James David 2
Baldree, Ernest Orville 115
Banda, Esequel 103
Barber, Danny Lee 169
Barefield, John Kennedy 109
Barefoot, Thomas Andy 4
Barnard, Harold Amos 72
Barnes, Jr., Odell 209
Barnes, Willis Jay 187
Barney, Jeffrey Allen 12
Bass, Charles William 11
Beathard, James 197
Beavers, Richard Lee 74
Beets, Betty Lou 208
Behringer, Earl Russell 128
Belyeu, Clifton Eugene 118
Bird, Jerry Joe 40
Black, Jr., Robert 50
Blackmon, Ricky Don 181
Boggess, Clifford 153
Bonham, Antonio Nathaniel 69
Boyd, Charles Anthony 182
Boyle, Benjamin H. 114
Briddle, James Michael 104
Bridge, Warren Eugene 83
Brimage, Jr., Richard 108
Brock, Kenneth 15
Brooks, Jr., Charlie 1
Burks, John Albert 220
Butler, Jerome 34
Buxton, Lawrence Lee 38
Callins, Bruce Edwin 121
Camacho, Jr., Genaro 156
Cannon, Joseph John 148
Cantu, Andrew 170
Cantu, Jr., Domingo 192
Cantu, Ruben Montoya 66
Carter, Robert Anthony 151

Carter, Robert Earl 218
Castillo, David Allen 158
Clark, David M. 45
Clark, Jr., Herman Robert Charles 84
Clayton, James Edward 217
Cockrum, John William 136
Coleman, Clydell 176
Cook, Anthony Quinn 70
Cordova, George 168
Cordova, Joe Angel 43
Corwin, Daniel Lee 162
Crane, Alvin 190
Crank, Denton 78
Cruz, Javier 159
Cuevas, Ignacio 39
Davis, James Carl Lee 133
Davis, William Prince 188
De la Cruz, Jose 175
De la Rosa, Jesse 7
De Luna, Carlos 33
Demouchette, James 52
Derrick, Mikel James 37
Drew, Robert Nelson 79
Drinkard, Richard G. 119
Duff-Smith, Markum 60
Dunn, Kenneth 183
Earheart, James Otto 184
Ellis, Edward 46
Emery, Jeff 163
Esquivel, Rudy Ramos 14
Evans, Michael Wayne 19
Farris, Troy Dale 166
Faulder, Joseph Stanley 178
Fearance, John W. 96
Felder, Jr., Sammie 199
Foster, Richard Donald 216
Foust, Aaron Christopher 174
Franklin, Donald Gene 28
Fuller, Aaron Lee 141
Fuller, Tyrone Leroy 180
Gardner, Billy Conn 91
Garrett, Johnny Frank 44
Gentry, Kenneth Edward 113
Gonzalez, Jr., Joe Fedelfido 107
Goodman, Spencer Corey 201

Gosch, Lesley Lee 149
Goss, Cornelius 207
Graham, Gary Lee 222
Granviel, Kenneth 106
Green, G. W. 42
Green, Norman Evans 171
Green, Ricky Lee 138
Gribble, Timothy 211
Griffin, Jeffery 53
Gutierrez, Jesse 80
Gutierrez, Jose 195
Hammond, Karl 97
Harris, Curtis Paul 61
Harris, Danny Ray 62
Harris, Kenneth Bernard 125
Hawkins, Samuel 92
Heiselbetz, Jr., Earl Carl 200
Herman, David Lee 110
Hernandez, Ramon 21
Herrera, Leonel Torres 58
Hicks, David 202
Hogue, Jerry Lee 147
Holland, David 64
Hughes, Jr., Billy George 204
Jackson, Tommy Ray 212
Jacobs, Jesse Dewayne 86
James, Johnny 68
Jenkins, Jr., Leo Ernest 105
Jennings, Desmond 193
Jernigan, Joseph Paul 63
Johnson, Carl 99
Johnson, Curtis L. 51
Johnson, Jr., Dorsie 126
Johnson, Eddie James 130
Johnson, Elliot Rod 24
Jones, Raymond 186
Kelly, Carl E. 65
King, Leon Rutherford 30
Kinnamon, Raymond 85
Kitchens, William Joseph 213
Lackey, Clarence Allen 120
Lamb, John 194
Landry, Raymond 29
Lane, Harold 100
Lauti, Aua 140